40,000 MILES
IN A CANOE
and *SEA QUEEN*

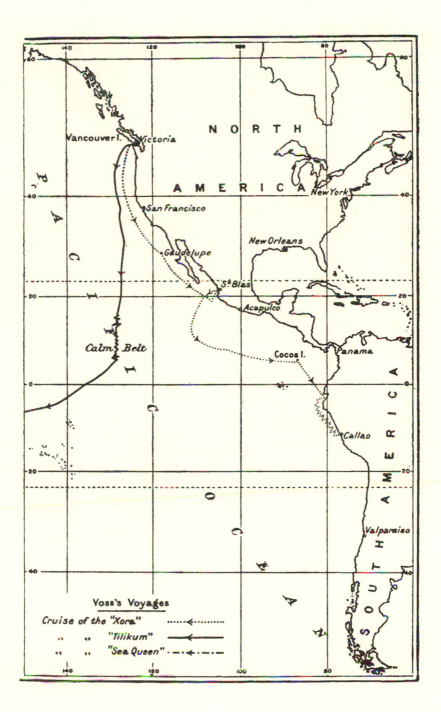

60

140   120   100   80

N O R T H

60

P A C I F I C

A M E R I C A

Vancouver I.   Victoria

New York   40

40

San Francisco

New Orleans

Gaudelupe

St Blas

20   20

Acapulco

Calm Belt

Cocos I.   Panama

0

Callao

S O U T H   A M E R I C A

20   20

Valparaiso

40   40

O C E A N

Voss's Voyages

Cruise of the "Xora" ....◄............

"   "   "Tilikum"   ——————◄——————

"   "   "Sea Queen" —·—◄—·—·—

140   120   100   80

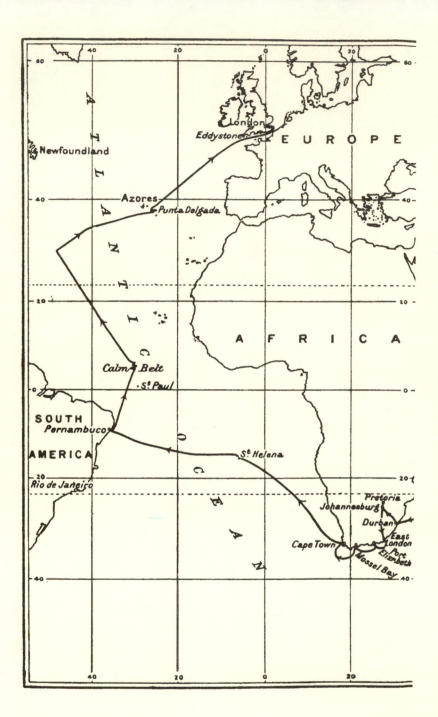

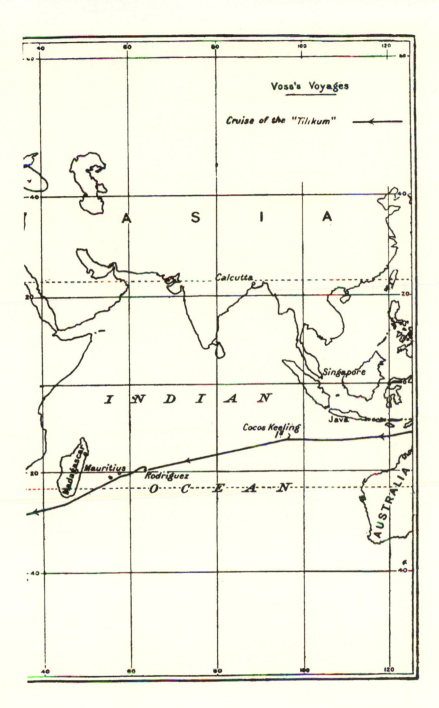

Voss's Voyages

Cruise of the "Tilikum" ←

ASIA

Calcutta

INDIAN

Singapore

Cocos Keeling

Java

INDIAN

Madagascar Mauritius

Rodriguez

OCEAN

AUSTRALIA

40,000 MILES
IN A CANOE
and *SEA QUEEN*

J. C. Voss

Introduction by Jonathan Raban

INTERNATIONAL MARINE / McGRAW-HILL

Camden, Maine • New York • San Francisco • Washington, D.C. • Auckland •
Bogotá • Caracas • Lisbon • London • Madrid • Mexico City •
Milan • Montreal • New Delhi • San Juan • Singapore • Sydney •
Tokyo • Toronto

Other titles in The Sailor's Classics series:

Gipsy Moth Circles the World, *Sir Francis Chichester*
The Saga of Cimba, *Richard Maury*
The Strange Last Voyage of Donald Crowhurst, *Nicholas Tomalin
and Ron Hall*

International Marine
A Division of The McGraw-Hill Companies

10 9 8 7 6 5 4 3 2 1
Introduction © 2001 Jonathan Raban

Library of Congress Cataloging-in-Publication Data

Voss, John Claus, 1838–1922.
   40,000 miles in a canoe and Sea Queen / J.C. Voss ; introduction by Jonathan Raban.
      p.   cm.
   First published: The venturesome voyages of Captain Voss. Yokohama, 1913.
   ISBN 0-07-137333-0 (alk. paper).
      1. Voss, John Claus, 1838–1922—Journeys. 2. Voyages and travels.
   3.Tilikum (Canoe). 4. Sea Queen (Ship). I. Title: Forty thousand miles in a canoe and Sea Queen. II. Voss, John Claus. 1838–1922. Venturesome voyages of Captain Voss. III. Title.
   G530.V78V67 2001
   910.4'5   00-050593

Printed on 55# Sebago by R. R. Donnelley, Crawfordsville IN
Design by Dennis Anderson
Page layout by Nancy Benner
Production management and photo layout by Janet Robbins

CONTENTS

SEA QUEEN

MAPS AND PHOTOGRAPHS

Maps

Photographs

INTRODUCTION TO THE SAILOR'S CLASSICS EDITION
Jonathan Raban

IT IS THE VOICE of Captain Voss that stops you in your tracks, like Coleridge's wedding guest detained by the Ancient Mariner; a gruff, bewhiskered, seadog's voice, rich in experience and personality. There's liquor on his breath, and a singular glitter in his eye. So it comes as a surprise to discover that Voss the man is a creature of supposition and rumor, his existence barely verifiable at all. He was born in 1854 (according to Richard Hughes, who wrote an introduction to an earlier edition of this book), though Voss himself (in the first chapter of "Sea Queen") says he was born on August 6th, 1858; while another writer asserts that he was born in 1861. He was a Newfoundlander, a Dane, a Swede, a German—or maybe none of those; it depends on whatever scanty account of his life you happen to be reading. He may or may not have escaped from a Californian penitentiary where he may have been jailed for smuggling Chinese immigrants. It's possible that he was lost at sea in 1913, aboard a yawl that sailed out of Yokohama, or that he died of pneumonia in 1922, in Tracy, California, where he may have ended his days as a cabdriver.

One or two facts about him are reasonably clear. He was a strikingly short man (this comes from Weston Martyr, the well-known maritime writer, who met Voss in Cape Town in 1903, then spent much time in his company in Yokohama in 1912 and 1913). In the 1870s and 1880s, Captain Voss was at sea. It seems that, like Captain Slocum, he was a professional sailor who was driven ashore by the rise of steam. By the late 1890s, Voss was owner, or co-owner, of a hotel, or hotels, in Victoria, British Columbia, where *Tilikum* was fitted out for its great voyage around the world. Ambiguous and obscure pasts have always been common in the far West, where rolling stones and men from nowhere have naturally gravitated in order to build themselves new lives from scratch. It seems likely that Voss was twice married, and probably the father of three children; in fin de siècle Victoria he would have fitted happily into that society of rainbow-chasers with doubtful histories for whom the West might have been deliberately invented.

What is certain is that for a brief period, from 1901 to 1903, this pint-sized character with close-cropped hair and belligerent walrus mustache (two more ascertainable facts there) emerged from obscurity to seek fame and substance for himself with one of the great seafaring stunts of all time—a global voyage in a sailing canoe.

Joshua Slocum's *Sailing Alone around the World* had recently been published (in serial form in 1899, and as a book in 1900), and Slocum's exploits had made him briefly world-famous. On his voyage, which lasted from 1895 to 1899, Slocum made headlines at every port of call. In Australia, he was feted with reams of bad poetry; in South Africa, hauled off for an audience with President Kruger. In the new world of mass-circulation popular newspapers, there was ready money for true-life tales of death-defying adventure. After Slocum's circumnavigation, intrepid yachtsmen began to share the limelight with explorer-heroes like Amundsen, Scott, and Shackleton.

The *Tilikum* voyage was conceived, in Slocum's wake, by a young Canadian journalist—Norman Luxton, who was born in Winnipeg and had worked as a cub reporter on the *Calgary Herald* and *Vancouver Sun*. Luxton's idea was simply to sail round the world in a boat visibly (i.e., photographically) smaller than Slocum's 37-foot *Spray*. Voss—who agreed to skipper Luxton's voyage—went one better. He selected, then created, a vessel so weird-looking, so seemingly unsuited to its task, that it was guaranteed to bring newspaper photographers rushing at every port into which it sailed.

Tilikum was the first forerunner of all the bathtubs, pedalos, and other eccentric contrivances in which people have put to sea in order to make a big splash in the media. If your voyage is unoriginal in itself, you can compensate with the novelty of the craft in which it is undertaken. The most recent example at the time of writing is the fifty-year-old Alsatian man, of no previous distinction, who tried to propel himself into fame by walking across the Pacific Ocean on a pair of pontoon-skis. He set off from Los Angeles in March 2000, and managed to get thirty miles offshore before he had to be rescued by the U.S. Coast Guard.

But Captain Voss (and this is the most salient single fact of his life) had a genius for practical seamanship, and knew very well what he was doing. *Tilikum* looked queer, but was every bit as capable and seaworthy as *Spray*. The west coast of Vancouver Island, where the Nootka Indians fished, fought, and went whaling for several thousand years, is exposed to the full force of the Pacific Ocean. It is a sea-area of 10-meter swells and regular, sometimes daily, gales. The canoes built by the Nootkans, each hollowed from a single massive log of red cedar, were prized by neighboring tribes, like the Makahs to the south. Unlike any vessel built by whites, *Tilikum* had perfect hull-integrity, with no seams to open, no planks to spring. Its vernacular design, developed over millennia, was efficient, stable, and sea-kindly.

Voss gave his Indian canoe a shallow keel, raised its freeboard by several inches, decked it over, built a coachhouse-cabin and cockpit, then rigged it with three stubby masts. His most innovative touch was to lead all the running rigging aft, so that every sail could be raised or lowered from the safety of the cockpit. When he was finished, he had an eye-catching hybrid boat; no longer a canoe, exactly, it might have been named a *yanoe*, or, perhaps, a *canacht*.

On its first sailing trials in the Strait of Juan de Fuca, *Tilikum* performed beautifully. Norman Luxton's brother George reported to his mother:

> She sails like a fish . . . She stands rough weather fine. Before we got back to Victoria the wind was blowing something terrible, the waves were rolling something awful, we rolled up and down as if we were on a gigantic rocking horse. Sometimes the boat would nearly stand on end, but we did not take any water and we could not upset because we had so much ballast on board. Oh! It was just fine, so exhilarating.

One thinks of Francis Chichester trying out *Gipsy Moth IV* in the Solent—a puff of wind laying the boat over—and marvels at Voss's success at converting his canoe into a fast, safe, snug sailing machine. *Tilikum* possessed the enormous—and newsworthy—virtue of looking quite mad but being extremely sane.

UNDER THE TERMS of their original agreement, Voss was to captain *Tilikum*, with Luxton acting as mate. Luxton would pay the bills, and write a best-seller about their adventure. In the event, Luxton got off the boat at Suva in Fiji (where, thirty years later, Richard Maury's *Cimba* would end her classic voyage), while Voss continued round the world. Voss wrote the book, which he published in Yokohama in 1913; Luxton, meanwhile, nursed his grievances against his former skipper, and, a quarter century after his passage from Victoria to Fiji, wrote his own account of the voyage in 1927–28.*

Most yachting literature has been written in the uncontested first person. Frequently the writer is the only person who was aboard the boat, so that we have to trust him or her for the veracity of those forty-foot waves (all high waves in yachting lit are conventionally estimated at forty feet, no more, no less) and sixty-knot winds. We may suspect, but cannot directly challenge, Slocum's tale of *Spray's* astounding ability to sail herself (2700 miles in twenty-three days, with Slocum on the helm for only

---

*Eleanor Georgina Luxton (ed.), *Luxton's Pacific Crossing*, Sidney, B.C., 1971.

three hours of that time . . .). Solo voyagers are at liberty to tell their readers pretty much anything they choose, and small-boat cruises are littered with events that tax the reader's credulity to the point where several such books have landed up in my own wastepaper basket.

In the case of the *Tilikum* voyage, we have two narrators for the first, long stretch of the passage. Voss says one thing, Luxton quite another, giving a rare binocular view of events. The unexpected result is that Luxton's story, intended to discredit Voss's, makes one trust Voss all the more on the seagoing essentials of "Forty Thousand Miles in a Canoe."

Luxton accused Voss of being a thief and a murderer. Voss had broken his agreement with Luxton "by stealing the *Tilikum*'s story across the Pacific." More seriously, Luxton asserted that his own replacement as *Tilikum*'s mate, Louis Begent, had not been lost overboard as claimed by Voss in his book, but had been killed by Voss in a drunken assault. The trouble is that Luxton, an imprecise and naive writer, does not cut much ice with his charges, though he throws many incidental sidelights on Captain Voss's temperament and character.

Writing "Forty Thousand Miles in a Canoe," Voss used Norman Luxton as a stooge. Voss's narrative requires that Luxton appear as an innocent greenhorn, to be taught lessons by his captain, the wily old man of the sea. "Did you not tell me some time ago that you have never been to sea, and have not had any experience in sailing boats?" inquires Voss on the first page of the book; "I did," replies Luxton-as-rendered-by-Voss. Luxton, writing in his own voice, claims otherwise:

> My experience at sea was of course limited compared to Voss's. A time or two around Vancouver Island, with many short trips, and two trips into Bering Sea, were all I had ever had in sailing boats.

Having myself tried to circumnavigate Vancouver Island, in a sailboat with a 50 hp auxiliary diesel, and been beaten back by heavy weather, I find that "time or two around Vancouver

Island" a shade too airy to be true. We're not speaking here of, say, the Isle of Wight, but of an island 180 nautical miles long and 60 nautical miles wide, nearly half of it a treacherous lee shore open to everything the North Pacific can unleash on it, which is a lot by any standards. As for the Bering Sea . . .

One of the most revealing moments in Luxton's story is when, becalmed in the Doldrums, he and Voss see a sea-monster.

> This animal or mammal had never been classified in any natural history I had ever read . . . It was longer than any sailing ship I had ever seen . . . It did not appear to be at all stiff in the water like the body of a whale, it seemed to move at will, and carried its head, which was on the end of a huge neck, well out of the water. Fins or flukes we could not see, and its colours were all dark or greys. Out of the unknown it came like one of the storm's evil spirits, and into the darkest point of the stormy horizon it disappeared . . .

Luxton is on watch when the monster shows itself on *Tilikum*'s port side, and he summons Voss to see this horrid marvel of the deep.

> No one said a word. I silently pointed. To this day Jack has never spoken a dozen words about what we saw, though he did admit seeing the same thing once before. Jack never spoke about it because he said quite truthfully, no one would ever believe it, so why tell the truth and be a liar?

Voss is the realist. He knows what the market can stand. The sea-monster would undermine the plausibility of his narrative, so there is no mention of the beast in "Forty Thousand Miles in a Canoe." Unwittingly, Luxton has exposed Voss's strength (and his own weakness) as a writer. Where Luxton's account belongs to the genre of yarning romance, Voss's is factual, hardbitten, and eminently believable—which does not, of course, mean that it is necessarily true.

So when Luxton tells of the row that led to his quitting the boat in Fiji, he turns it into a boyish tale of blood-and-thunder, with himself as the clean-limbed young hero. According to Luxton, Voss "told me I would sail the way he wanted or else he would kill me, saying that he could easily throw me overboard and report me as missing at his next port of call." Whereupon (it is a very "whereupon" sort of story) Luxton reaches for his trusty .22 Stevens long-target pistol, points it at Voss's head, and orders him below. "I told him to go and to go fast, and Jack went and went fast." Luxton padlocks Voss into the cabin, opening it only to allow the captain to pass out a hot meal for the helmsman. Later, "Playing the old game, I hove to, hung up a lantern in the main mast, locked Voss in the cabin, threw out the anchor, and went to sleep." None of this exactly resounds with likeliness.

The episode is meant to prepare the reader for Luxton's suggestion that Voss killed Begent, for which his best evidence is the visit of an "infallible" fortune-teller to *Tilikum* in Sydney Harbour, where Luxton had gone to meet Voss—and, as he expected, Begent—on their arrival.

> In the most minute detail, [Mrs X.] described a fight taking place in the cockpit of the *Tilikum*, and so harrowing was it that my flesh went all goosey.

Poor Luxton. He fatally lacks the gift for carrying his readers with him. Interestingly Voss too mentions the visit of the fortune-teller:

> My old mate, Mr. Luxton . . . told me that the best fortune-teller in Australia had asked him to inform me that I should under no circumstances sail in the *Tilikum* to Melbourne, as, if I did, something very serious would happen; but as I had made up my mind to see Melbourne, which city I was informed was the finest south of the equator, I told Mr. Luxton that if nothing more serious than a fortune-teller would oppose my sailing to Melbourne, I would certainly sail.

There speaks the trustworthy realist, who admits to believing in neither sea-monsters nor seers. On the murder charge, Captain Voss handsomely carries the day.

Given Luxton's desire to inflict damage on Voss's reputation, it

is remarkable how the bulk of his narrative serves only to rein-
force Voss's in every detail of chronology, weather, sea-conditions,
and seamanship. Even as he is trying to frame Voss for Begent's
murder, he remarks: "Jack Voss, without doubt, had the most
wonderful store of sailing knowledge ever in one man's brain of
this day and age." Most surprisingly, in view of his portrait of
Voss as a raging madman when drunk (and Voss, by his own
admission, was certainly fond of the bottle), Luxton ends his
story with these sentences:

> "Would you repeat the trip again?" I am often asked. Quite candidly
> and truly *NO*, but not for anything would I have missed it. Under
> different circumstances, with a larger boat, the voyage would have
> been divine, and in such a boat if Voss were master, I would not
> have hesitated to go anywhere the winds and storms would drive.

Norman Luxton was by no means alone in his exalted esti-
mation of Voss's great abilities as a sailor. Weston Martyr claimed
that he thought Captain Voss a "most monumental liar" when he
first ran into him on the beach at Table Bay. But disbelief swiftly
turned into veneration. Martyr wrote:

> I have found every word of Voss's concerning ships and the sea to be
> pure gold; and I have treasured them accordingly. The success
> which, so far, has attended such ocean passages in small craft as I
> have made, I attribute solely to the fact that I religiously followed
> Voss's teaching. To this teaching I know I owe, at any rate, my life.

Martyr, I suspect, may have had a hand in the preparation of
Voss's book. The two men were much together in Yokohama in
the year preceding the book's publication, and there are some
oddly professional flourishes in Captain Voss's prose (like the
handling of dialogue designed to teach a lesson with the sug-
ared pill of salty direct speech) which hardly seem to match the
man described here by the fluent and prolific Martyr:

> Like most men who have *done* great things, Voss was not a satisfy-
> ing talker. He had been much too busy doing things all his life to
> have time to acquire those qualities which we more leisured, softer

and less effectual folk call refinement and culture. A gentle lady snugly wrapped, say, in a sealskin coat would doubtless have considered Voss a rough and vulgar person; forgetting that, but for the work of such men as he, it would be necessary for gentle ladies to walk through this life entirely naked. Be this as it may, a little "culture" is very helpful in enabling one to express one's thoughts, and expressing his thoughts was not, at the time I speak of, one of Voss's strong points.

I'm inclined to take this as a broad hint that Martyr helped to supply Voss with the "little 'culture'" needed for the composition of his genial and swift-moving book. But the voyage and the voice are clearly Voss's alone, and one reads the book not for its stylistic eloquence but for the pleasure of keeping the company of an astonishingly able and experienced seaman as he confides his knowledge to the reader.

On one level, "Forty Thousand Miles in a Canoe" is *the* classic primer on small-boat handling under all imaginable conditions. What do you do if the compass binnacle is swept overboard, and you are miles from anywhere under an overcast sky? It's in here. For many years—until the 1970s, when Bernard Moitessier challenged Voss's practice—Voss On the Sea-Anchor had the status of Biblical writ, and it still has its passionate disciples. There are hints and tips on almost every page—about weather, navigation, steering, sail-adjustment. To possess the book is to have your own compact fount of growling sea-wisdom at your elbow.

On another level, it has the structure of a familiar kind of Victorian novel. The hero (though, unlike in the novel, the hero of this book is born old) begins in disrepute—a reprobate from whom little good can ever be expected. After an epic series of trials and vicissitudes, he at last earns an honored place in society (in the novel, of course, he wins the hand of the beautiful girl who will bear his children, which is not quite Voss's style). So the voyage of *Tilikum* begins with the criminal plundering of an Indian burial site on Vancouver Island. Voss and Luxton, primed on a local trader's "very good Scotch whisky," rob a cave at Dodges Cove (now Ucluelet) of skulls and "curios." They are a pair of ruffians, and after reading of their behavior towards the Indians, some modern readers might well wish to see *Tilikum* swamped and sunk by the next available big wave. Yet John Voss's character is annealed by the process of the voyage. The central hinge of the narrative is located in Melbourne, site of the fortune-teller prophecy, where *Tilikum* is "smashed to pieces" on dry land by some careless work by the employees of a truck company. It is Voss's fortitude, as he lovingly repairs his broken boat, that begins to endear him to the reader, and from Melbourne onwards, he is on the upward path that will lead him to social redemption. At the end of the book, in London, he meets—or nearly meets, for the sentence has to be read carefully—Sir Alfred Harmsworth, the press lord and owner of the *Daily Mail*; he shakes the hand of Lieutenant—later Sir Ernest—Shackleton; and in the final, triumphant words of the book, "[I] was honoured by being elected a Fellow of the Royal Geographical Society in London."

From grave-robber to a man who can put the letters F.R.G.S. after his name . . . here is the Victorian novel come true. That Voss should set such store by this honor is perhaps a measure of how much he wanted his voyage to carry him from dark obscurity to officially sanctioned social respectability. He was, in the world's terms, a nobody who very badly wanted to be a Somebody.

It is a touching story, and it is made more touching, I think, by the fact that there is a slight snag in it. Though Captain John Claus Voss was twice proposed for a fellowship of the Royal Geographical Society, he was never elected to one. No one could have been more richly deserving of that rather modest accolade, but Captain Voss, "a rough and vulgar person," in Martyr's imaginary lady's words, failed to pass muster with the stern gentry of the committee.

Never mind. Most of the people who could legitimately put
F.R.G.S. after their names lie unregarded in their graves, but Voss
lives on, in his tobacco-roughened, whisky-scented, infinitely
knowledgeable voice:

> It is an ancient Mariner,
> And he stoppeth one of three.
> "By thy long grey beard and glittering eye,
> Now wherefore stopp'st thou me?"

40,000 MILES IN A CANOE

ONE

AN ADVENTUROUS PROPOSITION

IT WAS DURING the Spring of 1901, in Victoria, BC, that Mr Luxton, a Canadian journalist, asked me if I thought I could accomplish a voyage round the world in a smaller vessel than the American yawl *Spray*, in which Captain Slocum, an American citizen, had successfully circumnavigated the globe.

'What were the dimensions of the *Spray*,' I enquired.

'About twelve tons,' Mr Luxton replied.

'Well, I think we can go one better,' said I.

'There is five thousand dollars in it, out of which you will receive two thousand five hundred if we cross the three oceans,' Mr Luxton told me, 'and apart from that I shall publish an illustrated book after we complete the voyage, and you shall have half of what we make out of it.'

'Do I understand, Mr Luxton,' I said, 'that you intend to go yourself on the cruise you are speaking about?'

'I certainly do,' was the reply. 'How otherwise could I publish a book?'

'Did you not tell me some time ago that you have never been to sea, and have not had any experience in sailing boats?'

'I did. But did you not tell me at the time that you could sail a boat round the world by yourself? I therefore call upon you now to prove your statement. Instead of making the trip alone, as you said you could, you might just as well take me along, and I give you my word now that I shall do my best to help you in sailing the boat.'

I had been acquainted with Mr Luxton for some time, and knew him to be a temperate man, full of ambition, and his word as good as his bond. I accepted his proposal.

Mr Luxton having had no experience with boats, it was left to me to secure a suitable vessel and outfit for our intended cruise, and while I was looking round about the east coast of Vancouver Island, where there are boats of all sizes and build, I came across an Indian village where I saw a fairly good-looking canoe lying on the beach. It struck me at once that if we could make our proposed voyage in an Indian canoe we would not only make a world's record for the smallest vessel but also the only canoe that had ever circumnavigated the globe. I at once proceeded to examine and take dimensions of the canoe, and soon satisfied myself that she was solid, and also large enough to hold the provisions and other articles we would have to carry on our cruise.

While I was looking over the canoe an old Indian came along and gave me to understand, in very broken English, that he was the owner of the vessel and was willing to sell her. Now, when purchasing anything from Indians on Vancouver Island a drop out of a flask, the label on which reads 'Old Rye', goes a long way, because it makes them good natured and liberal. I know that if my old friend 'Pat Dasy', the Indian Inspector, had caught me in the act he would have given me three months in which to repent. But business is business, and with the aid of my flask I secured the canoe for a reasonable price. As the bargain, and probably, also, the little drop of whisky, had made the old fellow feel pretty good, he presented me with a human skull, which he claimed was that of his father, who had built the canoe fifty years previously.

Whether there was any truth in his statement I do not pretend to know, as these Indians are apt to tell a white man anything as long as they think there is a chance of getting something out of him, and I am inclined to doubt it very much. However, the canoe was sound and answered my purpose admirably, and as the skull was one of the real old flat heads I accepted it to take along as a curio. I then brought her to a small boat-building yard where I put her in such condition as I thought necessary for my purpose.

The canoe as I bought her was made out of one solid red cedar log; in other words, she was a proper 'dugout', as used by the Indians for travelling about, propelled by means of paddles, and at times, when the wind and weather were in their favour, a small square sail was used. Red cedar is very durable, but soft and easily split. I was therefore obliged to take great precautions in strengthening her so that she would be able to withstand the rolling and tumbling about in hard sailing or probably in the heavy gales she would most likely encounter during our trip. To put the little vessel in a seaworthy condition I bent, twenty-four inches apart, one-inch square oak frames inside the hull from one end to the other, fastened with galvanised iron nails, and as the canoe was not quite deep enough for my purpose I built up her sides seven inches. Inside of the vessel I fastened two-by-four-inch floor timbers, over which I placed a kelson of similar measurement, and fastened the same with bolts to a three-by-eight-inch keel. On the bottom of the keel I fastened three hundred pounds of lead. She was then decked over, and I built a five-by-eight-feet cabin in her and a cockpit for steering, after which I rigged her with three small masts and four small fore and aft sails, spreading in all two hundred and thirty square feet of canvas. The masts were stayed with small wire, and all running gear led to the cockpit, from where the man at the helm could set or take in all sails.

When all was ready I broke a bottle of wine over her figurehead and called her *Tilikum*, an Indian name the meaning of which is 'Friend'. The *Tilikum*'s dimensions were then as follows:

Length over all, including figurehead	38 ft
Length on bottom	30 ft
Main breadth	5 ft 6 in
Breadth, water-line	4 ft 6 in
Breadth, bottom	3 ft 6 in

I then put on board half a ton of ballast, which was placed between the floor timbers and securely boarded down, and four hundred pounds of sand in four bags was used as shifting ballast to keep the boat in good sailing trim. About one hundred gallons of fresh water in two galvanised iron tanks were placed under the cockpit. Three months' provisions, consisting mostly of tinned goods; one camera; two rifles; one double-barrelled shot gun; one revolver; ammunition; barometer and navigating instruments completed our equipment. With everything on board, including ourselves, she drew twenty-four inches aft and twenty-two inches forward.

TWO

VANCOUVER ISLAND

On May 20th the *Tilikum* was lying in the harbour at Victoria, ready for sea. The little vessel was inspected by many people, and the general opinion was that we should never get beyond Cape Flattery, but if that was accomplished we should never get back to land. Hundreds of different opinions were expressed in regard to our intended voyage, each spelled disaster for the *Tilikum* and her crew. However, my mate and I had made up our minds that nothing should stop us from making at least a good attempt at a successful voyage.

The following morning at six o'clock the weather was fine, so we pulled up our little twenty-five-pound anchor, and, with a light easterly breeze, sailed out of Victoria Harbour and shaped our course for the Straits of Juan de Fuca. The easterly breeze followed us until we rounded Race Rock, about nine miles from Victoria, when the wind hauled into the west, and as the tide was also against us our progress was very slow. We made tack for tack during the day with little or no progress, and anchored in a small bay a few miles west of Race Rock for the night.

At daybreak the wind was in the eastern quadrant again, so we hove up anchor, set all sail, and once more sailed before the wind, this time heading for the Pacific Ocean. During the afternoon the wind increased to a fresh breeze, and at three o'clock we were down to Cape Flattery, where the blue bosom of the great ocean lay before us. The wind hauling into the south-west, with threatening-looking weather, we kept off for Port San Juan, where we remained a few days weather bound.

At six o'clock on the morning of May 27th another start was made. The wind was from the north-east, with fine clear weather, and under all sail the *Tilikum* was headed for the open sea. The wind being off shore the water was fairly smooth, and with the fresh breeze blowing our canoe went along at the rate of six knots an hour, the mountains on Vancouver Island sinking lower and lower in the sea behind us. At half-past ten the wind hauled into the south-east, accompanied by thick and rainy weather, and the land was soon lost to sight. The wind kept increasing, and half an hour later it was blowing a gale, with the *Tilikum* lying under small sails. Just before the land disappeared I took a bearing of the south-west point of Vancouver Island.

It was my mate's first voyage at sea, and consequently he was not feeling too well! In addition to this, the weather looked very threatening. I therefore decided to make for a small bay near Cape Beal Lighthouse, and rounding the point at nine o'clock we anchored for the night.

The little bay was calm when we dropped the hook, and as my mate and I were hungry, besides being wet through from both rain and spray, we changed our garments and had a bite to eat. By ten o'clock we were sound asleep in our cabin. Mr Luxton occupied the only little bunk we had, and I took a small seat on the other side of the cabin. The space between the bunk and seat was only ten inches. The bunk was large enough for a man of moderate size to sleep comfortably in, but the seat, or top of the locker, where I had to rest, was only fourteen inches wide, and I therefore had to lie very quiet to keep from rolling off. We both slept soundly till all at once the *Tilikum* gave a quick lurch, which tumbled me up against the mainmast, between the bunk and locker, but my head struck on the cabin floor, which not only woke me up but nearly knocked my brains out. However, I got up quickly, and on looking out of the cabin door, in spite of the darkness I could see sharp breaking seas rolling one after the other into the bay, with a fresh breeze blowing at the same time. I advised Mr Luxton to get up quickly, for I realised that we must change our position. No sooner had I spoken the word than he was on deck. A few minutes afterwards we had our anchor up and all sail set, and out we sailed into open water. At daybreak the weather cleared up nicely and we sailed into the harbour at Dodges Cove, where there was quite a large Indian village.

Quite early in the morning we dropped anchor, and soon after the Indians came off in their canoes and asked us if we had any whisky for sale. I told them that we were not in that line of business, but had just come in weather bound. The Indians did not seem to believe our statement at first, as they offered us ten dollars a bottle. However, we at last made them understand that we had no whisky of any kind on board, at the same time trying to be friendly with them, in which we were eventually successful.

Dodges Cove is located about five miles north-west of Cape Beal, and is a safe little harbour for small vessels, which can lie between two little islands, and on either side there is quite a large Indian village. The houses are built along the water's edge with a fine sand beach in front of them. This beach was covered with canoes of all sizes. In the vicinity of Dodges Cove, and not very far off, are all kinds of small islands, covered with trees and intersected by small bays and inlets, where game and wild birds, principally ducks, abound, and the waters are full of fish.

During the forenoon an old gentleman came alongside our boat in a small canoe, and introduced himself as McKenzie, the store-keeper of the village. We invited him to come on board. In the course of our conversation Mr McKenzie told us he had been keeping a store there for a number of years, and from the way he spoke led us to understand he had made quite a pile.

'It seems to me that this is rather a lonely place in which to live. Wouldn't you rather live in a city?' I asked.

'City? No, not for me,' he replied. 'City life is not to be compared with life on the west coast of Vancouver Island, with its fresh, pure air and mild climate. The land is full of timber and game, and the water covered with wild birds of all descriptions. Yes,' he continued, 'and besides all that, when the tide is low the table is set.'

Mr McKenzie was a real good old fellow, as the Scots generally are, and said, 'Come up to my house and stop with me for a few days, and I will show you how we live on Vancouver Island.'

We accepted the hearty invitation, and after anchoring the *Tilikum* where we could see her from his house, went with him in his canoe. McKenzie's residence and store were about a hundred feet from the water's edge, He was a bachelor, and did all his own work, including the cooking—and a first-class housekeeper and cook he was. He also had some very good Scotch whisky on his shelf.

It was about ten o'clock when we got to McKenzie's house, and after we had sampled the whisky our host said, 'I presume you people are hungry, so I will get something ready to eat.'

It happened to be low water, so I said, 'Mr McKenzie, I heard you saying a while ago that when the tide was low the table was set. What about that?'

'I will show you,' said McKenzie.

He thereupon took a tin bucket and spade, and went down to the beach. After throwing up a few shovelfuls of sand we picked up clams enough in five minutes to fill the bucket, and at noon we had the finest clam chowder I ever had in my life.

The next morning my mate and I slept rather late. About seven o'clock we heard our host shouting, 'Breakfast ready.'

We were soon up and dressed and sat down to breakfast. There was some fine fresh red salmon on the table, and I asked Mac where he obtained it.

'I went trawling this morning and got seven in less than half an hour,' he said.

Our meal over, we went out to shoot ducks, and came home with a load before noon. The next day we shot five deer. I certainly agreed with Mac when he said that the west coast of Vancouver Island was a paradise.

Our friend was a very busy man. Most of his time was, of course, taken up in his store selling goods to the Indians, and they were very slow in buying. The women particularly would look at an article that cost about five or ten cents for an hour, and then go away without buying it. An old Indian woman came in one day and after pricing everything in the store finally left without spending five cents. Mac said she was nothing but an old hag, but I think she understood Mac, for she turned round and said something in her own language which I did not understand, though Mac apparently did, for he kept very quiet until she got outside. Then he said some more things.

THREE

WITH THE INDIANS

WE HAD BEEN with our host nearly a week, when I said to my mate, 'Look here, Luxton, we have a long way to go yet, so had better make another start.' But Luxton was anxious to get some Indian curios before we sailed.

Mac said, 'Stop till to-morrow, for it is the Sabbath and we will go to church.'

So we decided to stay, on my part chiefly, because I thought Mac had a little religious feeling in him, and therefore would like our company to church.

The place was crowded with Indian men and women, both old and young. The missionary was an Englishman, an earnest, good man, who tried his very best to make the Indians understand. Unfortunately, he was not well versed in the language, and as the Indians did not understand much English he was obliged to mix the two a little to make himself understood.

During this particular morning he was trying to explain what a sinner was, which he found very difficult to do. All at once, the old woman whom Mac had called an old hag the day before, got up from the very front bench and without saying a word came down to where we were sitting. Pointing her finger at McKenzie she looked at the missionary and said, 'That is one.'

Mac was one of those long-whiskered old Scotchmen and very good natured. All he said was, 'I will get even with her the next time she wants to buy a new dress.'

The bad weather returned for a few days. The wind was in the south-west and we were therefore obliged to wait a little longer for better weather. One day I stopped on board to do a little work that had to be done, and my mate went out hunting, returning, a little before dark, with a bag full of birds. After we had finished our supper he said to me confidentially, 'Say, John, I have made some great discoveries to-day. I have found a place where we can get a boat-load of all kinds of Indian curios, the best in the land; but we must keep it from old Mac, as he would not like it.'

'Where is it?' I asked, 'and why wouldn't Mac like us to get them?'

'Because it is in an Indian graveyard, and we will have to go there at night.'

I wanted some curios myself—but to rob a graveyard at night! Why, it gave me the shivers to think of it.

Next morning we went out hunting, and after a little while reached the graveyard. Instead of proper graves, the dead bodies had been put in all kinds of old boxes and left above the ground. Some of them were even placed in tops of trees, and all kinds of Indian tools, baskets, spears, old guns, mats, etc., were piled upon the coffins. On and round one I counted fifteen bags of flour. I found out later that it was a custom among the Indians when one of them dies that most if not all his belongings go with the body to the graveyard.

There was one large cave leading from a gravel beach about four hundred feet into a small mountain, apparently washed in years ago by large seas coming in from the Pacific Ocean. But at the time of my visit the cave was quite an appreciable height above the high-water mark. The mouth of this cave must have been about forty feet in diameter, the shape nearly round, and getting gradually smaller and smaller from the mouth.

My mate and I walked up to the innermost end. It was as dark as night, and we were obliged to strike a match to see. There we found dead bodies all wrapped up in some kind of Indian blanket. In some of the blankets nothing was left but human bones. We helped ourselves to some of the old flat-head skulls, which we were destined, however, to leave behind on our way out, for when we got to the entrance of the cave we saw some Indians outside apparently waiting for us to come out. As they were armed we dropped the skulls and walked out to meet them. They appeared to be very angry with us for going into the cave, but upon our assuring them that we did not know of the cemetery inside the cave they let us off with a warning. We went back a few nights later and got some curios.

We also became acquainted with the Indian chief, who invited us to come with him in his canoe on the next calm day to catch a whale. Hunting whales in a canoe was something I had never seen before, so I accepted the chief's invitation, but as it could only be done on a calm day we were obliged to wait some time before the weather was fine. Three canoes were got ready one afternoon. The Indians put on board each canoe whale spears, long lines and large sea-lion's bladders, together with some provisions and blankets, and the next morning at one o'clock we started off with three men in each canoe, except the one I was in, which had four. Of course I was only a passenger.

The distance from Dodges Cove to the ocean is only a few miles, but we went about ten miles off the coast before we sighted a whale, and a big one at that. The three canoes went along abreast, about five hundred yards apart. I was in the middle one. The canoe on our right sighted the whale, and after giving the signal all three rushed after the monster. It was some time before we got near him. The canoe on my left got in the first and only spear, but was apparently too near when the harpoon struck. The whale gave just one slap with his tail which smashed the canoe to pieces. The three men swam for dear life, while the whale, with the harpoon inside him, rushed along at full speed. A long line was fastened to the spear, to which were attached three sea-lion bladders, and as these floated on the surface we could see the direction he took. After picking up the three Indians, we went after him, but it seems that the whale got too much of a start, as we lost sight of the bladders and never saw the whale again. We then returned to get another canoe.

As the weather kept calm we went out again the next morning, this time with better success. We were only about five miles off the coast when we sighted two large whales, and in a very short time one of the canoes was fast to one of them. The whale travelled so rapidly that the Indians had to let him go with the line and bladders, after which all three canoes put after him, following the bladders, which were sometimes on top of the water and sometimes lost to view, though only just for a second, when he would come up again.

After the whale had gone quite a distance, with the heavy drag of the bladders behind him, he slackened his speed and the canoes gradually came up with him. They then drove two more spears into his body, which urged him to make another start; but the canoes stuck to him, and the Indians, continually throwing spears, soon had him conquered.

It seemed to me as if the sea monster knew that he had lost the battle as he gradually came under the control of the Indians. With one canoe on each side of him, and one behind, they led him along under his own power towards a sand beach near Dodges Cove, where they wished to cut him up. When we got about a mile from the beach the whale gradually stopped headway. The chief told me that he was dying. The Indians then fastened all the bladders on to the whale to stop him from sinking, after which the three canoes got ahead of him and towed him in. He was then placed on the sand beach at high tide, and when the tide was low and the whale high and dry nearly all the natives from Dodges Cove, old and young, cut him up, after which the Indians held a great feast, where the whale meat was equally divided among all the inhabitants. The chief gave me a piece of the whale meat, which I cut up in strips and fried, and it turned out to be excellent steak.

FOUR

INTO THE WIDE PACIFIC—SEA-GOING QUALITIES OF THE TILIKUM

BETWEEN OLD MAC, the Indians, fishing, war dances, canoe racing and our own hunting and fishing, it was made so pleasant for us that we stopped at Dodges Cove till July 6th.

Of course everything had been ready for sea for some time, and both of us slept on board that night. I got up early next morning, and found the weather was fine, with a gentle breeze blowing off the land. I said to my mate, 'All hands on deck, heave up anchor and set sail'; and in a few minutes we were under all sail and heading out towards the ocean.

The light wind, which was from the north-east, gradually hauled into the north-west, increasing as we got further off the land. We shaped our course to the south, as our plan was to cross the equator in one hundred and twenty-five degrees west longitude and make the Marquesas Islands our first place of call. During the middle part of the day we had a fresh north-westerly breeze, and at three o'clock, when the mountain tops on Vancouver Island sank very low, I was sitting in the cockpit steering, when I saw, quite a long way from us, a splash of water thrown up in the air. I kept watching that place for a little while, and then saw that it was a whale spouting. I knew from former experience that that part of the ocean was full of whales, but as my mate had never seen one spouting, and was at that time down in the cabin making afternoon tea, I called him up to have a look at the sight. While both of us were watching the whale we noticed that he was coming towards us, and every few minutes throwing more than half of his large body out of the water, and then falling back again, which latter caused the splash. The big sea monster came nearer and nearer to us, and we soon discovered that he was trying to get away from the killers, which are the worst enemy of the whale. The whale was doing his best to get away, swinging his large flippers about, his only means of defence, but, whenever he came to the surface, the killers, sometimes as many as half a dozen, would jump on top of him, while others underneath ripped him up with their large fins. It was a battle for life, but we could see plainly that the whale, large as he was, weakened fast from the awful punishment his enemies inflicted upon him. The last time the combatants showed themselves they were only about a hundred yards from us, and as we had our rifles all ready we fired a few shots among them, after which they all disappeared.

The weather kept fine and clear all day, and with a fresh breeze the *Tilikum* went along like a little ship. That night before dark we lost sight of land, which we did not see again for fifty-eight days. We were now in the open ocean, and running into harbour for the night, or tying the *Tilikum* up to a tree, was out of the question. We were now obliged to stay at sea by night as well as day and take the bitter with the sweet. Not only that, we also had to keep under sail and steer the boat on her course, as we had a straight course of at least four thousand miles to travel before seeing land again, and to make four thousand miles on the ocean in a small boat a man must keep his eyes open. Therefore, the very first thing which I had to teach my companion was how to look after the *Tilikum* while I slept.

My mate was a man of good commonsense, and as the weather kept fine for several days I had no trouble in teaching him enough seamanship to take care of the *Tilikum* at night as well as day. From that time we took turn about on deck, and we also regulated our meal hours as follows: breakfast at seven o'clock, which consisted of porridge and condensed milk, sometimes boiled eggs, with coffee and hard tack; dinner at noon, at which we generally had boiled potatoes, tinned meat of different kinds, coffee and hard tack and butter; for supper, at six o'clock, we generally made some kind of stew from what was left over from dinner, finishing up with tea, hard tack and butter. The above is not much of a daily bill of fare, but we got along fine with it, and always kept in good condition. In cooking we also took turns.

The weather kept fine and the north-west wind moderate until July 11th, when it started to increase during the morning hours, accompanied by heavy passing clouds from the north-west. At noon the *Tilikum* was going along at her very best speed under all sail. The seas began to get larger, and at times some of the tops would come over just enough to give us a good soaking. As the wind and sea kept on increasing, I took in the mainsail and spanker, and under the foresail the *Tilikum* went along nicely. Still the wind kept on increasing, and at three o'clock in the afternoon it was blowing very hard, the seas getting dangerous for a small boat. I thought it best to heave to in time, which would simultaneously give me a chance to experiment with the boat to find out under what sails she would lay head to sea the best.

In preparing to bring the boat round head to sea, I first of all lowered all sail to make her go as slow as possible before the wind. I then told my mate to go forward, hold on to the foremast and stand by to drop the sea anchor overboard when I said the word. To my great surprise he refused to do this, telling me that he would not do it for his grandmother. The *Tilikum* was going along under bare poles before the wind and sea quite comfortably, now and then taking a little spray over, and as there was no particular hurry to heave to, I called to him to come out in the cockpit and sit down alongside me while I gave him a little advice; but instead of coming out as I asked him he just put his head out of the cabin door and listened to what I had to say.

'Look here, Norman,' I said, 'I want to give you a little explanation of the danger of running before a breaking sea. Many large vessels are sent to the bottom with one breaking sea by keeping the vessel running before a gale too long, and where would the *Tilikum* and you and I be if we let her run before a heavy gale. This is not a heavy gale yet, but it will be by to-night, and therefore we must put our boat in safety before the seas get too large.'

'Is it not much better and safer to let the boat run along with the seas? She will then go nearly as fast as the waves, and I should think, therefore, that the seas would have no power on her and the boat be much safer,' my mate replied.

'It probably looks that way to you, but the reverse is the case. To begin with, waves (which seamen generally call seas) in a gale run at a speed of about twenty-seven to twenty-eight miles an hour. Our boat at the very best can make only eight miles an hour, and the eight miles are mostly made when she is on top of the seas, because when the boat is between the seas the wind blows over her and she consequently loses headway. As long as there is no break on the seas we are quite safe in letting her go as fast as she likes, but when the seas are breaking we run a great risk by allowing the boat to run before them. The seas are starting to break now, so we must prepare to heave to.'

'I fail to see the point yet,' my mate contended, 'as to why a boat should be safer with her headway stopped than when she is sailing along the sea and wind.'

'Look here, Norman,' I replied, 'I should like you to be perfectly satisfied on this point, for then I know you will have more confidence in our boat. I will therefore explain to you where the danger comes in with running before breaking seas. When a vessel runs before breaking seas her stern is pulled down by suction of the water, and the faster she sails the greater is the suction in this case, and when a breaking sea overtakes the boat, and her stern is held down by suction, the breaker will go over the top of her with tremendous force. One breaking sea of that kind may send a large vessel to the bottom; on the other hand, if the broken sea runs under her stern then the bow will be way down and the stern high up, and the rudder will have no control over the vessel. She will then come round sideways, and the same breaker will most likely turn her bottom upwards. But if a boat or ship in a heavy gale is stopped from going ahead through the water, she is free from suction and consequently will rise even to a breaking sea. It matters very little whether a vessel lays head on, stern on, or sideways, as long as her headway is stopped. There is only one way of stopping a sailing vessel from going ahead in a heavy gale, and that is, to bring her head to wind and sea, and this is called "heaving to". Large sailing vessels hove to under storm sails and properly loaded as a rule lie very dry and comfortable. They may take quite a lot of water on board during a heavy gale, but water in a case of this kind just rolls over the rails and is harmless. If she does ship dangerous seas when hove to it is a sure sign that the vessel is carrying too much sail. Now, in our case, with our small vessel and only a three-quarter-inch cedar deck we cannot allow even one sea to board us, as one sea breaking over this vessel will most likely put us out of business. Therefore, to keep seas from breaking over us we must first of all heave to in time, and heave her to in such a way that she will not ship heavy water even in the worst gale; and that is what we are going to do right now. You understand me now, don't you?'

My mate looked at me and then at the waves, and I know he was wishing himself ashore. I then tied a life-line round his waist, and told him to go forward and stand by to drop the sea anchor over the bow when I gave the word. This time he obeyed my orders, as I assured him that I would pull him in again if he should get washed overboard. He managed to get forward on his hands and knees, and when forward held on to the foremast to wait for orders. By this time there was quite a large sea running, and some of the waves were breaking heavily. I waited for a fairly smooth sea to come along, and when she got on top I put the helm down, and as she came round inside of a few seconds, and just before swinging head to sea, I pulled the small sail down which I had set for that occasion.

When the boat got head to sea a breaker came up in front of her which for a few moments looked very much like a brick wall. I shouted at the top of my voice, 'Throw the sea anchor over,' but instead of doing this he dropped it on deck and climbed up the foremast, and owing to the smallness of the boat his weight on top of the mast almost caused her to turn over. I quickly took a pull on the life-line and told him to come down, and as the sea had passed the boat by that time he came down just about as quickly as he went up. After throwing the sea anchor over, the *Tilikum* drifted along with the wind and sea and soon tightened the anchor rope; then the boat lay about five points from the wind, and, considering the sea which was running at the time, was fairly comfortable and apparently out of danger. I thought that she would be more comfortable and safer if I could manage to get her to lay closer to the wind; I therefore set my leg-of-mutton spanker and hauled the sheet in flat, which made a riding sail instead of a driving sail out of it. No sooner was the sail set than she swung her head to the wind and seas to about two and a half points. The *Tilikum* certainly rode fine that way.

I then said to my mate, 'The *Tilikum* is all right now and we are as safe here as in the Victoria Hotel in Victoria, BC. Now, tell me, why did you climb the foremast instead of attending to the sea anchor when I asked you?'

'Well,' Luxton replied, 'when I saw that sea coming up in front of us I made sure it was coming clean on top of us!'

During the afternoon, while running before the strong wind and large seas, the boat had taken some spray over, and both my mate and myself got pretty wet; in fact, we were soaked to the skin; but now that she was hove to, the decks, with the exception of the forward end, were quite dry. We then changed our clothes, had our supper, and then both of us sat down in the cockpit to have a smoke and talk about the poor people on shore, who at that very moment might have trees and houses blown about their heads.

The wind and sea were increasing fast towards evening, but the bow of the *Tilikum* rose finely to every sea.

'By Jove, John,' said Luxton, at the same time tapping me on the shoulder, 'I thought sure it was all off with us when we hove to and I saw that big sea in front of us, but to see this little canoe going over the top of those big monsters without rolling or tumbling about is most wonderful. Well, if ever we do get back to land, when I publish our experiences in this gale, not one person in a hundred will believe my story.'

I may say that my mate, a young man, had never seen salt water until we went out in the *Tilikum*. Nevertheless he proved himself a first-class shipmate in every way, good sailor, good cook, and quick of action, but he acknowledges himself that the quickest move he ever made was in going up the mast.

At dark I put a light on deck, and one of us laid down in the bunk and the other one on the seat. The little vessel laid very comfortably during that heavy gale, in fact, well enough for both of us to go to sleep. Owing, however, to the wind keeping up its fury all night I got up every now and then and had a look out on deck. But the night was dark and the wind howling, so I could see nothing but the breaking water on top of the large seas, shining through the darkness, while the roaring noise of the breaking seas made us feel rather gloomy during that night.

We were very glad when daylight made its appearance on the eastern horizon. The wind kept up its fury all the forenoon, accompanied by heavy seas and passing clouds. At midday the sky was clear and the wind moderating, and by standing on top of the cabin deck and putting one arm round the mainmast to steady myself, and watching my chance when the boat was on top of a large sea, I managed to get a good observation of the noon sun. According to that observation our little vessel had drifted twenty-four miles to the southward in sixteen hours while she had been hove to under the sea anchor. The wind during that gale was from NNW.

During the afternoon the wind kept on lightening, the seas getting smaller, and the sky clearing, and the first gale of our long voyage was over. The *Tilikum* had weathered it without the least trouble, not losing as much as a ropeyarn; in fact, the gale had not left a trace of any kind either on the *Tilikum* or her crew. The only thing the gale had done was to give us great confidence in the *Tilikum*'s capability of carrying us to our appointed destination. During the afternoon the wind kept on decreasing. At four o'clock there was still a strong breeze blowing from the same direction as it had kept all day, but the seas had lost their dangerous breaking tops, and therefore the danger of the same had disappeared. I hauled down the small storm sail, took in the sea anchor, hoisted the staysail, and the *Tilikum* swung round before the wind and sea on her southerly course. I kept her going under small sails for a while, but at midnight we were spinning along once more under all sails.

FIVE

THE CALM BELT—LAND IN SIGHT!

AFTER THE GALE, the weather settled fine, and clear, with a nice, steady northerly sailing breeze, the *Tilikum* making from a hundred to a hundred and fifty miles a day. On July 17th, shortly after breakfast, we sighted a sail on our starboard bow, apparently a sailing vessel standing to the eastward. I changed our course to meet the stranger. The wind was rather light during the forenoon, and it took us quite a while till we met, which was about eleven o'clock. When alongside we found the vessel was the US barquantine *Mary Winkelman*, from Honolulu with a cargo of sugar, and bound for San Francisco. The captain and his wife invited us on board for dinner, but as there was quite a large sea running at the time, we were afraid of something happening to our little canoe if she was brought up against the side of the barquantine by one of the seas.

'Would you like to have some fresh bread?' the captain's wife asked us.

We gratefully accepted the offer and the captain lowered a few loaves.

After comparing longitudes we said good-bye, and I put the *Tilikum* on her southerly course. The place where we met the *Mary Winkelman* was three hundred and fifty miles south-west of San Francisco. Just as I swung the *Tilikum* on her course the captain shouted, 'I will report you when I get to San Francisco,' which he did, as I found out later. The wind kept light during the afternoon, but at three o'clock the barquantine was out of sight, and we were once more left by ourselves on the ocean,

Alone, alone, all, all alone,
Alone on a wide, wide sea!

The weather kept fine and clear day after day, and the wind kept light and variable from the north. Averaging about one hundred miles a day we soon got into the north-east trade wind, which was also moderate with fine clear weather. A fresh-water yachtsman could have sailed the *Tilikum* through that part of the Pacific. My mate thought then that all our troubles were over, and that we had nothing but fine weather and smooth sailing before us. The weather was certainly fine and our sailing was as smooth as any sailing could possibly be, but as we were approaching the equator the weather got warmer and warmer every day. It finally got so hot that it was next to an impossibility to sleep in the cabin. As soon as we lay down, the sweat would just run out of us. Then, again, in sitting in the cockpit we could not keep our eyes open while steering. Still, the latter had to be done at all costs. One night, while I was asleep during my watch below, I heard the sails flapping and woke up. I said to myself, 'Hullo! My mate is asleep at the helm!' Thereupon I looked out of the cabin door and there he was, his head swinging from side to side, and the boat up in the wind.

'Wake up, out there,' I shouted.

He woke up all right, and then denied that he had been sleeping, and having no room for settling arguments on the *Tilikum* I dropped the matter.

Day after day the north-east wind kept light, and some days we only made about fifty miles. The weather also kept pretty warm. About a week later my mate again fell asleep at the rudder, and the flapping of the sails woke me up. Looking out of the companionway, I saw him in the same condition as before. The night was dark and cloudy, and he could not see me from the outside, so I took a bucketful of sea water and from the inside of the cabin poured the water over his head and laid down again, without him seeing me. As I said before, my mate was a newspaper man, and therefore knew how to string language, but I don't think Mr Luxton would like to see in print the language he used, so I shall keep it out just to oblige him.

About three hours later I got up, and as usual said, 'Good morning, Norman.' He did not speak, but looked very cross at me.

'What is the matter, Norman; don't you feel well?' I asked him.

'Look here, John,' he said, 'this boat should be put in a glass case instead of on the sea.'

'Why?' I asked.

'A vessel that ships seas in this kind of weather should never sail outside of a millpond,' and then he used some more of his own special brand of language.

I don't think he knew that I had thrown the water, but by considering it, later on, he thought differently, for some nights afterwards I got the same kind of a sea over me, but all I said the next morning was, 'I agree with what you said, Norman, this boat should be in a glass case or on a millpond.'

In the latter part of July, when in latitude seventeen degrees north and longitude one hundred and twenty-five west, the trade wind became very light, and the sky cloudy. At three o'clock in the afternoon a heavy westerly squall, accompanied by rain, struck the *Tilikum*, which made us take in sail pretty quickly. The squall was short and sweet, but I knew then, by the way the weather acted, that we had sailed out of the north-east trade wind and got into what is called the calm belt or Doldrums. It is rather unusual, and certainly very unlucky, to lose the north-east trade wind as soon as that, as it generally means a long spell of dirty and contrary weather, which we certainly got. Why that part of the ocean is called the calm belt I don't understand, because, from the trouble we had there with the *Tilikum*, and also from former experiences, I should call it anything but that. 'The belt of the seamen's trouble' would be a far more suitable name. For sixteen long days and nights we had nothing but trouble with the weather and the sails; it was up sails and down sails, hauling in sheets or slacking them, all the time. During that time, we experienced about fifty changes of weather every day. It would be pouring with rain for a little while, and then the sun would blaze down on us. The next thing would be a heavy squall of wind and rain combined, but my mate and I stuck to it. I don't think either of us ever dozed at the rudder while going through this belt of trouble. The distance to the nearest land about the time we were going through all that drilling was about fifteen hundred miles, so there was no chance of running in somewhere and tying up to a tree as we did on Vancouver Island.

One day a heavy squall of wind and rain came in from the south-west, which made me take in every sail when it struck us, but in about ten minutes' time the squall hauled round by the way of north, east, and then south-east, after which the rain stopped, the sky cleared, and the wind became a steady fresh breeze, which soon convinced me that we were now in the south-east trade wind. We were then in about five degrees north latitude and one hundred and twenty-eight degrees west longitude, and our course to the Marquesas Islands about SSW, distant one thousand miles. In sailing by the wind we could have made the Marquesas Islands all right, but owing to the wind being too strong, almost too strong for the *Tilikum* to sail by the wind, we changed our minds, and instead of steering for the Marquesas, shaped our course for Penrhyn Island in latitude eight degrees fifty-five minutes south and longitude one hundred and fifty-eight degrees six minutes west. The south-east trade wind was a good leading wind for us to Penrhyn, and as it gradually hauled into the ESE, it was still better, for this gave us the wind on the port quarter, which the *Tilikum* liked best of all. In a few days we crossed the equator, after which we had about as much wind as we could take care of.

Under all sail we were running off one hundred and fifty to one hundred and seventy miles a day, and the best day's run we got out of the *Tilikum*, which was also the record for the whole voyage, was one hundred and seventy-seven miles. My mate was by that time an excellent helmsman, otherwise we could never have done it, for we had to keep her going every minute to get that distance out of her. The strong trade wind threw up a large sea, which sometimes would break quite heavily, and when a breaker came along with its roaring noise, my mate would twist his head from one side to the other, watching it coming. Now and then he would say, 'John, I think we had better heave her to, I don't like this. I'm getting nervous.'

'No time to heave to round here,' I said. 'Just watch the forward end of the boat and the compass and keep her on her course, and you will be all right.'

There was no time for dozing at the rudder then, as careless-ness in steering just about that time would have had a bad effect, but as long as she was kept on her course the *Tilikum* was quite safe. Of course at times the water would wash over the deck, and at times it would even come into the cockpit and give us a good soaking, but the weather being warm, we did not mind that in the least. At any rate we kept the *Tilikum* sailing on her western course till September 1st, at dark, when according to my reck-oning we should be very near Penrhyn Island. We hove to for the night and waited for daylight next morning, after which we kept her before the south-east trade wind again.

At seven o'clock, as usual, we had our breakfast, and while we were eating, my mate said, 'I bet that old Waltham watch of yours got out of time and we will not be able to find the island.' At that time, according to my reckoning, we should only be about twelve miles from the island, and I was just about thinking myself that there was something wrong with my navigation. Still, I did not want to let on to my mate what I apprehended. That morning we had been fifty-eight days at sea, and both of us felt we would like to get on solid land once more and stretch our legs.

Penrhyn Island was given in my sailing directory as a low island about eight miles wide, which could be seen from a ship's deck about eight or nine miles distant. By being a little out in navigation we might have sailed by without seeing it, but still, as our distance was not quite up I was in hopes of making it. At any rate, I kept steering the same course as before. My mate was in the cabin washing the breakfast dishes, at the same time grum-bling and growling about my only taking an ordinary Waltham watch for a chronometer, and what would become of us if we did not make land, etc. I could not help listening to him grumbling, but at the same time was almost looking the eyes out of my head trying to find the land. The sky was as clear as could be, and my mate was still at the dishes when I thought I saw something ahead of me that looked like land. But it had disappeared again just as fast as it had appeared above the horizon. I kept looking in that direction, and in a minute or two I saw the same again.

'Land ahead,' I shouted.

In a second my mate was alongside me, saying 'Where?' It had disappeared again, and as my mate could not see it he looked at me; but before he said what he intended I saw it again.

'There it is,' I said; and this time we both saw it and also knew it was real land.

SIX

PENRHYN ISLAND

ON SEEING THE LAND, my mate got so excited that he threw his hat up in the air, and gave three cheers for old Canada. Unfortunately, the hat went overboard, and I had to tack ship to pick it up.

When we got near the island, we saw that it was very small and, being covered with cocoanut trees, it looked rather wild. My South Pacific sailing directory said that the natives on Penrhyn were not to be trusted, and as we were only two in a very small boat I must frankly admit that I did not care about making a landing on that lonely little out-of-the-way island in the great Pacific Ocean, and amongst a lot of dark people who were perhaps cannibals. Therefore I told my mate we had better keep on sailing till we came to Samoa. I surely thought that this advice would have found favour with Luxton, but instead of that he blew up like a stick of dynamite.

'What do you mean by suggesting that we pass by an island like this, the most interesting place we can go to. Never; we must go in at all costs. That is what I have come out for, to see small, out-of-the-way islands and people, and if you look at your agreement you will find it is so. No, John, don't talk to me like that.'

Of course I knew that our agreement called for visiting small inhabited and uninhabited islands, and also that my mate had made up his mind to call in, and it was of no use for me to say any more about it. So I said, 'Well, all right, Norman, we will go in, but by all means let us go about it in a careful way,' to which he readily agreed.

The island was described in the sailing directory as being a low round-shaped lagoon island and inhabited by four hundred South

Sea Islanders, who were not to be trusted, and that there were several entrances into the lagoon, one in particular on the east and another on the north side. With the fresh ESE trade wind we steered for the eastern entrance, and I said to myself, 'If the natives do get after us, the easterly wind will also be a fair wind to take us through the lagoon and out of the northern channel.'

With our four one-hundred-pound bags of sand, which we used as shifting ballast, we fortified ourselves in the cockpit, and with all our firearms loaded and lying alongside us, ready for instant use, we sailed in for the east end of the island. We soon got near the east coast, but could not see the entrance into the lagoon. We then shaped our course along the coast to the northward, and saw two wrecks of large sailing vessels lying in amongst the rocks and breakers. They were lying abeam a quarter of a mile apart. One of them was pretty well broken up, but the other was lying on her side, with the hull apparently still in fairly good condition. Shortly after passing the two ill-fated vessels we saw the roofs of some buildings quite a way in amongst the cocoanut trees, but so far no entrance to the lagoon. We kept on following the coast to the northward, and finally reached the gap we were looking for. It was about half a mile wide, and there were large breakers at the entrance. We could see from the outside, while still sailing amongst the large seas, the perfectly smooth shining water of the lagoon, and as we got nearer and nearer could see small boats and canoes sailing on the lagoon. My mate said, 'Now just look at that picture. It is the finest I have ever seen. See that fine smooth piece of water with small boats sailing about in different directions, while the bright morning sun shining on all of it gives the water a silvery colour. Just look at the sails of the boats and canoes as white as snow, with all kinds of tropical birds flying about; and all this surrounded by a ring of green cocoanut trees! Well, John,' he continued, 'there is no artist in the world that could make a picture look so beautiful as this; and to think that you wanted to pass this place without calling in!'

'You may change your mind when you meet the natives,' I replied.

As we still had the strong ENE trade wind driving us along we soon got out of the large seas and into smooth water. The strip of land round the lagoon was only about half a mile wide, and as soon as we got through the entrance we changed our course along the land towards the south, where we had seen signs of habitation shortly before. While sailing along near the land we saw several native men among the cocoanut trees with very scanty clothing on.

I said to my mate, 'Those fellows may have us for supper to-night.'

'If they do they will have to fight hard for it,' he replied.

We continued sailing along the land, and soon saw some houses near the water's edge. Next the village came into full view, and not far from the village lay a fine-looking schooner, painted white. To all appearances it was a European vessel, and to make sure we hoisted our little Canadian flag, which was answered at once from the schooner, which proved to be a Frenchman. Neither of us could speak a word of French, but, as I told my mate, in all my travels I have been on vessels of every nation, and have never yet found a ship on which there wasn't someone who could speak English. At any rate, we changed our course and steered for the schooner, and in about fifteen minutes were alongside her.

The first words we heard from the French vessel were, in plain English, 'Take your sails in and we will give you a line to tie up with.' With that, one of the sailors threw a line across our bow. We soon lowered our sails and made fast to the schooner.

'Where are you from?' was the next question from the deck of the schooner.

'From Victoria, BC,' I answered.

'Come on board,' the same voice said. One of the seamen put a ladder over the side of the schooner, and both of us clambered up.

The first to greet us was a strong, heavy set man. He shook hands with us, and said, in good English, 'My name is Dexter. Allow me to welcome you gentlemen on board my vessel.'

Captain Dexter then introduced us to Mr Winchester. Dexter, an American, and Winchester, an Englishman, were partners in the schooner, and were trading among the South Pacific Islands.

We were hardly on board the schooner when the chief of the village came off to welcome us to his island. Soon after that, natives, old and young, came off in their canoes and boats to get a glimpse of the strangers. The natives certainly looked very much better than I had pictured them in my mind. They were quite tall and well built, and apparently very polite. Some of the women with long black hair hanging down their backs were exceedingly pretty, and all wore calico dresses, which were as white as snow.

During the afternoon Captain Dexter took us on shore to the house of the chief, who treated us to some cocoanut milk served in cocoanut shell, after which we were conducted through the village. The houses, which were built of wood and covered with dried cocoanut leaves, were mostly situated along the water front.

'Where do you get all the North American pine from?' I said, seeing that all the houses were built of that lumber.

'Did you see the two wrecks just outside the entrance when you came in?' Captain Dexter asked.

I replied in the affirmative.

'Well,' he said, 'one of them came along here a few years ago with a cargo of lumber for Australia, and got stranded here. The crew managed to get ashore, and as the vessel broke up, the lumber drifted in and naturally the natives helped themselves. The crew stopped here three months, waiting for a vessel to come along to take them off. But they waited in vain. Eventually they decked over the lifeboats which they had saved from the wreck and sailed to Samoa in them. From Samoa they took a steamer for Sydney, where the loss of the ship and cargo was reported. The captain's wife also got lost in the wreck. She was lost because her husband had the same idea as I had—that the natives were murderers and cannibals. When the vessel struck the boats were lowered, and, to keep out of the hands of the natives, the captain ordered the crew to pull to sea, instead of for the shore. The boat which held the captain and his wife was overturned in the breakers, and the poor woman was drowned. All the rest got ashore and were received with open arms by the natives on the island. The owners of the lost cargo at once sent for a duplicate cargo, and a vessel was chartered. After the cargo was put on board she set sail for Australia, but she also only got as far as Penrhyn Island, where she piled up on a dark night alongside the other one.'

No doubt many of my readers will think this is a most wonderful story, and so I did. When I got to London I went to the trouble of seeing the secretary of Lloyd's, who assured me that the story was correct.

These were the two wrecks we saw when coming in, and from which the natives got the lumber to build their town. I asked Captain Dexter how the natives made a living, to which he replied, that the natives of the South Sea in their own way are the most independent people in the world.

'To start with,' he continued, 'you see for yourself that this, like all the rest of the low islands, is covered with cocoanut trees, which are the most profitable tree they have. The wood is hard and can be used for any kind of woodwork. The leaves are used to make different kinds of plain and fancy hats, cloths, mats, baskets, brooms, scrubbers, house roofing, fish corrals, and to make large "flareups" for the purpose of attracting flying-fish to the canoes, in which they set out to catch them.'

The sap of the tree is obtained from the blossom, and as much as a gallon and a half can be extracted from a single tree. This sap when fresh tastes like excellent cool cider. If left standing for a day it turns into syrup, and in two or three days it becomes a liquor similar to rum, and very little of it will make a man intoxicated.

If the sap is not drawn out of the tree it will grow cocoanuts. Each full-grown tree will have about one hundred nuts. There are four different kinds of trees, bearing the red, white, blue, and sweet cocoanuts. The latter is the most profitable, as the nut husk, when green, is very good eating. Its taste is very much like sugar cane. All cocoanuts, when green, are full of milk. The milk itself is a sweet, cool drink and must be very nutritious. While I was cruising round the South Sea Islands I drank nothing else, and never felt better in my life. When the nuts are soft they are also very good eating. The husk of the ripe cocoanut is splendid fuel, and it will also make good rope, fishing lines and nets. The shells can be used for all kinds of drinking vessels and dishes. When the nut is ripe the kernel is taken from the shell and ground up fine, after which it is pressed and a liquor is extracted which tastes very much like cow's milk. On boiling the liquor is transformed into a white oil, and can be utilised for cooking and illuminating purposes. It is also used by the native women for hair oil, and if rubbed into the skin will repel all kinds of insects. It has also excellent healing properties. Besides all this, the nut is converted into copra by drying, and shiploads of this material are sent to Europe and the United States, where it is manufactured into soap and other articles.

When a cocoanut is ripe it will drop to the ground. If left lying on a moist ground the nut will quickly sprout from one of the eyes, one part descending into the ground to form the roots and the other part, growing upwards, in about six years develops into a full-grown tree. If the sprout is removed and the cocoanut opened, instead of the nut, what looks and tastes very much like sponge cake will be found, and one of them is just about enough to make a meal.

Bread-fruit and other tropical fruits are scarce on the low coral islands of the South Pacific. Besides the cocoanut, there are the arrowroot, yam and taro, the latter plant growing to a very large size. The pigs and poultry on the islands are chiefly raised on cocoanuts.

The waters, both in the lagoon and along the outside coast, are full of fish. The natives catch many by building a fire on the beach, towards which the fish will swim, only to be captured with a dip net. Some are caught by nets, or hooks made of pearl shell.

The best sport of all is catching flying-fish. To do this, three natives take a canoe outside the lagoon. One of the three sits in the stern and paddles her along; the second stands up in the middle of the boat, holding up a large flare, made of dried cocoanut leaves, and the third man, in the front end of the canoe, stands with a long-handled dip net, and is kept busy catching the flying-fish on the wing as they make for the fire.

In the Penrhyn Island lagoon pearl oyster shell is also very plentiful, and is a good source of income to the natives who dispose of it to traders, the proceeds of which are nearly equally shared amongst all the inhabitants of the island. The land, also, is divided in the same way. Some of the islands have a king, and others call their leader chief, but both have full power over the natives and are very much respected.

Only on one occasion have I seen a South Sea Islander drunk, the chief of the island being very severe with those found guilty of this weakness; his best friends got hold of the man before the chief got to hear about it, and took him down to the beach, where, in spite of all his kicking and shouting, they put him under the water and held him there till I felt sure the poor fellow was drowned. After a while they made him stand up, but, following a period of sniffing and blowing, he started to kick up 'Old Harry' again. So down he went once more under water. The next time they pulled him up he behaved a little more civilly, but was not quiet enough to suit his friends, who thought it advisable to give him another ducking. This time when he rose, or rather, was raised, they took him to the beach, and after rolling the water out of him, he appeared to be very weak, but quite sober, and without a word to say. I thought to myself that if a similar remedy could be applied to some people I know of, what a blessing it would prove to be to themselves and to others! I was told by the natives that three dips is a sure cure (for dipsomania).

We stopped only one day at the eastern village, as the next morning Captain Dexter sailed across the lagoon, a distance of about seven miles, to the village on the west side of the island, and we went along with the schooner.

The lagoon is very deep in places, but there are also plenty of spots where coral rocks are just high enough to make it dangerous for vessels to sail about, but at the same time they can easily be avoided by sailing through after ten o'clock in the morning, when the sun is well up. By keeping a good lookout from the bow, or better still, from the end of the jibboom or masthead, with the sun at your back, the rocks can be seen a long way off.

We dropped anchor at the western village about an hour after leaving the other one. This village was similar in appearance, the houses being also built along the shore of the lagoon. The chief came on board our little vessel, and asked if I would like to have her taken out of the water and cleaned up. I stated that it was my intention to give her a good cleaning and painting before we sailed. The next morning the chief sent natives down to me to take on shore all the stores and ballast, after which they pulled the *Tilikum* out of the water and placed her high and dry amongst the cocoanut trees. They then scrubbed her inside and out, and after she was properly clean and dry again, painted her.

The third day after our arrival at the western village, the British cruiser *Torch* arrived, and after dropping anchor outside of the western bay, Commander McAllister came on shore with some of the officers and men. Penrhyn Island is under British protection, and a cruiser calls there once a year to see that everything is all right. Commander McAllister, during his short stay of two days at the island, inspected the *Tilikum*, and also some of my charts. I was only in possession of one blue-backed chart of the South Pacific Ocean. Commander McAllister told me I had not sufficient charts to sail through the South Pacific, and as I was unable to buy any charts at the island, he was good enough to present me with several, which were very valuable to me later on in making certain islands.

After the *Torch* left, Captain Dexter sailed across the lagoon to the eastern village where he had some business to look after, and as he was only to be away for a few days, my mate went along and I stopped with the *Tilikum* till the schooner came back, which was on September 17th. The next day the *Tilikum* was put into the water, the ballast and stores placed on board again, and she was ready for sea.

On the morning of September 19th I got up at daybreak to get things ready for an early start. I saw the natives rushing about, and bringing cocoanuts down to the *Tilikum*, and if I had left them alone, they would, I think, have sunk our little vessel with cocoanuts and other eatables. However, when I considered she was deep enough loaded, I told the good chief that the boat could not possibly take any more. We thanked him for all his kindness, and while saying good-bye the tears came to his eyes. After shaking hands with all the natives, my mate and I stepped on board, set all sails, and with our little Canadian flag on the mizzen, we took our departure from Penrhyn Island. The natives gave us three cheers in true English style as we slowly sailed away from the village, which we answered by three dips of our flag as a final farewell.

SEVEN

MANAHIKI

IT WAS A BEAUTIFUL clear morning, with a moderate breeze from the ESE, and in a little while we sailed through the channel near the western village into the Pacific Ocean, after which we changed our course for the Island of Manahiki, or, as it is called in English, Humphrey Island, distant about two hundred miles. The wind freshened as we got away from the land, and a short time before the island dropped out of sight a heavy squall struck the *Tilikum*, which forced us to take in all sail; but it only lasted a few minutes, after which the weather cleared up and the wind moderated again. We then set all our sails, and with a fresh breeze reeled off the miles in fine style, and the following night at nine o'clock we sighted the Island of Manahiki. The wind keeping fresh from the ESE we soon closed in with the coast. At eleven o'clock we rounded the north-west point of the island, and as all villages of the small South Sea Islands that have no harbour are on the west side, which is the lee side for the easterly trade wind that blows nearly all the year round, we commenced to look for the village, which should be, according to directions given me by Captain Dexter, on the west side just after rounding the north-west point. Sure enough, after rounding the point, we saw lights on shore, but as I was also told by Captain Dexter that the safest anchorage was at the other village, which was four miles further along (Manahiki also has two villages), we followed the coast. It was a fine clear night, and being on the lee side of the island, the wind was light and the sea smooth. We had nearly reached the first village, when we heard all kinds of shouting and noise coming from its direction. I was about to change our course for the open ocean again when we were surrounded by several canoes full of natives shouting at us to stop.

In a second we had our firearms up, and were ready for action, at the same time keeping the *Tilikum* on her westerly course, but as the wind was rather light they could paddle faster than we were sailing, and in a very short time one of the canoes was alongside of us, in which one of the natives spoke a little English, saying, 'Cabten, me chief, me speak you.'

'What do you want?' I demanded.

'Stop, me want speak.'

With that I let the *Tilikum* come up to the wind and stopped her headway, allowing the canoe to come alongside.

Without any invitation, the man who called himself the chief came on board and offered to shake hands, saying again, 'Me chief.' The old man told us in very broken English, but plainly enough for us to understand, that the *Torch* had called there on the way from the Penrhyn, and had told them all about us; and since that time they had been watching for us night and day, and as we had arrived now they wanted us to stop. However, we had made up our minds to go to the other village, so we told the old chief that we would come and see him and his people before we sailed from the island for the west, after which they left us, and a little after midnight we anchored at the western village, where we had another reception somewhat similar to the one we had previously experienced, but no one came on board.

At sunrise the next morning a canoe came alongside us, with three men in her. One of them, speaking good English, introduced himself as Mr Williams, the trader of the island. Mr Williams then introduced one of the other men in the canoe as the King of the Island, I asked his Royal Highness (who was barefooted and without a hat) to come on board with Mr Williams, and after I had given the gentlemen a short explanation of our doings, the king invited us on shore.

At eleven o'clock we both went on shore, and were received by the king and queen and two fine-looking young princesses, but as neither could speak a word of English, they had the trader, Mr Williams, there as an interpreter, who, on behalf of the royal family, asked us to accompany the party to the town hall. On arriving at the building, which was only about a hundred yards from where we had landed, I saw a long table covered with all kinds of eatables. Mr Williams informed us that the table was set for us, and asked us to sit down and help ourselves. Both of us were seated on a wooden bench, behind the table. The royal family sat at one end of the table, to our right, and Mr Williams also sat there to do the interpreting. After this, all the natives of the village, men, women and children, came in. It took quite a time for the hall to fill, and during the interval I took an observation of our surroundings.

The hall, or rather building, in which this gathering took place was about thirty feet wide by about seventy feet long, built of rough lumber, and roofed with dried cocoanut leaves.

The table was spread for just the two of us. One roasted pig, weighing about one hundred and fifty pounds, was placed on the middle of the table, and at either side were flying-fish, about half a dozen roasted chickens, and yams, arrowroot, taro, cocoanuts and other made-up dishes. Comparatively speaking, there was enough there for a hundred people to make a good, square meal!

When all the natives had arrived and were seated, the king rose and made a speech to them about our voyage, after which they all clapped their hands. After his discourse the king whispered to Mr Williams, and then Mr Williams told us to help ourselves, and that the king and all his people wished us a pleasant voyage and a safe return to our home.

As there were only two places set, we knew very well that they were intended for us, and the pig being too large for us to tackle, we started on the chickens and taro. No sooner had we started eating, than the two princesses got up, and one of them placed a fine-woven panama hat, nicely decorated with different coloured ribbons, on my mate's head, and the other princess did the same to me. Mr Luxton certainly looked queer with his head decorated, and I presume I did also. We stared at each other for a minute, and then my mate said, 'These two young girls must be partly gone on us.'

By that time, the two princesses had taken their seats, and two more young ladies came along with more hats of the same description, took off the ones we had, and replaced them with theirs. Immediately after, two more young ladies came along, and repeated the performance. That was as much as my mate could stand. He got up and said, 'Mr Williams, will you please tell these young ladies for me, that the next one that comes along and changes my hat is going to be kissed.' Of course the word was sent along by Mr Williams, after which they all started to laugh and chat about something. I told my mate that he had put his foot into it. The next thing we saw, the oldest woman of the lot (she must have been about a hundred years of age, for she was all doubled up and could hardly walk) came along with a straw hat, and as she got nearer Mr Luxton turned pale. I said, 'Courage, Norman, courage: don't go back on your word'; but I am sorry to say that my mate did on that occasion. However, the young ladies and hats continued arriving, and by the time we got through with our feast, we had quite a few hats.

Later in the afternoon we were taken to the king's palace, where we dined with the royal family. The dinner was something similar to what we had in the hall. The king's residence was built on the same principle as the hall, only smaller. The furniture consisted of two double sleeping places, which were made out of one-inch boards, covered with mats, and raised about a foot above the ground, one table and two wooden benches. Apparently the King of Manahiki didn't care for very much ceremony.

Dinner over, the royal family accompanied us to the beach where our boat was anchored. We found, to our great surprise, that our little vessel was decorated with long ribbons of various colours hanging from the tops of the masts, down to the deck and the water, and the decks covered with fancy mats. The decorating had been done by the same young ladies who had presented us with the fancy hats. Some of them were still on board the *Tilikum*, and others were alongside her in their canoes. When we got on board, we found that all the hats, chickens, pig, and everything that we had left on the table had been carefully wrapped up in green leaves and put in our cabin, which was so full that we could not get into it ourselves! I told the trader to thank the natives, on our behalf, for all their kindness, but that it would be impossible for us to keep everything they had given us on board. In the first place, we had no room for it, and in the second place the meat would spoil in a day or two. But the trader, Mr Williams, informed us that all the natives would take it as an insult if we asked them to take it back, and advised us to keep it, and throw it overboard during the night, which, to my sorrow, we were obliged to do.

The following morning I awoke to the sound of drums and bells, and on looking out of the cabin saw Mr Williams standing near the beach. Asking him what was the matter, he informed me that the sound of drums and bells was to call the natives to get ready for a dance, at the same time asking us to come ashore by seven o'clock. On landing, we found the natives all gathered round the town hall, about seven or eight of them playing different home-made instruments. They were playing a native tune, and about twelve young ladies, ranging in age from seventeen to twenty, lined up in a double row and danced to the music. The king's two daughters also took part in the dancing. The lady dancers kept it up for quite a while, after which their places were taken by twelve young men. After the men had finished their places were taken by young girls from ten to sixteen years of age; and so they kept changing about. Children of seven years and upwards could certainly dance wonderfully. Sometimes men and women danced together. It was continued the whole day, and when they got hungry or thirsty some of the young men would climb cocoanut trees and get some green sweet cocoanuts and eat the husk, the soft and sweet tasting kernels, and drink the nice cool milk.

The dancing was kept up till dark, after which they retired into their singing hall, where the men squatted down at one end and the women at the other end of the hall facing each other, with the band-master standing in the middle. And it was certainly some of the sweetest music that I ever listened to. This was kept up till after midnight; then all retired, and we joined our ship.

The next day we took a small boat and sailed through the lagoon to call on the chief and his people as promised. Arriving at the village we were met by the same old chief we had seen in his canoe when making the island. The old man could speak a little English, though not enough to make himself plainly understood, but there was also a trader there who spoke English. He asked this man to tell us that he would be very much obliged if we would come again in our own boat, when they would receive us just as well as the king and his people had done. As the people at the other village had treated us so well, and on finding out that this chief and his people had been watching for us for many nights past to get us to anchor at their village so that they would be the first to give a reception, we agreed to do as the chief asked. We thereupon returned to the village from whence we had come, and, in company of the two princesses, sailed for the old chief's village next morning at about seven o'clock, arriving there an hour later. We could see the natives, young and old, lined up along the beach, and when within about two hundred yards of the shore the old chief jumped into the water and swam towards us, and by the time we had our anchor down he was on board the canoe to welcome us to his town. We then went ashore and had just about as good a time as we had had in the other village.

Just before dark we returned to the western village, as we had promised the king and queen to bring their daughters back that night. When we got there both of us felt inclined to give up the cruise, and make this place our home for the remainder of our lives.

The Island of Manahiki is, like Penrhyn, a coral lagoon island, but is not quite so large, as the lagoon is only five miles in diameter, and there is no entrance, not even for small boats. The ring of land, which is also covered with cocoanut trees, seems to be wider than that of Penrhyn. The natives of Manahiki look like the Penrhyn people, but are much more pleasant, and are lovers of sport.

EIGHT

DANGER ISLAND—SAMOA

ON THE MORNING of September 25th, after saying good-bye to all the natives on shore, including the two young princesses, we went on board to take our departure. A good many of the natives came in their canoes to see us off.

In trying to get our anchor up, we found that it had got foul of the bottom, and we were therefore unable to move it. The native bandmaster, who was one of those who had come to see us off, went ashore in his canoe, and in a minute or two was back with a water telescope, with which he went overboard, and by swimming around for a little while, and surveying the bottom through the telescope, he soon located the anchor. He then pushed the telescope aside, and down he went. He must have been under water nearly a minute when he came up with the *Tilikum*'s largest anchor in his hand, swam alongside and passed it on board. I offered to pay him for his service, but it was not accepted. We thanked him, and once more saying good-bye to the people who came on board to see us off, they re-entered their canoes and we set sail and shaped our course for Danger Island, distant about three hundred miles.

The weather was clear and the wind moderate from the ESE, but as we got away from the lee of the island, it increased to a fresh breeze, and by noon the island was out of sight. While I was steering I asked my mate to open the parcel that the two princesses had brought on board just before we sailed, which he did, and found two roasted chickens in it. Needless to say, we had roast chicken for lunch.

The three hundred miles to Danger Island, owing to a rather mild trade wind, took us three days to cover, during which time we had fine weather, and nothing unusual happened with the exception of our catching quite a few flying-fish at night. This was done by putting a bright light on deck, to which they will fly, and very often strike the sail and fall on deck. The flying-fish is one of the best eating fish to be found in salt water, so we made good use of them.

September 28th, a little before dark, we sighted the island, but dreading the name Danger on the chart we hove to for the night, and the next morning, at daybreak, set sail and steered in for it. As we got near the land we could see three small and apparently separated islands, which we ascertained were connected and surrounded by low coral reefs, on which the seas were breaking heavily. We kept the island, reefs and breakers on our port side, and with a fresh breeze followed the breakers round till we got to the westernmost island. At Danger Island, as there is no lagoon or harbour for a vessel to go in, the villages are on the west side. When we arrived at a favourable position we shaped our course for a village we espied amongst the cocoanut trees, and as we neared the land I took soundings for an anchorage, but found deep water right up to the beach. A good many natives came running towards us, and one of them, who spoke a little English, told us that the water was too deep to anchor, but that by putting our anchor on the beach the wind would keep the boat from swinging on to the shore. With that we did as the natives advised, and apparently the *Tilikum* laid there quite safely.

This native then introduced himself as the chief of Danger Island, and invited us to come on shore to the village. Not caring to leave the *Tilikum* at such a poor anchorage I declined the invitation. It was then about two o'clock, and, owing to the dangerous sailing round Danger Island, I told the chief that we wished to get under weigh again so as to be clear of the surrounding reefs before dark. The chief did not seem to like this, but seeing that we would not stay, asked us to remain for one hour, which we agreed to do. He at once sent two of his men to the village, and in about an hour they came back loaded with cocoanuts and eggs. We thanked him and took our departure, and rounding a long coral reef running quite a way into the north-westward, shaped our course for Samoa, about four hundred miles, which we made in three days, experiencing similar wind and weather as we had had all the way from the Penrhyn Island. On nearing the harbour we saw flags flying at half-mast all over the town, and the first news we got was that President McKinley of the United States had been assassinated about a week previously, but Samoa had only received the sad news that very morning. Apia was the first port which we were obliged to enter and clear in the same manner as any other deep-water vessel, but Mr Reinhart, the collector of customs, after coming on board and noting the size and build of our vessel (saying with a smile that he would not cross a millpond in the *Tilikum*) freed us of all harbour dues.

We remained several days in Apia, during which time we made the acquaintance of the ex-King of Samoa, and some of the leading citizens honoured us with a Samoan dinner, of which the serving of kava was the most interesting part. A root, of which the kava is made, was brought in, cut to pieces and given to three Samoan beauties, and after my mate had examined their teeth, and reported them as clean and polished, all three sat on a clean mat round a kava bowl, and chewed the root into a juicy mass. When sufficient root had been prepared it was put in the kava bowl half filled with water, in which it was washed and squeezed with the hands until every drop of the juice was extracted and mixed with water; after straining it through a clean linen cloth, it appeared of a whitish colour. It was then served in cocoanut shell, and to me the taste was anything but pleasant; still, as a matter of courtesy, I, like the rest, drank to the dregs without a pause. The cups were at once refilled, and the ceremony repeated several times, so that by the time we were ready to return I felt somewhat weak in the knees, and in a little while I got so shaky in the legs that I was quite unable to walk! I then discovered that kava is an intoxicating drink, but that instead of going to a man's head like other strong spirits, it mainly affects his lower extremities.

The Samoan Islands, the natives and their habits have been so often described that I omit that part, and proceed with my voyage.

NINE

NIUA-FU—FIJI ISLANDS

AFTER SEVERAL DAYS rest in Samoa we set sail for the Fiji Islands, a distance of about six hundred miles to the westward, and as the easterly trade wind was strong we soon put the high mountains below the horizon. On the third day we sighted at daybreak the island of Niua-fu, and as it was right in our track we sailed round the north side of it, and beheld quite a large village on the western side. We at once altered our course for the village, and on reaching it found a good anchorage in fifteen fathoms, with perfectly smooth water.

The chief came to pay us a visit in a canoe while other natives swam, and amongst the swimmers was a young native girl. The *Tilikum* was anchored about two hundred yards from the shore, and the young woman swam that distance in no time. When the fair maiden reached our vessel she took hold of the rail and raised herself to the deck in true athletic fashion. She then sat down and said something which I did not understand at first, but later discovered she was asking for tobacco. I gave her a plug of T. and B., which she put in her long, dark hair, lowered herself into the water, and went back the same way she had come.

The natives of Niua-fu and their habits are very similar to those of Samoa, but their skin is darker in colour. The island is about five miles in diameter, with heights of five thousand feet, and all kinds of tropical plants grow in profusion. The treatment we received was similar to that extended by the inhabitants of the other islands.

Having stayed one day in Niua-fu we sailed for the Fiji Islands, and sighted the northern part after a two days' voyage with a strong south-east trade wind. The first island we came to was a small low coral reef, covered with cocoanut trees, on which the seas were breaking heavily. After passing the south-west end, we saw smooth water on the western side, where we dropped anchor in three feet of water. It was nine o'clock in the morning when we anchored, and my mate at once took a gun and a camera and waded ashore. I stopped on board to clean things up a little, at the same time cooking some dinner. At noon I fired a few signal shots to let my mate know that dinner was ready, for he was one of those men that never think of eating when out shooting. I waited a little while, and as he did not put in an appearance fired another double shot, but got no answer. I had a trifle to eat, and then took my gun and went ashore. The place where I landed was a fine coral beach, from the water to the cocoanut trees about three hundred feet wide. I walked across the beach, and was soon amongst the cocoanut trees , where the ground was covered with a kind of coarse grass, and through it ran what looked to me like an old footpath, which led to the interior of the island. Nothing could be heard around except the song of the tropical birds. Still, I was satisfied in my own mind that people were or had been on the island not long before.

I fired a few more shots, but there was still no reply. I then continued in the same direction, and presently saw something amongst the trees that looked to me like a house. I stopped and looked, but could not see anything moving, neither could I hear any sound, but as I had ten shots in my rifle I picked up courage and walked up to the house. There was no sign of either my mate or anybody else. The little house proved to be one of the real old native huts, and near by was lying a pile of human bones.

The Fiji natives were, not long ago, considered the worst cannibals in the South Pacific Ocean, and I think the little house on the island must have been a feasting place. After seeing that I walked back towards the beach, and collected a few shells. At four o'clock, while about to board the canoe, I saw a shark coming along with his back fin out of the water, and once more I made for the beach. This gentleman was one of the yellow-striped tiger variety, the worst and about the only real man-eating shark there is. He kept swimming round and round the boat. Mr Shark was not more than seven to eight feet long, but I knew that if he ever got hold of me he could make it pretty warm! I watched him for a while, and by and by took a shot at him, making a hole through his back fin, after which he left in a hurry, and I returned to the *Tilikum* unmolested. No sooner was I on board than he was alongside the boat again. I then got my shark hook over the side with a piece of bacon fat attached to it, and the next minute I had him on the hook. As the man-eater kept very quiet I raised him level with the water, and in that position put a bullet through his head, killing him instantly. After getting the hook out of his mouth, he sank to the bottom. In a very short while the water all around was red with blood, and I saw sharks, large and small, coming along with their fins out of the water, all making for the carcase. The latter was torn to pieces in no time and eaten by his brothers, after which they all left for deep water again.

About six o'clock my mate returned with a load of birds.

The next morning, at daybreak, we set sail for Suva. The weather was fine and clear, and as the south-east trade wind still continued to aid us we passed island after island during the afternoon. The same afternoon we sighted a vessel on our starboard bow. We watched her for a while, and as she did not change her position we altered our course to have a closer look. After a while we saw that the vessel was stranded. She proved to be a large sailing vessel, but as she was surrounded by reefs and large breakers dashing all over her, we were unable to get any particulars.

On October 17th, at nine o'clock at night, we arrived at the entrance of Suva Harbour, but it being a dark and stormy night, hove to outside and sailed in at daybreak. On entering Suva Bay we were met by a steam launch. The man in charge was Captain Clark, harbour master of Suva, and with him was the Reverend Mr Williams, of New Zealand. I invited the two gentlemen on board. Captain Clark, being a seaman, took into account the size of the *Tilikum* and stepped into the middle of the cockpit, for which the boat hardly moved. But the reverend gentleman from

New Zealand, nearly three hundred pounds in weight, instead of stepping on board in the same way placed his foot on the gunwale. The *Tilikum* at once gave way under the weight and put her deck under water. Mr Williams made a quick step back into the launch, saying he could see quite enough of the *Tilikum* from there. After conversing a little while, Captain Clark took us in tow, and anchored us at the landing-place.

Suva, which is the capital of the Fiji Islands, is a nice clean little town with a population, I was told, of about six hundred Europeans. There, as in Samoa, we were cleared of all harbour dues. We dined that day at the MacDonnel Hotel, and during the afternoon went to see a dance performed by the native men and women of the Solomon Islands. The dancing and music was a good deal like that I had witnessed in Manahiki and Samoa, but the Solomon natives were not so good looking as the former. They are of a dark, shiny colour, with black, curly hair. There were also quite a few Fiji natives. These are of very strong and powerful build.

TEN

TO THE AUSTRALIAN CONTINENT— DISASTROUS VOYAGE

ON OCTOBER 20TH Mr Luxton came to me and said, 'Look here, John, I have got a good seaman to take my place for the run with you to Sydney, and if you are willing to take him along I propose to take passage on a steamship, and on your arrival there I will join you again and complete the voyage, as I am satisfied now that the *Tilikum* is quite able to make it.'

I accepted his proposal, and the next morning my new mate came on board. By the looks of him he appeared to be what he later on proved himself, a first-class seaman. His name was Louis Begent, aged thirty-one, a native of Louchester, Tasmania. I told Begent to go to work and get the boat ready for sea, saying that we were going to sail during the afternoon. However, having made quite a few friends in Fiji, we did not get away till the following afternoon at three o'clock. Captain Clark was good enough to give us a tow out as far as the lighthouse. An hour later he turned back with his launch, and we, with a moderate south-easterly breeze, shaped our course for Sydney, a distance of about eighteen hundred miles. Just about sunset, about seven miles outside the bay, we got into a channel between two islands, and as this looked very dangerous for navigation, I ran close to a beach in smooth water and anchored.

The following morning, at daybreak, when we were in the act of getting under sail again, we found that our anchor was foul of the bottom, and were therefore unable to get it up. My mate offered to dive down to clear it, but as the water was full of sharks I cut the anchor rope instead, and with a fresh easterly breeze we steered again on our westerly course. The wind kept fresh and the weather clear until the morning of the 27th, when the sky became cloudy, and during the day the wind freshened up to a strong breeze. At ten o'clock that night, I took in the foresail and spanker, and under the mainsail and staysail, with a strong easterly wind, and steering south-west, the *Tilikum* went along quite comfortably, now and then taking over a little water, but nothing to speak of.

It was my watch on deck from eight till twelve, and about half an hour before midnight the compass light went out. As the night was quite clear, with a good many stars shining brightly in the south-west, I picked out one of the stars nearly ahead of the boat and steered by it till my watch came to an end, when I called my mate, who got up and took my place at the rudder. I told him to keep the boat going by the star ahead till the light was fixed up. I then took the box, which contained the compass and light, down to the cabin. My mate was well able to keep the canoe on her course by the stars, so there was no particular hurry about the compass, and instead of getting the lamp lit at once, I lit a cigar for myself, another for my mate, and passed it out to him. I then set to work on the compass light. While I was thus employed my mate was telling me how he enjoyed the sailing in the *Tilikum* and how he would like to make the trip to London in her.

'If we keep this wind,' he said, 'we will be in Sydney in time for the Melbourne Cup Race. I expect my brother-in-law to be in Melbourne by that time, perhaps you know him? His name is Castella, and he is in command of the American ship *Hawaiian Island*.'

'I am well acquainted with Captain Castella and his wife,' I answered. (The ship in question was at that time the largest and finest steel ship under the American flag.) After that I became very much interested in my mate, and for a minute forgot all about the compass, till he said, 'It is getting cloudy ahead of us, so will you pass the compass out?'

While we were chatting away the *Tilikum* went along at her best, answering her helm beautifully. I had lit the lamp and handed the binnacle out to my mate, who, for a second, let go the tiller in order to place it in front of him on the seat of the cockpit, and just as he put the binnacle back in its place, I saw a large breaking sea coming up near the stern of the boat. Knowing by the appearance of the sea that it was a bad one, I shouted loudly, 'Hold on'; but before I had the words out of my mouth the breaker had struck us.

I had braced myself in the cabin door to keep the water out, but when the sea struck it knocked me down. However, I was up in a second to see if any damage had been done on deck. I could not see my mate, and the boat was just about half-way round coming up to the wind. I peered forward, thinking that my mate was getting the sea anchor out or doing some other kind of work, but he was not to be seen. I shouted, but got no answer. I knew then that he was overboard, and of course that he must be to windward, as the boat had been going very fast, and therefore must have left him some distance astern ere she came to the wind. To try and beat back to where he had gone overboard was an impossible task owing to the strong wind and large seas. Therefore I put the helm hard down, lowered the sails, and put the sea anchor out to prevent the boat drifting too much. Thinking that he might be able to swim to the boat, and that this was the only way his life could be saved, I continued calling him by name, but got no reply. All my shouting and calling, which I kept up for a long time, was in vain. Nothing but the sound of the wind, and now and then a breaking sea, was to be heard. Ten minutes passed; twenty minutes; thirty minutes; an hour; and still no sign of my unfortunate companion. Then I knew that he was dead.

The loss of my mate was partly due to negligence, as I always had a life-line, one end of which was fastened to the boat; the other end to be put round the helmsman's body. I told him, when he first came on board, never to neglect to put that life-line around himself whenever he took the rudder, as I always did, and if he had followed my advice he may have gone overboard from the effects of the sea, but would never have got away from the boat.

The sea that took my mate overboard was by no means very dangerous. Of course there was water enough in it to carry a man away if he was not holding on to anything. However, later on during the cruise the boat shipped larger seas than this one, but I never again had a deplorable accident of this kind.

After I had given up all hope of ever seeing my mate again I went down to the cabin, and there found everything afloat. The bedding was soaked and everything else in the cabin was very wet. I then baled the *Tilikum* out, after which I went on deck again, and sat down in the cockpit thinking over the loss I had sustained. I was approaching the southern limit of the south-east trade wind, but instead of a trade wind it developed into a howling gale during the morning hours. I was just going to have a look at the compass to see if the wind was still in the same direction when I discovered to my dismay that the compass and binnacle had gone too!

When daylight came, and the sun made its appearance on the eastern horizon, I got on top of the cabin deck and took a good look round for my missing mate. But there was nothing to be seen but the large seas with their breaking summits, and the passing clouds in the sky above, while the *Tilikum* under her sea anchor and a storm sail over the stern, rose bravely to every sea as it came along.

At eight o'clock I hoisted my little Canadian flag half-mast, and then proceeded to search for a small pocket compass, which I knew my former companion had, when we were hunting in the forest of Vancouver Island. Being unable to find it, it struck me that Mr Luxton kept the same in one of his valises, and doubtless without thinking of it took the compass with him when he left me in Suva. Consequently, I was alone at sea without a compass.

My position was then about six hundred miles south-west from Suva, and about twelve hundred from Sydney, isolated, no compass to steer by, everything soaking wet, and the boat hove to in a gale. For some time I was completely taken aback, and did not know what to do or what would become of me. The first thought that occurred to me was that I might wait there for a passing vessel. Then again, it struck me that I was out of the track of vessels and might lay there for months and not see one.

During the forenoon the wind abated somewhat. At midday the sun was shining brightly. I took my quadrant, and getting on top of the cabin deck, with one arm round the mast to prevent myself from falling overboard, tried to get the noon altitude. While standing there watching the sun slowly rising to the meridian to the north of me, I said to myself, 'Well, there is north.' By facing north the wind was about ten points to my right and the sea running from the same quarter, which of course made the direction of the wind and sea from the ESE. The latter observation almost satisfied me that I could make a fairly good course by steering in clear weather by the sun, moon or stars, and in thick weather do the best I could, steering by the ocean swell.

A little after noon the wind had moderated considerably and the seas had lost their breaking tops. I hauled in my sea anchor, and under the forestaysail swung the *Tilikum* on her course to the south-westward, steering by the ocean swell which was running from the ESE. By steering the boat so that the ESE swell would strike her two points abaft the port beam, was to give her a SW course.

The guides I had to steer by were the sun, moon, stars, and the ocean swell, but I soon discovered that the ocean swell was by far the best to keep the boat making a good course. Then, again, I was obliged to use the heavenly bodies to get the set of the swell. The only trouble I had in finding the course was when I got up from a sleep and found the weather thick and overcast. Still worse, when there was a cross swell I was helpless, and obliged to heave to until the weather cleared up.

For two days after the accident it kept blowing from the ESE, and as I was unable to sleep I kept her going night and day until the third day, when the wind died out and I lay becalmed.

From the time of the accident till the calm was two and a half days, during which time I had no sleep, and very little to eat, and that cold; I may say that I was just about played out. I therefore went to work and made myself some warm food, and after a fairly good meal, laid down to have a sleep. I laid in my little bunk for quite a while, turning from side to side and thinking over the past few days. However, I eventually dozed off only to dream about all kinds of things. I thought I saw my lost companion look in at the cabin door, and it gave me an awful start. On looking up the time I found to my surprise that I had only been asleep about ten minutes. I tried again and again to sleep, but in vain. However, I laid down for a few hours; then I fancied I felt a breeze come in through the cabin door, and sure enough when I got on deck there was a moderate breeze from the south. The great trouble was that whenever I retired to my bunk to sleep I could not do so, and when sailing, especially in light winds, I could not keep awake. Still, I set sail and did the best I could to keep the *Tilikum* going towards Sydney.

The wind and weather kept about the same till the following day. It was in the afternoon, while I was nearly asleep, when a heavy southerly squall struck the *Tilikum* under all sails, and over she went on her beam ends. So did I; it was only through a piece of luck that I did not go overboard, for the boat was on the port tack, with the sheets hauled by the wind. I was sitting on the port side dozing when she went over on her beam ends. Landing against the lee washboards, which kept me from going overboard, I nearly broke my neck. As luck happened the foremast snapped, and the boat righted at once.

From the fall I got a kink in the neck, and laid for a little while in the cockpit before I was able to realise what had happened. When I came to my proper senses, I looked round and saw the foresail, part of the foremast, forestaysail and all the head gear hanging overboard. The mainsail and mizzen were still set, and these, with the aid of the fore gear hanging overboard, kept the vessel nicely head to wind. After stripping her of the mainsail, and hauling in the mizzen sheet, the *Tilikum* laid as well as if she was riding to her sea anchor.

For the next few hours, while I was thinking of my miserable plight and what would next happen to the *Tilikum* and myself, I let her drift as she was. By and by I came to the conclusion that while there is life there is hope, and where there is a will there is a way; and being still in the possession of both, I went to work and picked up all the head gear and sails that were hanging over-board, secured them on deck, and as it kept blowing hard for two days I let the boat drift under her sea anchor and storm sail. All that time I was, of course, unable to do anything toward repairing the damage, but by keeping a riding light on deck during the night I got all the sleep I possibly could.

During the second night the wind gradually died out, and at daybreak the weather was calm and clear. After the large seas had gone down I went to work to splice the foremast and put everything back in its place, and in the afternoon I was ready for another breeze. I did not have to wait long for it, a moderate breeze coming up the same night. From then I experienced light winds and weather until October 14th, and when my position was about a hundred and fifty miles north-east from Sydney a strong breeze came in from the rear. I kept running before it as long as I thought it safe to do so, but when the wind increased to a howling gale and the seas commenced to break I hove to in the usual way. I put a light on deck, and then turned in 'all standing' (with all my clothes on). Now and then I would get up and see if the light on deck was burning.

About midnight I got up to see if the light was all right, but to my surprise it was extinguished, and, to make matters worse, a green, red and bright light appeared ahead. Of course, I knew at once that these were a steamer's lights, and that the vessel was coming straight towards me. There was no time to lose. I had to let the lookout on the steamer know that I was ahead of her or in another five minutes she would have run me down. I knew that I had no time to fix my light, so pulled off one of my socks, soaked it with kerosene, and set it ablaze. I felt a good deal better when I saw the green light disappearing from my sight. They had seen my signal, and in less than five minutes a large steamer passed by.

The gale kept up its fury for three days and nights, after which the wind moderated, but as I had seen neither sun, moon nor stars, and had completely lost my position, I kept the boat under her sea anchor till noon, when I got the position, which put me about a hundred miles south-east of Sydney. By that time the wind had died down and the sea became quite calm. Two hours later the sky was as clear as crystal, with the exception of a very heavy cloud rising from the south-west. I watched this as it grew larger and larger. In a little while, when it rose to about forty-five degrees above the horizon, it looked like a huge arch supported on the bosom of the ocean, one abutment in the south-west and the other in the south-east, and it certainly appeared as if I was getting into another heavy gale. I therefore secured all my sails and prepared for the storm; but the cloud rose no higher, and while I was looking at it I saw what appeared to be a long, sharp point forming underneath the centre of the span, which was gradually approached by a similar point rising out of the ocean, and as soon as the two points met they formed a large water-spout. I at once made a dive down into my cabin to get my rifle on deck, which did not take longer than half a minute, and by the time I was on deck again there were two. Then, one after the other they formed until, in a very short time, there were six, the nearest at the very most, one mile from me; but there they stopped, and owing to the perfect calm I could hear the water rushing up in the cloud, which sounded something like a distant waterfall. Shortly afterwards one of the spouts broke; then another; then another would rise; and so they kept on rising and falling, one after the other, for about three hours. The cloud got larger and larger till six o'clock, when the last spout dropped.

I may mention here that I had sailed across the South Pacific several times, and on different occasions I have seen water-spouts, but never, before or since, have I witnessed spouts of the same nature. All other water-spouts I have seen moved more or less in a slanting position, while those in question were all perfectly vertical.

During the afternoon, from about three till six o'clock, there must have been at least thirty spouts that I saw from my boat, and the nearest at any time I should judge was about a mile distant. I fired several shots at the spouts, and one of them broke shortly after I fired, but whether it broke from the effects of the vibration of the shot or from natural consequences I cannot say.

I have been told by ship-masters who have had experience with water-spouts that they will break every time from the vibration of a gun-shot, if it is discharged within two hundred yards. I, however, was well pleased that they kept where they were, as, had they come near my vessel, and had I been unable to break them with my gun, the *Tilikum* and I might still be sailing in the sky.

At six o'clock the bank that had up to then formed a large arch, and by the looks of it had imbibed from the ocean thousands upon thousands of tons of water, broke up and covered the sky in a few minutes with dark and threatening clouds. At the same time the weather still kept calm, but I heard light thunder; then a flash of lightning was followed by a loud peal of thunder, and I then experienced a very severe thunderstorm. There was no wind with it, but occasionally very heavy rain squalls. The lightning was apparently very near my boat, for it would make the dark and cloudy night as bright as day. I knew I was absolutely unable to prevent the lightning from striking my boat, so went below and laid down in my bunk to await further developments.

The thunderbolts seemed to be very close to the *Tilikum*, and I was apprehensive that the next flash of lightning would strike the canoe and put the two of us out of existence. However, nothing happened to me or my boat, and later the thunder diminished, until at midnight it stopped altogether. I got up, opened the cabin door, and took a look round. There was then no cloud to be seen anywhere, and the sky was dotted with stars. There was also a light breeze from the south-east, and as I had all the stars I wanted to guide me on my way, I at once got sails on the *Tilikum* and directed my course for Sydney.

The south-easterly breeze kept light during the night, but freshened in the morning. At noon I had as much wind as she could stand under all sails, and this condition continued until dark, when the breeze gradually moderated, and at nine o'clock I said to myself, 'If my reckoning is right I should see the Sydney light before long.'

From that time I kept looking for the light, and in fifteen minutes sighted it.

ELEVEN

SYDNEY

THE WIND FELL very light towards midnight, and an hour later I was becalmed. Lowering all sails, I laid down in my little bunk and slept till daybreak, when I awoke to the sound of a whistle. I got up, and there was a large tug alongside me. The captain of the tug told me that he had read in the Sydney papers that the *Tilikum* had left Suva, but owing to the bad weather that had been prevailing on the coast, she had been given up for lost. The captain then asked me if I had seen any vessels outside, and when I answered 'No,' he said that he was going out to look for some. He surmised that there would most likely be an easterly breeze at about ten o'clock, and then proceeded seaward.

My position at that time was about fifteen miles from the lighthouse. As the captain had anticipated it breezed up from the east, and at two o'clock in the afternoon I sailed through the entrance of Sydney Harbour, one of the most beautiful harbours in the world. I then shaped my course towards the town. The doctor's boat was soon alongside, and I reported the loss of my mate. He said he would like to come on board and look at my log book. As there was a strong wind at the time, the doctor did not care to trust himself on the *Tilikum*. However, after I assured him that I had come all the way from Victoria in her, and that she was quite safe in Sydney Harbour, he came on board, and after looking round said, 'Captain, this is the smallest deep-water ship that has ever entered Sydney Harbour. Some years ago Captain Slocum called here in the sloop *Spray*, on a voyage round the world. I thought then that she was a very small vessel to undertake such a cruise, but you could have put this one in her cabin.'

I then showed him my log book and satisfied him that the loss of my mate had been an accident, pure and simple, and one that might have happened on the largest and best vessel afloat.

Shortly after the doctor left me I sailed into a small bay on the left-hand side going up towards Sydney, made the *Tilikum* fast to a yacht, and went on shore to look up Mr Luxton. Mr Luxton and I had an understanding in Suva that he would leave his address in the Sydney Post Office, and on enquiring there I found that he was at an hotel in Manly, which is about seven miles across the harbour from Sydney. A ferry boat leaves Sydney for Manly every thirty minutes, so I boarded the first one available, and met Mr Luxton the same afternoon.

On saying good-bye to Mr Luxton in Suva, I had told him that the distance to Sydney was about eighteen hundred miles, and that he could look for my arrival in about eighteen days from the time I left Suva; but as I was ten days overdue Mr Luxton had given me up for lost.

On meeting my old mate, he looked at me with astonishment, exclaiming, 'Is that really you, John? Are you still alive? Is it possible that you got safely through that bad weather? I thought once that we were going to get lost on the large steamer I came across in, and people here have already given you up.'

When I told Mr Luxton about losing the man who had taken his place in Suva for the run to Sydney, he looked at me for a while and then almost collapsed. When sufficiently recovered, he said, 'Well, John, if I had known that such a thing would happen, I would never have left you. I would far sooner have taken chances on my own life than to see someone else die for me. But, John,' he continued, 'after this accident we must put a stop to our adventure here, sell the boat and go back to Victoria.'

In a way I did not blame Mr Luxton for making such a proposal, and if the accident had happened a day or even a few days before my arrival in Sydney, I should certainly have agreed to his proposal. As it was, I felt so bad after the accident that if a vessel had come along I would have been only too glad to part with my little craft on the high seas and board her, but owing to the fact that I was all that time alone, and had managed to bring the *Tilikum* safely to land, in spite of the bad weather, I had gained so much confidence in her that I felt in my own mind that I should go on and complete the voyage I had undertaken. I told Mr Luxton that accidents would happen to the best of ships afloat, and as the *Tilikum* had proved her seaworthiness in all kinds of weather I could not agree to such a proposal, and asked him to fulfil his agreement.

Mr Luxton was a good shipmate in every way, and was also a very careful man on board the boat, and I am quite certain that if he had remained on the vessel in Suva and made the trip with me to Sydney, the accident would not have happened. I therefore urged him to continue the voyage to Europe, but in spite of all my pleading he refused to go on, and so I became the sole owner of the *Tilikum* and all her fittings. My trouble did not end here, however, as I needed provisions and another mate, and to get these more money than I was in possession of at the time was necessary. After considering the matter, I decided to place my boat and the curios I had collected in Indian villages on the west coast of Vancouver Island and the South Sea Islands on exhibition.

I certainly had luck when the Mayor of Manly granted me permission to place my outfit on exhibition in Manly Park, near the landing-place, where thousands upon thousands of sightseers arrive on the Sydney ferry boats every day, and within twenty-four hours I had sailed my little vessel across Sydney Harbour to Manly, conveyed her to the park, put a canvas tent around her, placed my collection of curios alongside the boat, and there I was, ready for business. I got all the advertising I wanted from the Sydney papers, and so I thought everything would surely be all right.

The next morning at nine o'clock I opened the door and hung up a notice that the *Tilikum* was on exhibition, admission sixpence. To make the exhibition look attractive I hung hundreds of photographs of the natives of the South Sea Islands which we had taken all around the outside of the canvas, and decorated the place with flags. The next thing I had to do was to act the part of a showman, and this I soon found was the hardest proposition that I had tackled so far on the cruise, and I very nearly gave it up at the beginning.

There was very little doing the first morning. The only customer I had was a woman of I don't know how many winters. She was one of those short, stout ladies, and after paying her sixpence she stepped on board and sat down in the cockpit. After she had been there for some time I took heart enough to speak the first word, saying, 'Well, madam, how do you like my little boat?'

'Like what?' she said.

'My little boat,' I repeated.

'I don't see anything to like about your little boat,' she replied; 'but when is she going to start?'

'Start for where?' I asked.

'I don't know,' she retorted; 'you ought to know; I paid you sixpence for a boat ride, and I'm going to have it.'

'Madam,' I explained, 'you are mistaken; this boat is not here to ride about on, but on exhibition as a novelty.'

To my great surprise the good old lady went off like a stick of dynamite.

'Boat on exhibition as a novelty! You must think I'm crazy. I can see hundreds of boats every day in Sydney Harbour for nothing, and you are very much mistaken if you think I have come here to pay you sixpence to see your old boat!'

The lady kept the floor for quite a while, calling me all kinds of pet names. I stood there listening quietly, for I had an idea that if I said anything it would only make matters worse. When she got tired of talking I was only too glad to return her sixpence, which she accepted, and then went out looking as angry as an old hen. This person certainly made me think that I was out of place as a showman, and that the best thing I could do was to sell my outfit and go home with Mr Luxton. However, the same afternoon at three o'clock the Sydney boat came alongside the wharf just loaded down with people, and about five minutes later there was hardly standing room left in my place of exhibition. Some of them told me that they had read with great interest in the daily papers all about my adventures.

The same night, when I counted my takings for the day, I was quite satisfied that everything would come right, which proved true later on. Before I took my departure from Sydney I made up my mind that I would not go direct to Europe in my boat, but would also visit some of the largest cities of Australia, New Zealand, Africa, South America, and then proceed to Europe, calling at different islands as I went along. I may say that I was so taken with Sydney that I stayed there till the middle of January.

As I had fully made up my mind to proceed on my voyage I advertised for a mate, thinking that it might be hard to get one, but to my great surprise I received dozens of applications from all types of men, and one woman even applied. The latter wrote me a very nice letter in which she told me that she had been to see the boat and myself, and that she would give almost anything to make the voyage to Europe in the *Tilikum*. I answered her letter to the effect that to make the voyage to Europe in the canoe would be very hard on a man, but it surely would be too much for a woman. A few days later I received another appeal, in which she said that she had been sailing boats in Sydney Harbour for several years and that she knew all about a boat and the sailing of one, and pleaded hard that I should take her as my mate. I, however, was obdurate, and engaged a young man of the same type as Mr Luxton.

While I was busy getting ready to sail I received a letter from the secretary of the Sydney Harbour Board, asking me to call at his office, which I did the following day. On entering and introducing myself, the good gentleman presented me with a bill for five pounds, representing pilot dues for entering and leaving the harbour, and three shillings and some pence for dues. I told this gentleman that I had found my way into Sydney Harbour without a pilot and that I thought I could find my way out again unassisted.

'Pilotage is compulsory,' he said, 'and it must be paid before you can sail out of this harbour.'

I promised the secretary I would be in next day to pay the bill. The following morning I called at the office and said to the secretary, 'I think I owe you two pounds ten for pilotage and three shillings and a few pence for harbour dues.' With that I placed the money on his desk.

The secretary looked at me, and added, 'Two pounds ten shillings more for going out.'

'I will pay you that amount before I sail out of your harbour,' I assured him.

After a few words he gave a receipt for the money I offered him; I reassured him that I would pay the balance of the pilot dues before sailing out of Sydney Harbour, bade him good day and left the office. A few days later I took the train for Newcastle, taking my boat along as baggage, and during my stay there got a permit from headquarters to the effect that I could sail in and out of any Australasian port at any time, free of charge.

I soon discovered that taking the boat overland was a losing proposition in regard to its exhibition. In the first place the papers would say nothing about my arrival, and as a consequence the exhibition in Newcastle was a complete failure. Of course, on Saturday night, when the town was full of miners, a good many came in just to see what there was to be seen, and when I related that I had crossed the Pacific Ocean in the *Tilikum* they told me that it very much looked to them as if I had crossed the Pacific in her in the same way as I had come from Sydney. I made up my mind there and then that I would never take my boat overland again to a place I could reach by water.

I then prepared to sail for Melbourne. Shortly before my departure from Newcastle I met my old mate, Mr Luxton, who told me that the best fortune-teller in Australia had asked him to inform me that I should under no circumstances sail in the *Tilikum* to Melbourne, as, if I did, something very serious would happen; but as I had made up my mind to see Melbourne, which city I was informed was the finest south of the equator, I told Mr Luxton that if nothing more serious than a fortune-teller would oppose my sailing to Melbourne, I would certainly sail. As soon as the *Tilikum* was ready for sea, I took my departure from Newcastle for the Queen City of the south.

Top: *John Voss, age 22.*
Bottom: *Captain Voss.*
(Maritime Museum of British Columbia)

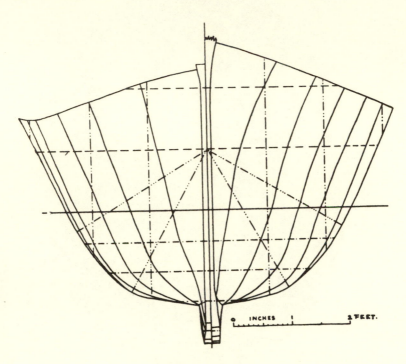

Tilikum *body plan*.

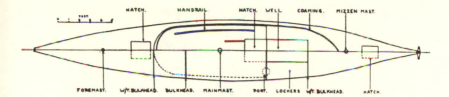

FEET

HATCH. HANDRAIL. HATCH. WELL COAMING. MIZZEN MAST.

FOREMAST. W/T. BULKHEAD. BULKHEAD. MAINMAST. PORT. LOCKERS W/T. BULKHEAD. HATCH.

Tilikum *deck plan and interior arrangement.*

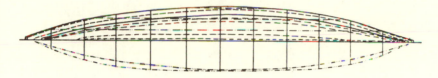

FEET

Tilikum *half-deck plan and diagonal plan.*

FEET

Tilikum *sheer plan.*

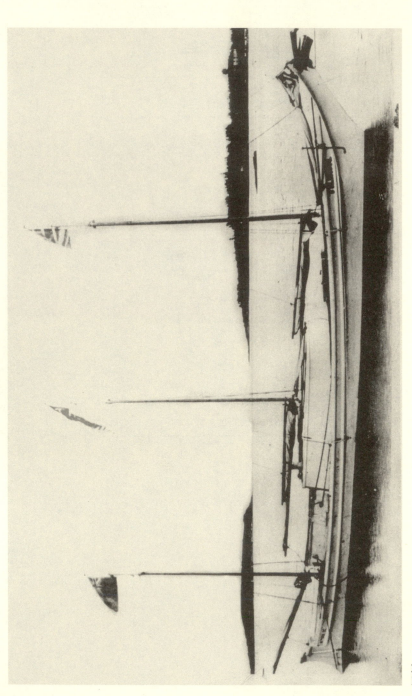

Tilikum. (BC Archives F-07473)

The departure of Tilikum *from Oak Bay, Victoria, British Columbia, May 20, 1901. Mrs. Voss and family are in the foreground. In the back, left to right, are O. B. Ormond, Norman Luxton, and Voss.* (MARITIME MUSEUM OF BRITISH COLUMBIA)

Tilikum *under sail at Galiano Island, British Columbia, 1901.* (BC ARCHIVES E-04094)

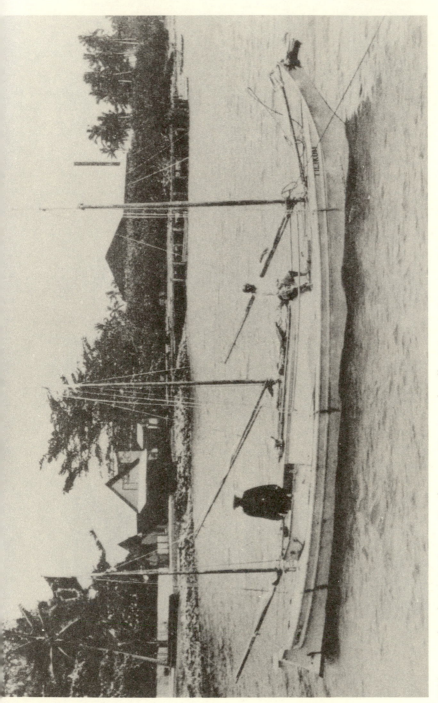

Tilikum *anchored at Apia, Samoa, October 1901. Voss is at the tiller.* (Maritime Museum of British Columbia)

TWELVE

A GENUINE FORTUNE-TELLER

I SET SAIL EARLY in the morning of February 10th, 1902, and with a fresh southerly breeze sailed through the harbour of New-castle toward Nobby Head lighthouse. After rounding the head, my course was south, but the wind being from the southward, I put her about seventy-five miles on the land and took advantage of the Australian stream, which was quite a help to me.

The quick motion of the *Tilikum* was too much for my new mate's stomach, and he soon hung his head over the rail. I advised him to take a good drink of salt water and he would soon be all right, but somehow he could not get the salt water down, and kept sick day after day, being therefore of very little use. The wind remained in the south day after day at times varying a little to the east or west, of which I took advantage in tacking about, and between that and the southerly current I gradually worked my way down as far as Cape How, the south-east point of Aus-tralia, where I had to alter my course to the south-westward for Bass Straits. But as bad luck would have it, not alone did the wind haul into the south-west but it started to blow a heavy gale, which lasted nearly two days, during which time we were hove to under a sea anchor, and drifted a long way out of our course.

That gale almost killed my mate. In my long career at sea I have found that, as a rule, if a person gets sea sick and takes a good drink or two of salt water, he soon gets over it, but my new mate was unable to swallow it at all, and as sea water is the only remedy I know of that does any good, I had to give him up as a bad job. I may say that nearly all through my voyage I took a drink of sea water every morning. That is about the only medicine I used, with few exceptions, which I will explain later on, and I was nearly always in excellent health.

After the south-westerly gale I was lucky in getting a leading all-sail breeze and soon got up to the west of Bass Straits, after which the wind hauled into the south-west again and increased fast, with threatening weather, so I was practically sure of another gale. It was fourteen days since I had sailed from Newcastle; my mate had been sick all the time, and I was afraid that if we should get into another south-westerly gale it might kill him.

My position was at that time a little to the south-east of Cape Liptrap, and according to a chart of the coast which I had there was a good-sized lagoon at the head of Liptrap Bay, about twenty miles distant in a northerly direction, to which there is an entrance for small vessels. As I had a strong south-westerly wind I kept off and steered for the lagoon. The wind was increasing fast, and in about three hours' time I could see the entrance, and sometimes, when my little vessel was on top of a sea, the smooth water in the lagoon; but at the same time I saw heavy surf breakers both before the entrance and also along the shore as far as the eye could reach. I realised at once that I had got into a very dangerous position, and could not think of allowing the boat to get into the breakers ahead of me; and as the place where I was formed a kind of horseshoe bight, with a strong wind and large sea making straight into it for the land, I hauled up to the wind at once and tried to beat out into the open sea again. I made tack for tack; but as the wind was increasing and the sea growing larger I was obliged to shorten sail. Nevertheless, instead of beating to the seaward, I drew ever nearer to the breakers, and thereby knew that it was impossible to keep clear of them. I therefore prepared to sail the *Tilikum* through the heavy breaking water.

I asked my mate if he was a good swimmer. He said that he was, but in the condition he was in at the time, would last but a very short while in the breakers. I had two small life-belts, and put one round my mate, advising him, if a breaker should turn the boat over, to be careful not to get underneath but to get away from the boat as quickly as possible, and then take his time in swimming ashore, as the life-belt would keep his head out of the water, and to let all the breakers pass over him. I then donned the other, and swung the *Tilikum* before the wind and sea and steered straight in for the breakers under small sails. I also put my sea anchor over the stern, with one line fastened to the mouth and the other to the point of it, and, as I was sailing towards the breakers, towed it along by the line which was fastened to the point. The sea anchor being light it slipped over the surface of the water without retarding the speed of the boat. In a minute or two we were in the midst of the surf. When I saw the first breaker overtaking the boat, and when it was within a short distance of the stern, I slacked the tripping line. As the line that was fastened at one end to the mouth of the sea anchor and at the other to the stern of the boat tightened, the sea anchor at once filled with water and stopped the headway of the vessel. The breakers would rush at us, but owing to the headway of the boat being stopped she would raise her stern to them splendidly, only taking a little spray over. When the stern of the boat was on top of the breaker the rudder was out of the water and, therefore, of no use; but the sea anchor took its place. It did not only prevent the boat from going ahead, and at the same time relieved her from suction by allowing the stern to rise when on top of a breaker, but it also kept the boat from broaching to while the rudder was out of action. As soon as the breaker got under the middle of the boat and her stern dipped the rudder took action in the water again. The boat being thus out of danger, I quickly pulled the tripping line, which turned the sea anchor over, point towards the boat. Thus we gathered headway again. I repeated the same manoeuvre with every breaker, and we crossed the surf with a minimum of trouble and taking over only a little spray.

The long beach was slowly shallowing, and before the *Tilikum* struck bottom we entered smooth water. When nearly half-way through the entrance we grounded, and owing to low water were obliged to remain there until the tide came in again. In a little while the water had left us high and dry, and after we had taken a run on the sandy beach my mate enjoyed a good meal for the first time in a fortnight.

We had hardly finished our dinner when the tide returned and the water rose very fast. The wind blew hard, also, and the water became choppy round the boat. As it rose, the waves grew larger, and before the boat was afloat they developed into small but swiftly-breaking seas which set the *Tilikum* rolling about on her keel. This stirred the sand up, and as the tide came running in fast and the seas rolled the boat about she gradually swung sideways, on to the wind and sea. Presently the sand began piling up on the lee side, and, the water rising, the breakers grew larger and larger. However, as the boat was lying sideways, thrust up against a sandbank which increased in height faster than the tide owing to drift sand in the current, we were absolutely helpless.

It was a most difficult position. The breakers would deliberately roll along and strike the boat on the starboard, hammering it sideways up against the sandbank, and at the same time sweeping over us. All we could do was to hold on, to prevent our being washed overboard. While in that awful predicament, thinking whether it would be advisable to give up the *Tilikum* the Sydney fortune-teller's prognostication came back to my mind.

At that critical moment I noticed four men running down the beach in our direction; but they could get only within about two hundred yards of us. There they stood, we could not hear their voices, but saw them waving their hats as if to invite us to leave our doomed vessel and come on shore.

I said to my mate, 'You go ashore, before the water gets too deep, and save your life. I am going to stay with the boat till she breaks up.'

'I will leave her when you do,' my mate turned round and replied.

Then, as a last resort, I hoisted the forestaysail and next the foresail, and when I hauled the foresheet in it put the boat almost on her beam ends. Just then a large breaking sea struck the boat with such a force that I thought it would dash her to pieces. But, contrary to my expectations, our boat was lifted, and the sails catching enough wind to put her over the sandbank the *Tilikum* was safe and sound once more in smooth water, out of all danger!

Sailing on to the beach where the four men who had been watching our struggle for some time were waiting to receive us, I jumped ashore and introduced myself. I then learned that the gap which we had passed through into the lagoon, and where we had encountered all the trouble, was not the proper entrance, it was simply an opening in the narrow low spit of land that framed the lagoon seawards. Large breaking seas during a heavy south-westerly gale had done this damage. The proper entrance lay a few miles more to the eastward.

We were congratulated upon our luck in successfully effecting a landing through that false entrance. On telling them what kind of trip we were on they said that they had read about the cruise in the Melbourne papers but never expected me to call at this remote place. However, we received a friendly welcome and were invited to their home which, they said, lay about four miles distant. It was also the nearest house to the spot, and we gladly accepted the invitation.

After changing our clothes and assuring ourselves that the *Tilikum* was well secured, we accompanied our newly-found friends up the beach towards a forest, where four saddle horses were hitched to a tree. My mate and myself were given a mount, and in company of two of our hosts rode for about two miles through the forest. Passing for a like distance over a stretch of grassland we finally arrived at a neat farmstead, which belonged to the two gentlemen who had guided us. They were brothers named Pinkerton.

Within a very short time of our arrival the table was spread with a sumptuous repast. After two weeks of fasting my mate, who had been compelled to part even with his last meal when the boat was bumping and rolling on the sandbar, certainly did full justice to the good things before him, and remarked at the conclusion of the meal that he felt as well as ever.

After dinner the farmers entertained us with songs and music. Hearing 'Life on the Ocean Wave,' 'When Ireland will have

Home Rule,' and 'Jig-jig with the Flap-flap' certainly made us feel that we were among friends and welcome, and when I hinted at nine o'clock that it was time for us to return to the boat, these kind people almost compelled us to stop for the night, and even went so far as to ask us to stay for a week or two. They offered us the use of their house and buggy for as long as we liked. We thanked them for their hospitality, but gave them to understand that we had to go down to look after our boat. We promised, however, to come back the next day.

When we bade them good night and opened the door we saw to our surprise three horses, saddled and ready to take us down to the beach. I mounted one, my mate another, and one of the farmers got astride the third one. Being a poor horseman I requested the farmer to take his time, and in the clear starlit night we rode slowly over the pastureland. In about half an hour we had reached the forest. The sky had become cloudy and overcast, so it was very dark under the trees. However, we made our way. I was just thinking how it would suit me to take a little more practice on horseback, and that I might eventually develop into a fairly good jockey and strike a job in Melbourne to ride one of the fast horses in the cup race. Possibly this mind-wandering caused me to be less careful, for somehow my horse had got off the cow trail which we were following along between the trees, and I was suddenly brought to my senses, only to lose them temporarily, by falling heavily from my mount and nearly breaking my neck. A stout bough had caught me in the chest. I lay on the ground for a few minutes, not unconscious, but thinking again of a certain fortune-teller.

On convincing my companions that I was unhurt I proclaimed that I would prefer walking the rest of the way. Thereupon, as my mate swore that, while he was not much of a sailor, he could, on the other hand, navigate through any forest in the southern part of Australia, our host returned to his farm with the three horses. So with my mate in the lead we resumed the cow trail which was to take us down to the beach. We chatted as we went along through the forest, and owing to the darkness made only slow progress.

Some considerable time had elapsed and my dead reckoning was up. So I ventured the opinion that we should be near the boat and I hoped we had not got on the wrong trail. My mate assured me that we were on the right course towards the boat and that we would soon drop anchor there. We therefore continued, but when I consulted my watch and discovered that over an hour had elapsed since we had left the horses I was quite sure that we had passed the place or got off the right trail. Now and then through an opening in the dense foliage overhead I could see the stars, which were gradually disappearing behind a bank of heavy clouds, and it looked to me like approaching rain.

'Back the mainyard and take a sounding. I should like to find out where we are,' I said as I struck a match to have a look at the trail. 'This don't look to me like a cow trail. At any rate it is not the one we came along this afternoon which showed bare ground, worn by the tracks of cattle. This place rather resembles a pasture lately grazed over.'

'Indeed,' my mate assented, 'you are right, but just follow me, and we will soon be on the cow trail again.'

By this time the stars had altogether disappeared and rain began to fall. We went along as best we could, my mate making full speed ahead, and owing to the darkness I lost sight of him. But as he unceasingly talked about his former bush travels in Australia I managed to keep track of him by following his voice. All of a sudden my pilot gave an abrupt yell, and called for help. I hurried to his rescue and, striking a match, found him lying in what he called a prickle bush. In my endeavours to free him from the rank undergrowth in which he was entangled, I received my share of the prickling. When I got him out of his unenviable position we started on our homeward journey again, this time for the most part on our hands and knees, feeling for the cow trail which we were unable to find.

The rain was increasing fast and soon poured down on us in torrents, and as it was so dark in the forest that we could not see a hand before our eyes, we were compelled to give up our journey and stop where we happened to be to wait for the daylight.

It was about eleven o'clock when we hove to in the heavy rain, which poured down on us for about five hours. We could not sit or lie down as the ground was flooded with water, and as it was not advisable to walk about, lest we should run into another tree or prickle bush, we had to stand like two statues. I did not say much during that time, my mind being occupied with Luxton's fortune-teller, in whose ability I gradually gained confidence.

We certainly felt gratified when the rain ceased at daybreak. As luck would have it, we were near the lagoon, and through the trees could see the water shimmering. A few minutes' walk brought us to the beach where the *Tilikum* lay high and dry on the sand: she had drifted up on the high tide during the night.

In about ten minutes we were on board, and after having changed our clothes built a large fire of drift-wood to dry our wet garments and cook breakfast. It was a beautiful morning, clear and warm, and we soon forgot our unpleasant experiences of the previous night. At nine o'clock two saddle horses were sent down by the brothers Pinkerton, on which we rode back to the farm. During our stay the good fellows treated us so well that I almost felt home-sick when we finally sailed for Melbourne, after having enjoyed their hospitality for a whole week.

On the day fixed for our departure, at one o'clock in the afternoon it was high water, and we tried to get under way before that time in order to cross the surf on the top of the tide; but owing to the farewell dinner with which we were honoured by our hosts we did not make a start until two hours later, and as the surf was breaking heavily outside the new entrance I made up my mind to pass it and leave the lagoon by the proper outlet, where, as the Pinkertons had told us, we would have no difficulty in reaching the open sea. A light breeze blew out of the lagoon, which afforded us a beam wind to sail to the eastward. But when abreast of the new entrance, which I remembered so dearly, the ebb tide went rushing through it with such a force that the *Tilikum* was drawn towards the treacherous gap at a rate of about six miles an hour. Face to face with the dangerous breakers which came rolling towards us, and knowing that in another five minutes we would be right in the midst of them if we did not succeed in stopping the boat, I dropped anchor and lowered the sails. The boat swung round, but the anchor did not take hold. So, as the boat kept on drifting, I pulled the anchor on board, swung the boat before the wind and with the light easterly breeze sailed straight into the roaring combers. I knew that between the wind and tide the boat would have headway enough to resist the breakers' fury, and prevent her being turned end over.

And then it came! In a minute we were in it. The first few breakers were small and only threw some spray over us, but now a large one towered above us, and in an instant the *Tilikum* and her crew were submerged. When the sea had passed over us I just had time enough to ascertain that the boat was all right, and no sooner had I announced another comber when it was on us with all its might. But as before, we stood the trial and got out safely. After that we met with quite a few smaller breakers, which, however, were not of a dangerous description, and as tide and a light northerly breeze took the boat in charge, we soon passed beyond all breaking water and entered the open sea.

In crossing the breakers no harm was done to the boat; but we obtained another good soaking and my mate turned seasick again, this time worse than ever. By four o'clock the farewell dinner, which he had enjoyed heartily, was overboard and he still retched, his head hanging over the rail.

The wind freshened up a little towards evening and about eight o'clock we rounded Cape Liptrap, whence we shaped a course for the entrance of Port Phillip Bay, reaching the same on the following night at about ten o'clock, but owing to a rumbling sound, apparently caused by the strong tide setting through the narrow entrance and thus forming a dangerous overfall, we kept off a little until the noise ceased. Then we sailed into the entrance and with a moderate southerly breeze made towards Melbourne, a distance of about thirty-seven miles, dropping anchor off St Kilda at five o'clock the following afternoon.

The next day the *Tilikum* was taken out of the water at Captain Canney's bathing establishment, and a few days later she was transported on wheels to Collance Street and exhibited there until Labour Day. She was then removed to the park and placed in the Melbourne exhibition building during the celebration, and at the conclusion of the latter she was taken out of the building to be transferred by the same wagon that had previously served for conveyance.

I had contracted with a truck and dray company for transporting the *Tilikum* wherever I wanted her. After removal from the exhibition building, and when ready to be put on the wagon, the same sheerlegs that previously had lowered her were used to raise her again. These were placed in position and two double-block tackles rove off with a three-inch rope. The top block was hooked on to the top of the sheerlegs and the lower block to a strop which ran around the boat. Then the hauling part of the tackle was passed to a winch, which itself was fastened to the lower end of the sheerlegs. As I directed the work myself I told the four men in attendance to heave away slowly. The *Tilikum* soon swung in the air, high enough to push the wagon underneath. But just when I said 'Stop heaving,' the boat dropped to the ground! As I stood right alongside she nearly fell upon me.

There she lay at my feet, smashed to pieces, after having successfully weathered all sorts of heavy gales and having carried me many thousand miles over the ocean. She had withstood all the tumbling about at the lagoon entrance near Cape Liptrap and the tremendous breakers at that unlucky place. Now on this bright morning, she lay there a total wreck, to all appearance; wrecked on dry land and in one of the finest places in Australia, surrounded by all the products of a refined civilisation, not to mention beautiful flowers and sweet singing birds!

Up to that time the *Tilikum*, from her keel to the top was a solid vessel, not a seam nor a split in her hull anywhere. After the smash-up, when I examined her, I found splits in five different places, one crack extending from the top and down the middle of the stern and along the bottom nearly as far as the forward end, and four more cracks, two on each side running from aft to forward to about the same length. Besides, there were several cross splits. Some of the splits were from one inch to two inches wide: in fact, the boat was all in pieces. In face of this calamity I arrived at the conclusion that I should have listened to Mr Luxton and his fortune-teller, when advising me to leave the 'Queen City of the South' out of my programme.

The breaking of the hook which held the top tackle caused the accident. The hook had snapped like a piece of glass, and as it dropped into the cockpit I picked it up and put it in my pocket. After having re-examined my little vessel carefully, I thought that I might be able to repair her and proceed with my voyage.

THIRTEEN

A LAWSUIT

THE CONTRACT which I had made with the manager of the carrier company was a verbal one only. However, I had informed that gentleman of the weight of my boat and also told him that she held the world's record for the only real canoe and the smallest vessel that ever crossed the Pacific Ocean. I had pointed out the fact that the *Tilikum* constituted my home and my existence, and as I considered her of great value to me I had urged him to employ the greatest care and good gear to avoid possible accidents; whereupon the manager had assured me that he would use the best appliances and that nothing would happen to my boat: and I had taken his promise as a guarantee.

The manager was not present when the unfortunate smash-up occurred, but I at once sent for him, not allowing anybody to touch the boat until after his arrival. I then asked the man whether he would be good enough to have the *Tilikum* repaired under my instruction, and 'Whether she proves seaworthy or not,' I said, 'we will call it square.'

'Captain,' he answered, 'I am very sorry; it is rather a sad accident, but I don't think I can do anything for you.'

'Mr X' (I refrain from mentioning the name for obvious reasons), I said, 'you will excuse me for correcting you. The breaking up of my boat was not an accident, but due to carelessness on your part. I repeat my offer. If you repair the boat under my instructions I will call it square and say no more about it.'

Mr X promised to send a carpenter, who came the next day. He offered to repair the boat for twenty-two pounds ten. Mr X now proposed to pay half of this sum on condition that I contributed the other half. But the carpenter acted in a way which gave me some reason to doubt his ability to restore my little vessel to a seaworthy condition. Therefore I asked Mr X to send another man of more experience, to which he agreed.

The following day the new man arrived to examine the boat. He was of middle age, and I could see at once that he knew his business; so I wished that Mr X would entrust him with the job. However, as he asked thirty-seven pounds for repairing the boat Mr X refused him and adhered to the original proposal. As I would not accept that a lawsuit followed, which kept me in Melbourne for several months longer than my programme provided for.

I was, of course, a perfect stranger in Melbourne, with the exception of a few friends whom I had made during my short stay. On the other hand, the firm with which I was to go to law had the reputation of being the largest truck and dray company in the city, and were very wealthy. When it became known, therefore, that I had sued the firm for damages, people advised me not to appeal to law, for the company would prove too strong for me, and that they would be sure to win eventually at my expense. Others came forward and even offered to pay for the repairs to my boat. In short, when I got into that trouble I discovered that I had a good many more friends than I had supposed. However, I declined all assistance, knowing from personal experience that British jurisdiction is fair for rich and poor alike, everyone getting his deserts.

I therefore took the advice of Mr C. McLoughlin, a member of the St Kilda Yacht Club, at whose house I was staying, and went to see Mr W. Wolcot, a Melbourne solicitor. After having stated my case, Mr Wolcot assured me that my claims were substantial, and consequently did not hesitate to file a suit for damages amounting to five hundred pounds. I told Mr Wolcot that I considered this sum to be excessive, inasmuch as I only wanted my boat restored to a sound condition. But he pointed out that I would have to suffer a loss of time amounting to three months, until the court sat, and that the delay might even exceed that time.

Mr J. E. Smith, a building inspector and Canadian by birth,

had, ever since my arrival at Melbourne, shown great interest in my voyage. He said he would like to see me complete the cruise, and was kind enough to offer me a vacant plot near his home to put my boat in order. This I accepted, and as I wanted to be near the *Tilikum*, I likewise took advantage of Mr and Mrs Smith's generous invitation to stay with them as a guest until the case should be decided in court. The people of Melbourne having treated me so hospitably, I naturally disliked the idea of taking action against a Melbourne firm. However, as my cause was just and I was advised by my new friends and the solicitor to go ahead, steps were taken and the case was called in the Melbourne county court.

The day came and I was present with Mr Wolcot and my barrister, Mr McArthur, when the court opened. There were three breach of promise cases ahead of mine, and they were settled in about two hours. I consequently thought that in another hour or two I should have my verdict, but in this I was very much mistaken, as my case required seven days in all! And because it took such a long time it may be interesting to the reader to learn the most important points on which I won and Mr X lost.

The defendants' lawyer took me under a crossfire which lasted nearly one whole day. But it only served to prove that practically the sole point of importance was the hook which broke and thus caused all the trouble. The lawyer asked me what I thought of the hook, to which I replied that it was no good. This seemed to upset the temper of my questioner, and he evidently thought that he had already cornered me. He looked at me, and then at the judge, and uttered in a harsh tone, 'Your opinion is that the hook was no good, but what will you say when Professor Curnow, who is an authority on iron and steel manufacture, will stand where you are now and declare under an oath that the hook in question was made of the very best Swedish iron?' Professor Curnow was considered the most prominent expert on iron and steel in Australia at that time, and he served as a witness to Mr X. I answered that in such a case I still would uphold what I had stated, viz., that the hook was no good. Then the lawyer looked at me and said, 'You are a most wonderful man.' At this juncture the judge intervened and asked me to explain why the hook was no good.

My contention was on these lines: To begin with, the iron of which the hook was made was probably good Swedish iron before it was shaped into the hook. But the blacksmith who manufactured the hook made a mistake, inasmuch as all hooks should be forged out of one single and solid piece of stock. In this case the eye and the hook proper have been made each separately, and then the two pieces were welded together at what is called the neck of the hook. Besides, as the fracture plainly shows, there existed at the inner side of the neck, where the welding was done, a flaw about one-sixteenth of an inch deep which extended half-way round the hook to the outside. And the brittle condition of the iron at the outer neck leaves no doubt that in welding the material had been overheated. In other words, the iron, through being overheated, became similar to cast iron. For when the hook broke, instead of straightening out at first before reaching the breaking-point, as it would have done under normal circumstances, it snapped like a piece of glass. Consequently, though good Swedish iron might have been employed, it was ruined through poor workmanship, leaving the finished hook unreliable and unsafe to use. Whereupon I produced the lower end of the hook to corroborate my statement.

The next man in the box was Mr X, and, like myself, he was kept there for the best part of a day, being cross-examined by my lawyer. The agreement between Mr X and myself with regard to moving the boat had been a verbal one only, as stated above; but in his evidence he acknowledged—which of course was bare truth—what I had said when accepting his tender for moving my boat—to wit, the weight of the boat was about three thousand pounds, that he should be sure to employ good gear in order to avoid accidents, and that the *Tilikum* was my home and means of livelihood. I do not think that Mr X treated me altogether properly when he refused to repair the boat, but he certainly proved himself a gentleman when acknowledging the above statement before the judge and jury.

The next to bear witness—also on behalf of Mr X—was the carpenter who had offered to repair the boat for thirty-seven pounds. Here I must premise that the three sheerlegs which were used for hoisting the boat off and on the wagon belonged to myself, and I had purchased them in Melbourne for the purpose. I had also supervised the moving operations, as already mentioned. The carpenter's evidence ran as follows: To lift any kind of heavy weight two sheerlegs, stayed by means of a guy-rope fastened to the top should be used instead of three sheerlegs, as employed on this occasion. Three sheerlegs, the witness claimed, were good enough to lift a few bags of potatoes or coal, but would never do for raising a heavy load, as they would shack and swing about when the strain was applied. This witness claimed to be a shipbuilder. The judge, who seemed much surprised at his statement, asked him what he was talking about. As to myself, having been previously informed of the evidence that was to be brought forward against me, I was prepared to meet the occasion. I had made three quarter-inch square sticks, two feet long, and to prove by actual demonstration that the witness was altogether wrong, with permission of the judge, I placed two of the sticks on a board like two sheerlegs, with a stay fastened to the top, just as the witness had described it. I then hung a small spring scale to the top of the two sheerlegs and slowly pulled it down. When the sheerlegs came to a breaking strain, the spring scale indicated six pounds. I then placed the third leg in position, removing the stayrope, and without altering the angle of the first two sheerlegs. Now the sheerlegs would come to a breaking strain when the scale showed fourteen pounds. Mr McArthur then told the shipbuilder that that was all he wanted from him.

The next witness for Mr X was Professor Curnow, and like the rest of the chief witnesses he was kept under direct cross-examination for the best part of a day. However, the gist of his evidence was that he had tested the lower hook of the tackle which did not break, and had ascertained a breaking strain of nearly four tons. He also stated that the hook was made of good iron. The Professor further admitted the existence of the flaw in the broken hook.

When all the evidence was gathered, I requested Mr McArthur to put it to Professor Curnow whether he would or would not use a hook like the one in question when about to lift a heavy and valuable load; to which he replied that he would not. In giving that answer Professor Curnow certainly confirmed my statement that the hook used with the tackle was inefficient. Several other witnesses were examined, whose evidence had less importance.

The case having been summed up the jury retired, and when returning, about half an hour later, judgment was given in my favour for two hundred pounds and costs. Mr X intended to appeal, but in order to avoid further loss of time I came to a private agreement with him. Thus the trouble was settled.

FOURTEEN

REPAIRING A WRECK—AN OVERLAND HAUL—WITH AN INTOXICATED CREW OFF FOR ADELAIDE

MEANTIME, the *Tilikum* lay at the vacant lot with all her bones broken, and by looking at her no one would have thought that she was good for anything but firewood. However, I did not abandon the idea that I would be able to fix her up and complete my voyage in her to London, and as I have some experience with tools, being a bit of a woodspoiler myself, I went to work to put her together and see her floating once more.

The first thing I did was to place the wreckage on blocks. I proceeded to screw here and there and all round until the boat had assumed its former shape. I then laid ropes all round and by means of Spanish windlasses tightened them. In this way I gradually closed the splits and brought all pieces together in their proper places. Thereupon I applied thin steel ribs from one end to the other, fastening the same with screw-bolts driven from the outside and set up with a nut inside. When I had all the steel ribs and bolts in place I removed the ropes and put a new keel under her. I then caulked all splits and fractures and finally put the fittings back in their respective places. After I had applied two coats of paint inside and outside, the *Tilikum* looked almost as well as when I left Victoria. The only difference was that with the exception of the top work not a split or seam could be seen in her when I set out, for she had not suffered as much as a scratch all the way to Melbourne. Now, I had but a patched-up canoe. However, I decided to give her another trial, and if she would stand the test, I was to proceed on my voyage.

During my stay in Melbourne I met people from Ballarat, an important mining town with a population of about forty thousand, situated at a distance of approximately one hundred miles from Melbourne. They asked me to bring my boat to their city. As I was desirous of seeing a little of the interior of Australia, I went up to Ballarat by train, via Geelong. Quite a surprise was in store for me on my arrival, for I had no idea that such a fine city existed in the interior. The main street compares favourably with any I have seen in other parts of the world. There is a reason for this, as Ballarat is surrounded by some of the best farming country found anywhere, besides being a great mining centre. It also derives fame from the fact that it is the only place in Australia where a battle between Europeans was fought. If I am not mistaken, this happened about 1849, when miners came into conflict with the police. Just outside Ballarat is a fine park, the centre of which is occupied by a beautiful lake, about a mile across. The view of this lake, surrounded by splendid trees and flowers of every description, and covered with pleasure-boats and yachts, with the bright sun shining over all, reminded me of Penrhyn Island and its lagoon. On that bright sheet of water, enlivened by all the splendour of a regatta day, I sailed the *Tilikum* among a crowd of yachts and pleasure-boats. Proudly she carried her new suit of sails, which was presented by the Ballarat yachtsmen. And the people told me that she was the first deep-sea vessel to sail on their lake.

My next move was to Geelong, where the *Tilikum* re-entered the briny. I was in need of a new mate, and several young Ballarat men had offered their services. After I had picked one of the number I took him to the Mayor to have him signed on for the trip to London. The Mayor of Ballarat, who had held that office for a good many years, was about sixty-five years of age, and the people looked upon him as a father. He told me, with tears in his eyes, that one of his sons had taken to the sea and was lost; he warned the young man to be careful. But when I had assured the old gentleman that after the accident which had befallen me I always made sure that a life-line was used he seemed to feel more satisfied. It was a day or two later that I took the *Tilikum* down to Geelong and put her in the water.

When everything was ready, a good strong breeze was blowing, which turned up a short, choppy sea. This gave me an excellent opportunity for a trial, and I went out sailing, accompanied by some of the Geelong yachts. I forced the boat as much as she could stand under all sail, and she sometimes put her bow clean under water. However, the trial proved successful as I could discover no sign of a leak. The only mischief that was done was the upsetting of my new mate's stomach, but I consoled him somewhat with the assurance that in a day or two he would get over that. At nightfall we anchored alongside the Geelong wharf again, and after advising my mate that we should sail the next morning at daybreak I went on shore to bid good-bye to some friends. When I returned to the boat next morning my mate was missing, and I have not seen him since.

I at once wired to the Seamen's Home at Melbourne for another man, and the following morning, while I stood on the wharf awaiting the arrival of my companion, I noticed a man walking towards me with a bag of clothes on his shoulder. He was very much intoxicated to all appearance, as at times the bag would overbalance him, and both bag and owner fell heavily to the ground. However, he managed to regain his feet each time, and by and by came near me. Then the fellow dropped his bag and said that he had just arrived from Melbourne and was going to join a vessel. He pointed at the same time to a barque which lay at anchor about three hundred yards distant. He showed me a letter which, he said, was addressed to the captain of the vessel he was hired for. I looked at it and saw my own name written thereon, and I knew at once that he was to be my mate. He then queried whether that was my boat, lying alongside the wharf. I replied in the affirmative, and added that it was the vessel he would go in. He was like all other men when they are intoxicated, full of arguments and foolish talk, and after some dispute I finally got him on board and he soon fell asleep in the cabin. I set all sail and losing no more time took my departure for Adelaide.

It was about four o'clock when the *Tilikum*, with a light easterly breeze, was gliding down Port Phillip Bay towards the ocean. But at sunset the wind lightened, so I dropped anchor for the night. My new mate was still sound asleep, in which condition he continued until the next morning at daybreak. When I got up and gave him a call he exhibited great surprise. He stared at me, then looked out on deck and asked, 'Where am I?'

'You are on board the *Tilikum* and bound for Shanghai,' I replied.

'Holy smoke, Shanghaied and bound for Shanghai,' the new-comer uttered.

When I had explained matters to him, and what kind of a job he had undertaken, he was not quite so dismayed. Only, he felt very bad, he said, and would give anything for a drink. But as his bottle was empty and I had no liquor of any kind on board I told him that a good draught of water was the best drink he could take to restore himself. We then got our anchor up and headed once more for the open sea. About midday we sailed through the entrance of Port Phillip Bay, and shaped a course along the coast for Port Adelaide, a distance of about five hundred miles. When my new mate had sobered up he proved himself a first-class seaman.

The wind was variable and moderate all the way, and nothing unusual happened during the trip. On the sixth day out we were becalmed near Kangaroo Island, and anchored there for the night. The next morning a light breeze blew from the south-west and we sailed with it up to Port Adelaide. There the *Tilikum* again was taken ashore and conveyed to the City of Adelaide, the capital of South Australia, where I stopped till December 28th. Thereafter I removed the boat to Glenell, a summer and pleasure resort eight miles out of Adelaide.

My mate was greatly addicted to alcoholic drinks, and I was obliged, therefore, to engage another man. When he was found, I sailed from Glenell on January 4th, 1903, for Hobart, Tasmania, a distance of about eight hundred miles, which was made in thirteen days with variable winds and good weather. The night before I was honoured with a banquet given by the Glenell yachtsmen who, when leaving, accompanied the *Tilikum* for some distance in their yachts.

On arrival at Hobart my new mate from Adelaide assured me that he had enjoyed the trip immensely and that he would like to accompany me to London in the *Tilikum*. His name was Ed. O. Donner, but he was better known as the 'Tattooed Man of Australia,' being tattooed all over his body. He was a good entertainer and knew how to while away the time pleasantly.

FIFTEEN

A SAD RECOLLECTION AT HOBART— RUNNING TOO LONG AND ITS CONSEQUENCE—THE ALBATROSS

HOBART IS the capital of Tasmania, and has a population of about forty-five thousand people. The city is picturesquely situated at the foot of Mount Wellington and on the River Derwent, about twelve miles from its mouth. Owing to its excellent climate, Hobart is visited during the summer by many holiday-makers from the Australian continent. The River Derwent and the Entrecasteaux Channel afford one of the most beautiful cruising grounds in the world, and many yachtsmen take full advantage of this.

While staying at Hobart, as in other places, I received many invitations to afternoon teas, dinners, etc. One afternoon, having accepted an invitation from a young married couple, I was shown some photographs. One of them represented a bright-looking young man, and it struck me that I had seen his face before. The lady of the house, who had passed me the picture and stood beside me, said, in a low voice: 'Do you recognise this photograph?' And when I looked up into her face, I saw tears in her eyes.

'I do,' I replied. 'It is a photograph of the young man whom I lost off the *Tilikum* on the night of October 27th, 1901!'

'Yes,' she said, 'that young man was my brother.'

Both the young lady and her husband must have noticed that I also was moved by the sudden recall of that sad accident. They assured me, however, that they did not think in the least of blaming me; they knew that it was a very common occurrence to lose lives from much larger vessels.

After a stay of a fortnight at Hobart, we sailed for the south end of New Zealand. I was advised by people at Hobart that I had better not take that course, as the weather most likely would prove too much for the *Tilikum*. But by that time I was fully convinced that the boat was as sound as she ever had been, and I felt as comfortable in her during a heavy gale as in a calm. I had made up my mind; so we set sail on January 27th and shaped a course for Invercargill, the southernmost city of New Zealand. The distance as the crow flies is about nine hundred miles.

We started with a light westerly breeze and under a clear sky. The wind freshened up towards night and we soon got into the open Pacific. For the first two days the westerly winds kept fresh and the *Tilikum* went along at her best. On the third day the wind gradually hauled into the north-eastward, and thereafter into the east. As I had reason to hope that it soon would haul into the westward, these being the average winds in that part of the world, I kept the boat on the port tack, thinking that in this way we would most likely secure a quick passage. But at the same time we were carried more and more to the south and got down nearly as far as the fiftieth degree, while the wind still blew from the east. I then put her on starboard tack and stood to the northward.

We always enjoyed a good strong breeze, just enough for the *Tilikum* to nicely put up with under all sail. Only at times, during the night, I shortened down. Having gone a few miles to the northward, the easterly wind became light and hauled into the westward; after which the force increased. I kept the *Tilikum* before it and steered for the south of New Zealand under all sail. Whenever a south-wester comes in after an easterly wind in that part of the world it very often develops into a gale; and so it did on this occasion.

The wind continued blowing and the boat increased her speed as it got stronger. I took in one sail after the other, until she was running under a mainsail only. I told my mate to put one shutter into the cabin door, as I intended doing a little sailing that afternoon. I do not like to press a small boat hard when sailing by the wind with a strong breeze and head sea on a long cruise such as we were on, because the jumping and pitching and the heavy spray which the boat will take on board under those circumstances is anything but pleasant. But it is certainly a pleasure to sail a boat with a free wind, or when she is running before it and has a good large sea in her favour. In running with wind and sea I could sit in the cockpit, with the tiller in my hand, hour upon hour, and watch her going along. When running hard, I mostly used the mainsail only. Sailing of this sort is a pleasure, and it seemed so fascinating to me that afternoon, that I would sit there, not conversing with my mate, but talking to the boat, after this style: 'That's right. Go it, go it, good old *Tilikum*. Get to New Zealand quickly and we will have a fine time!'

It was about four o'clock in the afternoon; the wind was increasing and the seas getting larger, and I was thinking to myself about heaving to, when all of a sudden I heard the noise of a breaking sea coming up behind us. 'Hullo,' I said to myself, 'there it is.' And by that time the sea certainly was there. It turned out to be a bad one and the boat was not quick enough to raise her stern to the occasion, so the sea broke over us. For a second, ship and crew were submerged. However, as we had one shutter in the door very little water penetrated into the cabin. But whatever little did get in, it must have entered like a shot; for my mate said afterwards, he had been sitting upright in the forepart of the cabin when the water, splashing over the top of the low shutter, struck him in the face. My chronometer watch, which hung in the same neighbourhood near the deck, had disappeared from its place—I found some pieces of it later on at the bottom of the boat. But apart from the watch and a few little things that got wet, there was no damage done.

This sea was much larger than the one which took my unfortunate mate and the compass overboard, and only the life-line which I had fastened to myself prevented me from going along with it. I managed to keep the vessel from broaching to when the sea broke over her, but, of course, after that reminder I hove to under sea anchor and riding sail.

Owing to our southerly position—we had almost reached the fiftieth degree—the weather was rather cold, and as both of us had got somewhat wet in the operation, we lit our little swinging stove (which was something like the sea anchor—it never failed to do its duty in any kind of weather), to make a cup of coffee which turned out to be, when finished, a 'number one and a half.' The stove could be utilised also for warming and drying the cabin, and we soon had everything shipshape again.

The gale proved to be one of the real 'Old Cape Horners,' accompanied as it was by genuine breaking seas. Apparently the *Tilikum* enjoyed it very much, raising her body over the large seas with almost as much ease as the albatross, of which an ample number swarmed round us. These great birds seemed to take much interest in the boat, probably because of the build, size and painting of the little vessel. There is no doubt that ever since the Southern Seas have been the home of the albatross, they have never seen a vessel of similar small size and curious form. They would glide close to the mast for hours, now and then describing a circle round the boat, and at the same time taking an investigating look at the figurehead, which very much resembled their own.

Some of the birds would alight near and alongside our boat and face those large approaching seas with their white foaming and roaring tops in the same manner as the *Tilikum*. But instead of riding every sea, as our vessel was obliged to do, the albatross, on the approach of a bad sea, would spread its white wings and, gracefully rising just high enough to let the breaker pass, alight again. This gentle seabird accompanied us all the way from Tasmania to New Zealand, and we felt sorry when we lost such company.

The gale kept up its fury for two days and nights, after which the wind moderated, and when the large seas had lost their breaking tops we hauled the sea anchor on board and swung the boat before the wind. Our chronometer was spoiled, but it was beyond doubt that our longitudinal position at that time lay somewhere south of the New Zealand coast. I therefore decided to sail to the northward until we reached the latitude of the south end of New Zealand, whereafter a course was to be shaped for Solander Island.

SIXTEEN

ARRIVAL AT NEW ZEALAND—OYSTERS AND WHAT THEY EFFECTED—THE CITY OF THE 'MAC'S'

THE WESTERLY WIND soon settled into a steady breeze, and on the morning of February 8th we sighted Solander. Although the wind lightened considerably during the day, we found ourselves towards evening right alongside. This is a small island, about a mile in length and half a mile wide, with heights of eleven hundred feet. It was too late that night to make Invercargill, on account of the dangerous navigation on New River, on the bank of which the city is situated. We therefore sailed round Solander looking for ambergris, but there was nothing doing in that line. We observed no signs of the island being inhabited, and aimed a few shots at the birds which were flying about in great numbers. At dark we shaped our course for New River, and at three o'clock next morning, when within about five miles of its mouth, we hove to and waited for daylight. After sunrise we sailed up the river, arriving at Invercargill about midday, with boat and crew in the best of condition.

Invercargill is a well-laid-out little city with a population of about fifteen thousand. I was assured by the people that no smaller vessel than the *Tilikum* had ever visited them, and both my mate and I received a very warm welcome.

A day or two later my mate came to me and said, 'Skipper, last night I went into a pop and called for a glass of beer, for which I paid threepence; and with it they gave me, free of charge, six great, big, fine, fresh, juicy oysters on a half shell! Truly, this New Zealand must be a great country.'

We remained a few days at Invercargill and then went round to Bluff Harbour, about eight miles distant, which serves as a port to the former place, New River being too shallow for vessels of greater draught. The small town situated on the south side of the harbour is Campbell, and I believe I am correct in saying that twenty-four hours after our arrival everybody there knew us, and we in turn knew everybody in Campbell. Owing to the kind treatment we received, we stopped for a few days longer than we should have done, and when sailing, the crew of the *Tilikum* was presented with a number of bags full of 'great, big, fine, fresh, juicy oysters,' which were in whole shell, and, needless to say, after my mate's heart.

Leaving Bluff Harbour with a moderate westerly breeze we followed the coast towards Dunedin, a distance of about a hundred and twenty miles. It is a pleasure on a fine clear day, with a moderate breeze off the land, to sail along the beautiful seaboard of New Zealand, and to make it all the more enjoyable we had oysters with every meal and a few between meals. My mate declared that he could slip down a dozen or two at any time.

However, the fine breeze did not last; on the following day, about noon, threatening clouds rose from the west, accompanied by a fast-increasing wind. This proved sufficiently that a westerly gale was approaching. As we were then too near the coast to ride out a gale, and no harbour was at hand in which to take shelter, I altered our course to the south-eastward in order to gain sea room. Having managed to get clear of the land for about fifteen miles, we were compelled to take in the last sail and heave to in the usual way. That night it blew very hard and we must have been in a tide rip, for the *Tilikum* rolled and tumbled about much more than in previous gales. My mate complained of the oysters he had eaten for supper, saying that they tried desperately to return to the ocean. I advised him to bite the heads off, whenever eating oysters at sea, as I did, and then they were quite dead. 'Bite their heads off,' he said, 'I should say I did, and bit their legs off too, but . . .' Something, not quite a groan, finished our conversation.

The gale lasted for two days and proved to be one of the hardest blows that I experienced on the *Tilikum*. In fact, the tumbling about and the oysters made my mate so sick of the sea that he gave me notice right there and then that there would be no more *Tilikum* and oysters for him once he put his foot ashore again.

Two days after, we arrived at Port Chalmers, about eight miles from Dunedin, where we remained for two days and then took the boat up to the latter place. This constitutes the 'Scotch City' of New Zealand and the headquarters of all the 'Mac's,' such as McDonald, McPherson, McKenzie, and many others. And we certainly found the Macs to be all right, and so was Piper Gray, though not a Mac himself. The latter was the proprietor of the hotel at which I stayed, and the very night of our arrival he and some of the Macs resolved that I could not run about in Dunedin as a plain Voss. Consequently my name had to be changed, and I at once was christened McVoss. If I remember rightly it was Piper Gray who sprinkled the water on my head.

I remained for twenty-two days at Dunedin. During that period, at the request of the city authorities, the *Tilikum* was removed on a wagon to the park to take part in a floral fête. There the ladies of Dunedin decorated her from her keel to the tops of the three masts!

When, on March 25th, I was obliged to tear myself away from the Macs and Piper Gray, at the same time rechristening myself plain Voss, it almost felt like leaving home. My only consolation was the old saying: 'The best of friends must part.' With Mr G. McDonald on board, who insisted on making a sea trip in the *Tilikum* and volunteered to go with me to Lyttelton, I set sail shortly after noon. Flags were flying all over the harbour, and thousands of people crowded the water front, waving handkerchiefs and hats and wishing us a safe voyage. We were taken in tow by a large river steamer, full of people, and, accompanied by another passenger boat and a fleet of Dunedin yachts, we proceeded down the bay towards the ocean, a distance of about eleven miles. The wind blowing lightly the yachts soon dropped behind, but the two steamers, with their decks crowded with passengers, escorted us all the way down. On arrival at the mouth of the river a nice south-easterly breeze induced us to set all sail, so the steamer let go and the people on board gave us three hearty cheers, which we answered by three dips of our flag on the mizzen. Then the steamers returned up river to Dunedin, while the *Tilikum* headed for the north.

New Zealand had so far afforded me a splendid reception, more than I could ever deserve. But as I am one of those who never get too much of a good thing, I made up my mind to enjoy that beautiful country as long as possible, and accordingly called in at nearly every port along the coast.

The next morning after leaving Dunedin we sighted Oamaru, a small town situated near the beach. Coming nearer, we saw an artificial breakwater, inside of which a large vessel lay alongside a wharf. Near that ship I brought the *Tilikum* up, and as place and people also looked inviting, we remained for a few days. Then we resumed our course northward and called in at Timaru, a town somewhat resembling Oamaru. After a short stop we sailed for Lyttelton. The distance between the two places is only about a hundred and twenty miles. But as we got mixed up in a north-easterly blow we were compelled to heave to under a sea anchor for about thirty-six hours, and consequently it took us three days to make Lyttelton. On our arrival there the *Tilikum* was transported by train to Christchurch, a distance of about eight miles.

SEVENTEEN

CHRISTCHURCH—A PRACTICAL DEMONSTRATION

AT CHRISTCHURCH many people came to inspect my boat. The first question, of course, always was: 'How do you manage your tiny vessel in heavy storms?'

On one occasion, a gentleman asked me the same question again and when I had explained matters to him, said: 'It is surprising indeed that you have come all the way from British Columbia and weathered all gales successfully in this little vessel. Only a few days ago two friends of mine entered Sumno in a launch much larger than your boat. In crossing the bar the launch was upset and one of the two, a particular friend of mine, who only recently had returned from the South African war, unfortunately was drowned, in spite of being a very good swimmer. The other was saved by the Sumno lifeboat.' I then related my experience near Melbourne, where I was compelled to run the *Tilikum* for half a mile through heavy surf breakers, explaining how I crossed the breakers by having a sea anchor over the stern. Now, that gentleman asked me whether I was willing to repeat the same manoeuvre on the Sumno bar. 'I am certain,' he said, 'the people of Christchurch would appreciate a practical demonstration, as we have had many accidents on the Sumno bar.'

I am always willing and ready to put into practice what I preach. I therefore agreed to give a demonstration before my departure from Christchurch.

'What kind of boat do you want to use?' he enquired.

'Any boat of, say, from eighteen to twenty feet in length,' I replied, 'and one that three men can handle.'

'I will get a boat of that description for you. What day do you choose?'

'Any time,' I said; and we fixed the day on the spot.

Crossing a breaking bar requires three men, two must be at the oars while one tends to the sea anchor. Mr McDonald, who had sailed with me from Dunedin, had left the boat already to return to that city. However, he was still in Christchurch, and as he had told me when we parted that he would go with me again, at any time and in any vessel, I notified him and he readily volunteered. The second man was Mr H. Buckridge, who had just returned from Captain Scott's South Pole Expedition on the relief ship *Morning* and who had taken Mr McDonald's place aboard the *Tilikum*.

We left Christchurch on April 28th at nine in the morning by tramcar for Sumno, which is about nine miles distant. On our arrival there we went down to the beach to have a look at the boat which we were to use for the demonstration. It turned out to be an ordinary eighteen-foot fishing boat with a sharp stern. The weather was fine, and the breakers, running in towards the beach and over the bar, were just about right to make things interesting both to the spectators and ourselves.

The demonstration on the bar was to take place at half-past two in the afternoon, but to get my two men into trim I went out with them for a drill at eleven o'clock. The boat lay a short distance from Sumno in a quiet little bay. My mates took the oars and I sat down in the stern holding the same sea anchor that had guided the *Tilikum* through several gales ready for instant use. We then rowed out into the open where long, big rollers came running in. Steering round, we rowed towards the shore where the rollers struck shallow water and, with an overfalling top, ran up the beach. Shortly before the boat entered the breaking seas I dropped the sea anchor over the stern and, instead of reversing it, as I had done near Melbourne, kept it full, and slowly and safely we crossed the surf breakers.

Just before the boat struck bottom I brought the sea anchor aboard and we backed the boat towards the ocean. That, however, was not quite so easy, as great care must be taken to meet every approaching breaker head on. And if a boat has got too much speed when meeting a comber the latter is sure to break over her and most likely will send her to the bottom. On the other hand, if a boat in that case has not enough headway, it may be turned end over. Therefore, it takes trained men to accomplish a feat of that sort. Both my mates were strong, able men and knew how to pull an oar. I watched the approaching breakers and advised them how to pull, and thus we managed to bring the boat back through the surf, but not without shipping her half full of water.

Having returned to the landing-place we changed our garments and went back to Sumno, where, to our surprise, we found the town already alive with people who had come from Christchurch, and still every tram running in was crowded.

At the stated time we manned our little boat again, and this time pulled in towards the bar. In coming near the breakers we saw the beach crowded with people, and just when we entered them a band, concealed in the crowd on shore, struck up 'Life on the Ocean Wave.' Then we passed over the roaring and foaming breakers only about a hundred yards distant from the beach, while over seven thousand people—a figure given me later on—waved their hats, caps, umbrellas, and handkerchiefs, shouting at the top of their voices: 'Well done! well done!'

Having thus crossed the bar breakers we got into smooth water, where the Sumno lifeboat lay with a crew of trained men on board, everyone with a lifebelt around him, ready to come to our rescue in case of emergency.

Our demonstration did not end when we had crossed the bar only once. We desired to take another round trip to give the spectators something for the money which they had spent on the tram from Christchurch. Crossing breakers seawards, as I have stated before, is much worse than coming in towards the shore, and on this occasion, as before, we did not succeed without shipping quite a lot of water. Nevertheless, after having reached the open and baled out our boat we stood in for the breakers again.

When we were half-way across and in the worst of it, approximately a hundred and fifty yards from the spectators, we stopped the boat's headway and let her lay to the sea anchor, and with the additional help of the oars we kept her heading the breakers. The boat was then dancing up and down as the waves passed under her. One moment she would stand on her head and the next on her stern, but she was entirely out of danger.

We in the boat enjoyed the sport very much, although in crossing the bar on our way out we got thoroughly wet. We imagined that, from the spectators' side, the operation must have looked somewhat monotonous. Therefore, in order to create some excitement and liven things up a little, Mr Buckridge, who was a first-class swimmer and diver, unobservedly tied a rope round his waist, the end of which I kept under control, and then simulated falling overboard. The moment he disappeared in the breakers the yell came from every mouth on shore 'Man overboard,' the band stopped playing, and the lifeboat crew came pulling along with all their might to the rescue. Buckridge kept out of sight until the lifeboat was within about fifty feet of us, and then pulling in the rope, I found him safe and sound at the end of it. The people on shore applauded and hurrahed, the lifeboat was taken back to the station, and the band once more tuned up a 'Life on the Ocean Wave.' We rowed our boat towards the shore into smooth water, and after that we crossed and recrossed the bar once more, and thus successfully completed our demonstration. However, the best part of it, as far as the demonstrators were concerned, followed the next day, when the manager of the tramcar company presented me with a cheque for nearly fifty pounds.

EIGHTEEN

WHERE IS THE LIGHT?—MY FIRST LECTURE—AN AMUSING INCIDENT— MEETING WITH MAORIS

SHORTLY AFTER the demonstration had come to an end the *Tilikum* was entrained again and taken down to Lyttelton. When afloat Mr Buckridge and myself went aboard and took our departure for Wellington, the capital of New Zealand, a distance of nearly two hundred miles. With a moderate westerly breeze we soon sailed the four miles down Lyttelton Bay, and once more the *Tilikum* poked her nose into the Pacific. The wind gradually hauled into the south-east and with a fresh breeze the boat went along flying towards Wellington. When we were nearly abreast of Cook Strait the wind changed to the north-east and forced us in toward Cape Campbell, whose white revolving light we sighted shortly after dark. Just about that time the wind returned to the original direction, and we shaped a course direct for Pencarrow Light, which stands at the eastern entrance of Port Nicholson.

The south-westerly wind became very strong towards midnight. Pencarrow Light towers over four hundred feet above the water and is visible at a distance of thirty miles; therefore, to my reckoning, we should have sighted it at about midnight. So I began to look for it, for it is one of my established rules to be on the lookout when, according to dead reckoning, land or a light should come in sight, and the vessel is shaping for it, and I never leave the deck until satisfied. But should the weather get thick and the likelihood of running into danger arise, I do what every careful navigator should do in unfamiliar surroundings, viz., put the vessel's head off shore and wait till the weather clears.

On this occasion, with the exception of a few clouds hanging about here and there, the weather was quite clear. Being sure that we were in sighting distance of the light but still unable to see it, I went to the forward end of the boat where the sails did not obstruct the view. My mate was steering and the *Tilikum* went along with the wind and a large sea right aft, at seven miles an hour. I stood there from one till five o'clock, when I thought that we should be within five miles of the light; but still I could not make it out. The morning hours were very dark and I considered the advisability of heaving to, to wait for daylight, when suddenly the light appeared right ahead of us and up in the sky!

Apparently the light in question stands too high to be seen in cloudy weather, as, owing to its lofty situation, dark clouds at times will accumulate and obscure it from view. Regarding lights that are visible for upwards of twenty-five miles, I may say that I have never recorded another incident of that kind. The night being dark, and both of us unacquainted with the locality, we hove to under small sail. When day broke we kept the boat before the wind, and with a strong southerly breeze sailed into Wellington Harbour, dropping anchor near Queen Street wharf.

Wellington is the capital of the Dominion of New Zealand, and its inhabitants very much resemble their fellow-countrymen in the other places where I had called: all had ample means of living, and seemed contented and happy, and as I was still hustling for the millions which I had failed to secure on Cocos Island, I took the *Tilikum* ashore and had her exhibited in a large hall.

It was for the first time in my life that I mounted a stage to address an audience, a task which so far had been out of my line. I shall never forget the moment when I stepped on to the stage and saw nearly six hundred people looking at me and watching every movement I made. Fortunately, the stage was strongly constructed, otherwise I think I should have fallen through it. A few days before the lecture was to take place an experienced speaker who instructed me in the art of lecturing warned me of stage fright. 'When you mount the stage,' he said, 'and see the audience in front of you, you might become nervous and won't be able to speak, as is frequently the case with beginners. If that should happen, just imagine that all the heads you see before you are nothing but a field of cabbages, and you soon will be all right!'

Now, to allow my imagination to run away with me in this manner was, for a man like me, who had met so many New Zealanders and had learned to like them, a little more than I thought I should be capable of, but as my instructor assured me it was part of the business it had to be so. So I spoke for about an hour, after which my mate, Mr Buckridge, took the floor and delivered a very interesting lecture on his experiences while with Captain Scott's South Pole Expedition in the *Discovery*. Among other occurrences, he related the jolly time they had when the vessel was frozen in during the dark and cold winter months, and how he and his comrades used to commandeer some excellent old Scotch from the officers' stateroom and hide it in the snow where it would freeze, and instead of drinking whisky in the ordinary way they would eat it as they would ice cream!

When Mr Buckridge had nearly finished his story, his voice suddenly dropped, his eyes widened, and he looked very much bewildered. At first, I thought he suffered from a sudden attack of heart failure; but he managed to finish his speech in a whisper which I am quite sure nobody could hear, then gave a little bow as if to say: 'That will be all you'll get from me to-night, my good people!' and thereupon received a deafening ovation from the audience. The latter then left their seats and crowded round the *Tilikum*, and I was just about to ask my mate whether he felt ill, when a tall, handsome young gentleman stepped up to the stage and, shaking hands with Buckridge, said with a smile: 'I could never understand what became of my whisky!' He was no other than Lieutenant Ernest Shackleton, of the *Discovery*, and Mr Buckridge happened to recognise his face amongst the audience immediately after telling of the 'iced whisky' he enjoyed so much in the frozen plains of the south!

Lieutenant Shackleton is now Sir Ernest, and judging from what I saw of him in Wellington, and later on in Scotland, and what I have read and heard about him since, all the harm I wish him is that he may become an admiral of the British fleet before reaching his fortieth year!

A splendid critique in the next morning's newspapers served as an instigation to us to speak on several succeeding occasions to full houses, and at the request of a white Maori chief from Palmerston North, a fair inland city, we put the boat on a train and, in company of the chief, journeyed overland to that place. In the country surrounding Palmerston live many Maori farmers who came to town by the hundred to give us a call. They were more than pleased to see a canoe which had crossed the ocean to their country, and the fact apparently strengthened their belief that in days of yore their ancestors had emigrated in large canoes to New Zealand from some distant region of the Pacific. One Maori, who spoke English fluently, told me that he had never credited the legend, as he thought it impossible to cross the ocean in such frail craft. 'And now, as I see with my own eyes that you have covered thousands of miles in this Indian canoe and have arrived safely on our shores, I do not longer question that my forefathers can have accomplished the same!'

NINETEEN

WANGANUI—LADIES ON BOARD—
A WET AFTERNOON

HAVING SPENT a few days at Palmerston North, we again
boarded the train and, making short stops at Fielding and other
country towns, proceeded down to Wanganui, which is a port of
considerable size, situated about four miles from the mouth of
the Wanganui River, one of the most beautiful streams in the
world. Across the mouth of the river lies a bar over which the sea
breaks very heavily at times, and as some Wanganui people had
read of our feat at Sumno, we were requested to repeat the performance. Consequently arrangements were made to give a
demonstration, this time in the *Tilikum* herself, and under sail.

While staying at Wanganui we had taken up quarters at an
hotel which was owned by a young couple who, like almost all
New Zealanders, were fond of sport. They asked me to be good
enough to give them a trip on the *Tilikum*, and I replied that on
the day fixed for the demonstration they were welcome to sail
with us as far as the river mouth. 'Oh, thank you,' the lady
exclaimed, 'that will be so nice!' I will try to describe to my readers how nice it turned out to be.

When the appointed day came, the landlord was unable to
leave his house for stress of business. So his place was taken by a
lady friend who joyfully agreed to accompany his wife, and in the
pleasant company of both ladies we sailed down the Wanganui.
When we arrived at the river mouth the wind had died out, and
in consequence the prospects for our performance became poor.
It was about two o'clock when large and heavy seas, which almost
broke on the bar, came running in towards us. Many people had

arrived from Wanganui by train to watch the *Tilikum* crossing the bar. But there being not the slightest breeze, the boat could not be sailed, and therefore those standing along the beach wore a disappointed look.

'Something must be done to create a little excitement,' I said to my mate, 'but how?' As luck would have it, just then a launch about thirty feet in length arrived from Wanganui with a dozen passengers on board, and as the bar was not breaking then the captain volunteered to tow us across. When everything was ready for the start I advised our two lady passengers to go ashore.

'No, please, Captain,' our landlady entreated, 'don't put us off now, when the real fun is to commence!'

'My good ladies,' I endeavoured to persuade, 'there will be not much fun if one of those high seas should happen to break on us when going out.'

'We won't mind that a bit,' the other assured me.

'And getting soaked with salt water; what about that?' I queried. 'Oh, that we would enjoy enormously!' they both asserted.

Feeling confident that nothing serious would happen, I made no further objection, and told the captain of the launch to go ahead. In a few minutes we were amongst the big, rolling seas.

Crossing the bar at a rate of six miles an hour, both boats rose comfortably to the seas as they came along, until we got about half-way across the bar, when an extra large sea broke between the launch and our boat. I knew at once what was going to happen, but it happened so quickly that the breaker was upon us ere we had time to hurry the ladies into the cabin. Before the breaker came over all four of us were sitting in the cockpit, and when the *Tilikum* dived into it our landlady clung to some ropes and cleats, whilst her companion, who was one of the belles of Wanganui, grabbed my mate round the neck and hung on for grim death. Even when all was over he could hardly induce her to let go again! Why our charming passenger should have cuddled my mate around the neck and squeezed him in the way she did, instead of me, I was at a loss to understand; for at the time when the breaker came down on us I was certainly much nearer. However, we succeeded in getting across the bar without further trouble. This was the only sea that broke upon us in going out, but nevertheless it was sufficient to give all a good soaking.

In returning we had a similar experience, but on this occasion we managed to shelter the two ladies in the cabin, shutting the door on them. When we were about the middle of the bar a large sea, as before, broke under the stern of the *Tilikum*. She took a little water over, but went along with the breaker at a tremendous speed, with the result that in a few minutes we were almost alongside the launch. Presently, the breaking sea passed under us and embraced the launch. As we had a hundred and fifty feet of towline out, a bight was formed alongside our boat, and the latter naturally stopped headway while the launch forged ahead with the breaker at a terrific speed. When the towline became taut it parted, causing the launch to broach to. Instantaneously the sea broke over her weather rail and almost resulted in her, with all on board, going to the bottom. As it was, the water she shipped stopped her engine, but luckily enough no more breaking seas came in and she was baled out and got safely into the river. The *Tilikum*, with her two lady passengers, who were now in a sorry plight, followed suit.

The breakers at Wanganui were then not nearly as high or so dangerous as were those we had experienced at the Sumno bar when crossing it six times in an open eighteen-foot boat, and the accident on this occasion could have been easily avoided if the launch had been allowed to go slow in crossing the bar, as I had advised the captain. Instead, she was driven full speed ahead, and consequently the accident happened as it will nine times out of ten when care is not taken, and possibly with more disastrous results. I told the captain afterwards that it was not his seamanship but the hand of Providence which had saved his vessel and the lives of those on board.

TWENTY

A GALE IN COOK STRAIT AND AN UNCOMFORTABLE NIGHT— NEW PLYMOUTH

THREE DAYS LATER we left Wanganui for New Plymouth, on the east coast, distant about one hundred miles. Cook Strait truly resembles its great namesake: like Captain Cook it is not to be trifled with. When it blows there it blows hard, and owing to shallows and currents a very bad sea is experienced. Sailing from Wanganui with a moderate easterly breeze, accompanied by a hazy sky, we directed our course to the south-west. This served our purpose by enabling us to obtain sea room to meet a possible gale.

We were no more than about twenty miles off the land when the wind hauled into the south-west with fast-increasing force. However, in order to clear the lee shore still further, we held our course until the wind and seas compelled us to take in the sails and heave to under sea anchor. To be only twenty miles off a lee shore in a heavy gale is rather risky, and we had gained little more. So to lessen the drift of our boat, we rigged a second sea anchor. For this purpose we employed our bunk boards, some old canvas and ropes, and one of our ordinary anchors. We discovered that with the two sea anchors the drift of our boat did not exceed three-quarters of a mile, and we therefore felt assured that the gale would have to blow quite a long time before the *Tilikum* would strike the rocks. Having a riding sail over the stern besides, and after putting a light on deck, we both sat down in the cabin, and over a comfortable smoke talked about our experiences on the Wanganui bar a few days previously.

Meantime the gale raged, and it proved to be the worst I experienced throughout my cruise in the *Tilikum*. It was accompanied by large, hollow-breaking seas, and our little vessel had to do all she could and tried strenuously to rise to the top of some of the high combers. She rolled and pitched and with heavy spray flying over her, sluggishly worked her way over the seas. It was the first gale my mate experienced in the *Tilikum*, and he complained of the continuous rolling and pitching, saying that it made him sick.

Before many hours had passed we were wishing for a change in the weather, but the wind did not moderate, and was later accompanied by heavy rain squalls. The night was so dark that we could not see a hand before our eyes. As we drifted more and more landward I commenced to feel a little uneasy; for I knew that if the gale lasted all day we would be smashed to pieces before nightfall. But a good shipmaster never reflects on danger until he be right near it. I stuck to the principle, and refrained from expressing my thoughts about the weather and the lee shore to my companion, but waited patiently for the change, which eventually came with unexpected suddenness. It was before daybreak, when the wind rapidly hauled into the south-east and the seas soon lost their dangerous breaking caps, when I steered the *Tilikum* to the westward. At seven o'clock the weather cleared up, our approximate position then being ten miles off the land and forty miles from Cape Egmont,

As a reminder of the previous night's gale, a large swell was still settling through from the south-west; but otherwise the wind and weather were all that one could wish, and helped my mate's stomach to recover its equilibrium. Early in the afternoon we rounded Cape Egmont and shaped our course for New Plymouth, which then was not more than twenty-five miles distant. However, the wind lightening during the night, we failed to reach port before the following morning.

New Plymouth is a nice little town of about five thousand inhabitants, and owing to the splendid farming country surrounding it, is named by the Maoris 'Taranaki,' *i.e.*, the garden of New Zealand. Mount Egmont, which rises approximately to a height of eight thousand six hundred feet above sea level, is clearly seen in fine weather, being only about fifteen miles distant from New Plymouth as the crow flies. It forms a most beautiful feature of the landscape, with its regular cone crowned with a white cap of snow. One great drawback to the city lies in the fact that there is no harbour. The 'Garden of New Zealand' is thickly populated with Maoris. When they discovered that we had come a long way in a canoe, they apparently felt, like their countrymen at Palmerston, reminded of the glorious days of the past, and honoured us with a welcome in Maori style. In crowds they flocked to town from the neighbouring districts to inspect our little vessel, and a song was given us in native language, followed by quite a long speech delivered by a chief. The natives then inspected the *Tilikum* inside and out, and having satisfied themselves that she was a real canoe, gave us three cheers before they departed.

TWENTY-ONE

NELSON—THE TILIKUM AS A MAIL-BOAT —'PELORUS JACK'

ON LEAVING New Plymouth we again rounded Cape Egmont and crossed Cook Strait to Nelson, a distance of about a hundred and twenty miles. Cook Strait this time was on good behaviour, and with a moderate north-westerly breeze we sailed across in a little less than twenty-four hours. Nelson also is a fine town, located at the head of Blind Bay and encompassed by high hills and mountain ranges. It possesses a pretty harbour, whilst the climate is excellent.

While in the South Pacific, the *Tilikum* had on various occasions carried mail matter from one island to another, but along the coast of New Zealand the people made her a regular mail-boat, for curiosity's sake, as will be well understood. And not only mails addressed to New Zealand ports were entrusted to our boat, but also many letters destined for Europe. Nelson was no exception, and we had a considerable mail taken on board here, mostly for Europe. The *Tilikum* was almost ready for sea, when an elderly, well-dressed lady brought down a tin box of ample dimensions and asked me to take it along to the Cocos Keeling Islands in the Indian Ocean, having been informed that our course laid that way.

'Madame,' I protested, 'you will please pardon me, but the box will take up too much space in our small vessel.' She then begged and pleaded with me, confiding that she had a son living on the islands who was employed in the British cable service, and that the box contained a fruit cake which was intended for a birthday present to him. My mate happened to be standing near by, and on hearing 'fruit cake'—later on he gave sufficient evidence that he liked fruit cakes quite as well as the ladies—whispered into my ear: 'Take it, Captain, take it; by all means take it along'; and as the good lady at the same time was appealing so insistently on behalf of her beloved son, I finally agreed and promised to do my best to deliver the parcel. My acquiescence nearly brought the tears into her eyes, and to show her thankfulness, shortly before we sailed she sent on board another cake for the entertainment of the crew of the *Tilikum.* Buckridge said that the second cake was to pay freight and insurance on the first one, but also sarcastically remarked that if fruit cakes were as scarce in the Indian Ocean as they were at the South Pole, something might happen to the mail before we reached the Cocos Keeling Islands! 'Look here, Buck'—I was wont to abbreviate his name for convenience' sake—'broaching cargo is prohibited on board the *Tilikum.*'

Leaving Nelson we sailed by way of the French Pass for Napier, which is situated on the east side of the northern island, at a distance of about three hundred miles. French Pass is the name given to a narrow strait separating the little island d'Urville from the main island, which here forms a small peninsula, some thirty miles out of Nelson.

French Pass is remarkable for the tremendously strong tides that rush through it at a rate of about nine miles an hour. It has further gained notoriety as the home of Pelorus Jack, the most wonderful fish in the world. This curious creature has a reputation for coming alongside every vessel passing the strait. It will accompany her for from five to twenty minutes and then disappear again into the deep.

Having heard a good deal about Pelorus Jack's peculiarities we anchored on the west side of the strait to wait for slack water with the turning of the tide, as nearly all vessels intending to make the passage do. It was a beautiful morning when we got under way at high water and with a light westerly breeze sailed through the narrow pass. We kept a sharp lookout for Jack, but he failed to put in an appearance. We cruised about the place where he is wont to make his calls, but were not honoured with a visit. Needless to say, the crew of the *Tilikum* felt highly insulted at this neglect.

On the east side of the pass we observed a nice little house, and as there was a good landing near by we ran the boat up the sandy beach and I jumped ashore. On walking towards the house I was met by a gentleman who introduced himself as Mr Brown, proprietor of the dwelling and the surrounding country site. Mr Brown said that he had met me a few days previously, at Nelson, but as I was introduced to so many people in ports of call I did not recognise his face at once. Now, we renewed the acquaintance. I told Mr Brown what I had heard of Pelorus Jack, and also of our vain endeavours to discover him, which had lasted for two hours. I added, furthermore, that in my opinion New Zealanders were pretty good story-tellers.

'It is a fish story all right,' Mr Brown replied, 'but nevertheless a true one. Jack calls on every vessel that goes through the pass and accompanies it for some time, with the exception of a certain steamship from which he was shot at. Ever since he has never been seen from the same vessel. Neither will he acknowledge small vessels such as yours.'

'That uncivil, self-conceited fellow,' I said: 'nearly every man, woman and child, including the Honourable R. Seddon, Premier of New Zealand, has come to see my boat, and this Pelorus Jack flatly refuses to pay any attention to her at all!'

'That question you must settle with Jack direct,' Mr Brown replied, 'but if you want to see him, wait till tomorrow, when a steamer will pass, and he is sure to come alongside her.'

Of course, I at once made up my mind to avail myself of the opportunity.

At ten o'clock the following morning a steamer entered the pass eastward bound, and Mr Brown took us off in his launch. Shortly after we had gone aboard and she had emerged from the narrows, a large fish of whitish colour made its appearance alongside the passing vessel. 'There he is!' came the yell from every passenger's lips. They crowded the deck and stretched their necks over the rail to obtain a glimpse of the unique fish.

Pelorus Jack first appeared about fifteen feet off the starboard quarter and went full speed ahead, gliding along in front of the steamer's bow, where he remained for a few minutes. Thereupon he made a dive under the vessel's bottom and showed up again off the port side, nearly abreast of the bridge. It was quite a sight in itself to watch the passengers, old and young, rushing about the deck to the various places wherever Jack performed his tricks. Jack kept up his manoeuvres for about fifteen minutes, and then suddenly disappeared from sight.

This far-famed wonder derives his name from the beautiful Pelorus Sound which forms the northern extremity of central New Zealand. This great and picturesque inlet branches into numerous arms and creeks, embracing altogether some two hundred and fifty miles of coast line; its waters are deep and sufficiently extensive to accommodate large vessels. There are said to exist thirty landlocked anchorages in all! French Pass constitutes the western-most part of the sound which Pelorus Jack has made his home, according to the natives' legend, many years before the arrival of white men.

Pelorus Jack is classed by zoologists as a dolphin, and thus in reality is not a fish but a mammal, for which, also, his highly-developed instinct and cleverness account. He measures about fifteen feet in length, his colour is nearly white, with a little admixture of grey and yellow, and an additional decoration of brown stripes. Jack shows a large head and massive shoulders, while the body tapers towards the tail. He possesses a scythe-shaped dorsal fin and a large horizontal tail, the latter very much resembling that of a finback whale. The animal is marvellously speedy, and will play around a steamer travelling at a rate of from fourteen to fifteen miles an hour, overtaking her with apparent ease, as if she was standing still! This wonderful creature serves as a great attraction, and doubtless forms an economic feature in New Zealand, drawing yearly crowds of holiday-makers and foreign tourists. Jack has thus become a foremost money-making concern and one of the wonders of the world. His equal in habits and colour is unknown, and his life is protected by the New Zealand Government.

As Pelorus Jack is the only known specimen of his kind, he is much esteemed by the population of New Zealand. He is treated with almost the same respect as a human being, and anyone guilty of detracting from his character is liable to get himself into trouble. About a year ago, while walking along Main Street, Yokohama, I happened to come across a passerby who wore a down-hearted look on his face, and whom I at once recognised as a New Zealander by his watch charm. It should here be mentioned that a green stone is found in New Zealand which is manufactured into a variety of ornaments and takes a high polish. Usually it is mounted in gold, and extensively worn by the people of that country. I addressed the gentleman and discovered that I had made no mistake. The interest I take in New Zealand generally is due to the splendid reception I received during my stay in that country, although I have, in this regard, no reason for complaint anywhere. On this occasion, upon enquiring how things were at home, I was told that the people of New Zealand were heart-broken and flags had been flying half-mast when he sailed from Wellington.

'What is the matter?' I enquired. 'Did the Governor die?'

'Not that,' the stranger replied; 'a Governor can always be replaced, but Pelorus Jack cannot; and he has abandoned his call and is given up for dead!'

Since then I have heard that the great fish had been missing for some time, but, fortunately, turned up again. Evidently, Jack had thought that after many years of continuous service he was entitled to a vacation which could not but be beneficial to his health, and my readers will agree with me that no one should blame the faithful old pilot!

TWENTY-TWO

HISTORICAL REMINISCENCES—
AUCKLAND—THE AMBITIONS OF MR
BUCKRIDGE—ENGAGING A FRESH MATE

THE WEATHER was fine when we sailed from French Pass in the latter part of June with a moderate westerly breeze and shaped our course across Cook Strait towards the southern end of the north island. Cook Strait during the winter months—May, June, and July—is frequented by heavy south-easterly gales, but we were favoured in that respect, the steady westerly breeze staying with us until we had rounded Cape Palliser, the southernmost point of the north island. Then the wind hauled into the south, and as the weather continued fine we made good headway, following the coast towards our next port of call.

However, when we reached Cape Kidnappers we got becalmed and drifted about for twenty-four hours near two white rocks, which looked very much like haystacks. Its name was applied to the cape by Captain Cook on his first exploring voyage, when many natives came off in a large canoe and tried to kidnap a little boy from his ship. Some of the natives lost their lives in the adventure.

The following day the wind came in from the east, and with its help we sailed into the little harbour of Napier. Here we remained for ten days, and after receiving a considerable consignment of letters for Europe we set sail for Auckland.

It was late in the evening when we sailed out of Napier Harbour, and when just clear of the land a fresh south-easterly breeze, accompanied by a short, choppy sea, made the *Tilikum* jump into the waves up to the foremast. Shortly before we left

Napier some of our hosts had treated us almost too kindly, and by urging me to 'Have another one,' 'Just one more,' 'I am sure you can stand another small bottle, Captain,' they had greatly over-estimated the capacity of my stomach and caused me to stow away more than I was accustomed to. The latter, however, revolted and was not satisfied until I relieved it from the extra pressure. My mate, Buck, showed his sympathy by saying, 'That serves you right. An old salt like you should know better than to get sea-sick in a little blow!'

During the night we crossed Hawke's Bay, which is about forty miles wide, from Napier Harbour to Portland Island, arriving at the latter place towards morning. A strong easterly wind made it difficult for us to weather the island, and we therefore anchored under the shelter of the west coast of Mahia Peninsula beyond it, in smooth water. There we lay waiting for more favourable wind and weather—and, incidentally, for my stomach to get into a seaworthy condition again.

Towards evening the wind hauled into the north-west and we resumed our voyage to Auckland. After rounding the point we shaped a course northward, and with a fresh breeze off the land followed the coast line until next morning when it hauled into the north-east, resulting in a dead headwind. We then put the boat on the starboard tack, and when under land we got becalmed near Poverty Bay.

While we drifted about and waited for wind, a canoe and three native men and a woman came alongside. One of the men, who had a good command of English, and acted as the speaker, offered his services as pilot to tow us into Poverty Bay for the sum of ten shillings, promising to conduct us to the very spot where Captain Cook had anchored on his discovery of New Zealand. I would have accepted the Maori's offer, but paying pilot fees and towage was against my principle in the *Tilikum*. Apart from this, my time was getting short and I was anxious to make Auckland, otherwise we would certainly have called in and availed ourselves of the opportunity to visit that historical place.

The south-west point of the bay near which we drifted is

called Young Nick's Head, named after a boy who belonged to the great navigator's crew and first saw the land. The small river Turango-nui flows into Poverty Bay, and this is the celebrated spot where Captain Cook first touched New Zealand soil. In the immediate surroundings of this place he met with inhospitable natives, and although he made them presents and employed every means to be friendly, they remained hostile, and the crew of the *Endeavour*, his ship, had on various occasions to resort to arms for protection. These unlucky circumstances and his unsuccessful attempt to obtain provisions caused him to apply the name 'Poverty Bay.' At the present time the flourishing town of Gisborne is situated on the shores of the bay, and the neighbourhood looks so prosperous that, judging from what I could see from a distance, it is about time to change the old name.

We had drifted about near Young Nick's Head for several hours, when a fresh breeze came in from the south-west which took us to the East Cape. Rounding the latter we shaped our course across the Bay of Plenty, named so by Captain Cook in March, 1770, because of the number of people seen on the fringing coast. The wind kept fair and fresh, and we soon passed Great Barrier Island on our starboard, and having crossed Hauraki Gulf arrived at Auckland on July 20th, 1903.

Auckland is the largest city in New Zealand, and at the time the *Tilikum* called had a population of about sixty-seven thousand. As at other places in Australasia at which I had called, almost every second man I met was interested in yachting. And if one considers the splendid sub-tropical climate and the great cruising grounds available, I think there is no place on the globe that surpasses Auckland in water-sport facilities. The cruising season here begins in September and ends in May. The other three months constitute the winter, during which period the yachts are hauled out of the water for repairing and cleaning. As our time of call coincided with the winter season I did not sail in one of the yachts. However, I was honoured by some of Auckland's yachtsmen, being taken round in a launch to various places where the yachts were hauled up, and considering the number of pleasure-boats and launches I saw that day it would seem that nearly every man, woman and child in that fair city must be devoted to yachting.

We had spent about a fortnight in Auckland, when my mate Buckridge suddenly announced, 'Captain, you better look for another mate, as I have to leave you.' This, of course, took me by surprise and I asked, 'What is the matter with you? Only a few days ago you told me that this is the best layout you ever got into, and now that we have passed through all that bad, dirty weather and intend to sail for the tropics you are going to leave me!' 'It is not that I am dissatisfied in any way,' he assured me, 'but I have made up my mind to build a boat of my own and of about the same size as the *Tilikum*, to race you to England.'

Buckridge was for his age a man of wide experience. As I have stated before, he took part in the South African campaign, and afterwards joined Captain Scott's Expedition to the South Pole. But he had no knowledge of navigation and very little practical seamanship. As I was well aware of his weak points in this respect I advised him strongly not to attempt such a voyage.

To make a cruise round the world in your own vessel and go as you please certainly looks most inviting, and for myself I do not hesitate to say that the three years spent in the *Tilikum*, in spite of her small dimensions, was the most enjoyable time of my life. But in order to make the cruise a success the man in charge requires an absolutely thorough knowledge of practical navigation and he must be able to handle a small vessel in all kinds of weather. And it is by no means sufficient for him to understand when a boat is correctly built, rigged, ballasted and provided with the proper sails and all gear necessary to weather heavy gales. He must also be a good judge of the weather, as barometers are very unreliable at times. More especially is this necessary when the boat is near land and there is no harbour in which to seek shelter from an approaching gale. The safety of the vessel and life may then depend on a quick decision to sail off the land in order to obtain sufficient sea room before the gale compels you to heave to. It is further essential that the boat be fitted with good water tanks to ensure an efficient supply of pure drinking water, and a complete list of stores must be secured as there are no 'road-houses' at sea. Apart from being an experienced seaman, the yachtsman who ventures on the high seas must also be a good cook; for, owing to the small dimensions of his boat, physical exercise is limited, and to keep in good condition all food must be intelligently selected and properly cooked. It is also a factor of considerable importance to adhere to regular meal hours in all kinds of weather. By understanding and attending to these points an ocean cruise is, in my opinion, the most enjoyable and healthy pastime a man could possibly choose. But it would be a fool-hardy undertaking for one who is not qualified or who is ignorant of the dangers involved to venture on his own account—a miserable spell would probably end in an early disaster!

As I have already observed, Mr Buckridge could not claim to be an experienced seaman; but ignoring my advice, he placed an order with a yacht builder in Auckland for a boat of about four tons, in which he proposed to proceed to England. Unfortunately, this left me again without a mate. However, I was lucky enough to pick a strong, healthy young man, whose name was W. Russell, from a number of applicants.

At this juncture it may be advisable to mention that the authorities of all ports I called at never interfered with me, and whenever I engaged a new mate the agreement was generally of a private character. My plan was to sail after leaving Auckland by way of some South Sea islands, through the Torres Strait and Arafura Sea, across the Indian Ocean to Durban, South Africa, *i.e.*, a distance of about fifteen thousand miles. Bearing in mind the length of the voyage, I was especially careful in selecting a reliable man and good companion. When Mr Russell applied in person I catechised him after this manner:

'Where were you born?'

'In Ireland.'

'How old are you?'

'Twenty-five years.'

'Have you ever been to sea as a sailor or in any other capacity?'

'As a passenger only.'

'What is your profession?'

'I was trained for the Church.'

'Are you still following that profession?'

'No; I lost my job some time ago.'

'Have you done any yacht sailing?'

'Yes.'

'Can you steer one?'

'Yes.'

'Can you tell a good story?' This was the last question put before the candidate, and as he answered it by telling me a real 'crackerjack' right on the spot Mr Russell was engaged for the voyage to South Africa.

To replace my broken chronometer I bought a new Waltham watch, which afterwards proved reliable and did excellent service throughout the remainder of my voyage.

In a city like Auckland, with its yachting population, pleasure and splendour, time quickly passes, and ere I realised it we were well into August, and it was time for the *Tilikum* to put to sea again. The little vessel had once more been favoured with a smile from the Goddess of Luck: some Auckland yachtsmen had kindly presented her with a set of new rigging, running gear and many other smaller articles which afterwards proved of value on the long voyage.

TWENTY-THREE

LEAVING NEW ZEALAND—A SEA OF ROCKS—CROSSING MY FORMER COURSE: FLAG HALF-MASTED—SAVAGE ISLANDS: MISSIONARY AND TRADER

On August 17th the *Tilikum* was moored near Queen Street wharf, ready for sea. In the early afternoon a large river passenger steamer, crowded with people who had come to see us off, took her in tow, and as we slowly drew away from the wharf we were cheered by thousands of onlookers, gathered in the neighbourhood of the harbour, who stretched their necks to obtain a last glimpse of the vessel. The day was fine and calm, and while our well-wishers on shore kept up their cheering, vessels lying at anchor in the harbour dipped their flags, and steamers tooted their sirens. All this was accompanied by the strains of a brass band on board our tow-boat which played the favourite piece, 'Life on the Ocean Wave.' By the time we left the harbour we had assumed full speed and the fine and hospitable city of Auckland soon dropped out of sight. At four o'clock the steamer blew three whistles to signify 'set sail and let go the towline.' This was done immediately, whereupon the steamer circled us twice, the passengers on deck shouting themselves hoarse with 'Good-bye' and 'Good luck,' the band played once more and the whistle tooted. Then our friends returned to their homes and the *Tilikum*, left alone with a long watery track before her, took advantage of a light southerly breeze and was headed for the north.

The wind remained rather light all the afternoon and the weather did not look any too propitious, so we anchored for the night under the lee of a small island. The following morning the weather was clear and a moderate breeze blew from the south. We got under way and bent a course towards Great Barrier Island. The wind freshened and at two o'clock in the afternoon we sailed through the channel between the Great and Little Barrier Islands, after which we stood out for the open ocean and shaped a course for the New Hebrides, a distance of about twelve hundred miles from Auckland.

My mate was a well-educated man of refined manners. It had struck me when we left Auckland that some of his friends in bidding good-bye had addressed him as MacMillen and others plainly Mac. On enquiry he told me that he had been known in New Zealand under that name and then we agreed that he would be 'Mac' also on board the *Tilikum*, for the sake of brevity.

It was about eleven in the forenoon on August 22nd. Land had been out of sight for some time; the wind had hauled into the east and with a beam wind our boat went along on her northerly course without the help of steering. It being a fine day, I availed myself of the opportunity to instruct my new mate in all particulars on board and how to keep everything in its place on deck. After that I said: 'Now, Mac, come down into the cabin and I will initiate you in the mysteries of cooking.' Mac had done a good deal of cruising in yachts and soon knew as much about sailing the *Tilikum* as I did myself, and when it came to cooking, he proved himself a first-rate hand. As it was drawing towards noon Mac enquired whether I had any flour and lard on board. 'Any amount of it,' I replied. 'Then let me show you how we manufacture pancakes in New Zealand,' he suggested. It was indeed surprising to see 'Father' Mac kneading the dough and then turning out cakes of regular form as if they were produced in a pastrycook's bake-house, and so tasty and light that they would almost melt on your tongue.

'Well done,' I said, 'you are the right man in the right place,' and he certainly was!

The easterly wind continued until we reached the latitude of the north of New Zealand, when it hauled into the north-east and started to blow. The wind thus being almost dead ahead we hove to in the approaching gale and took things easy. The gale was a heavy one, and abated only after the lapse of thirty-six hours, but the *Tilikum* rode through it as usual. Mac showed that he was a seaman in bad weather as well as on a fine day and that his stomach was sea-proof. Gales will sometimes blow at sea, the same as they do on shore, and generally a little harder, and naturally people who have crossed the ocean in large vessels will think that a yachtsman must experience an awful time in his small craft during a gale. But notwithstanding the great difference in size, such is not the case; one feels quite comfortable in a small boat when hove to, which may be further illustrated by my new mate's admiring exclamation in that first experience of his: 'This is like a real picnic!'

On the night of August 27th at ten o'clock we were in latitude twenty-nine twenty south by longitude one seventy-three east, and my mate was in charge of the deck while I slept in the cabin. Our boat went along with a light westerly breeze in a beautiful dreamy night, when, all of a sudden, I heard Mac shouting, 'Captain, hulloa, Captain; come up quickly; we are on shore!' Although sound asleep, this brought me to the deck in a few seconds. According to the observation of the previous noon our position should have been at least three hundred miles from the nearest land, viz., Norfolk Island. However, this startling news made me a little excited, and I got an extra move on myself. When I reached the deck the surroundings looked indeed as if we were on dry land. However, on a closer examination we discovered that we had sailed into a field of floating pumice stone! On picking up some of the pieces we found them very light in weight. In size they varied from a potato to a man's head. As the sea appeared to be literally covered with it, we took in our sail and waited for daylight.

When the sun rose under the clear sky of a bright morning a strange sight greeted us. As far as the eye could reach the surface of the ocean looked yellowish grey with the porous substance which, being almost like cork, followed every movement of the restless sea. A moderate breeze blew from the south, so we set sail and kept the boat on her northerly course again. As we sailed along we found that the pumice stone gathered in patches; some places were quite clear and had the appearance of pools, whilst at other points it was thickly massed, completely covering the surface of the water. At first it caused an apprehensive sensation to sail right into the 'rocks' after crossing one of the 'pools,' but we soon discovered that owing to the buoyancy of the material the boat cut through it with the greatest ease, and seemingly without losing any of her headway.

During the day the wind hauled into the east-south-east, and I knew that we had reached the region of the welcome trade winds. The *Tilikum* went along at five and a half miles an hour, and we expected soon to see the end of the tremendous field of pumice. On that day we made about sixty miles, and at dusk the patches of stone appeared as thick as ever, but as the boat did not suffer, not even the paint showing a mark, we kept northward on our course. The statement that our vessel was not injured by friction with the hard material, and that the speed was not affected, may seem an exaggeration; still it holds true. The parabolic wave caused by the stem in ploughing through the water would draw the floating stone sideways along with it, far enough to create sufficient clearance for the boat to pass without the sides coming in contact with the pumice.

August 30th found us in latitude twenty-two thirty south and longitude one hundred and seventy-two east, and still we were cutting through the pumice field, which, however, appeared to be thinning. It was on this day that we crossed the approximate position where on the unfortunate night of October 27th, 1901, I lost my unlucky mate. The weather was fine and a moderate breeze blew in from the south-east. Mac had proposed that we should pass Mr Begent's watery grave with our flag hoisted half-mast, and, accordingly, this was done. The flag was hoisted in the morning at eight o'clock and hauled down at sunset. The following is an extract from the log:

AUGUST 31st—Wind and weather the same. Pumice stone floating in patches and quite thick in places.
SEPTEMBER 1st—Wind and weather steady. Sailed through large
fields of pumice stone. Position at noon, one hundred miles SSE
from Aneityum Island.

On September 2nd, when enjoying my morning sleep in the
bunk, I was aroused at daybreak by a voice on deck: 'Land right
ahead.' Knowing by our previous day's observation what land it
was, and that we were still a long way off, I told my mate to notify
me before the *Tilikum* would run it down, after which I rolled
over and took another good sleep. At seven o'clock, when I got on
deck, Aneityum, the southernmost island of the New Hebrides,
could be distinctly seen about twenty-five miles to the NNW.
The wind was lightening when we approached the island and it
was not before three o'clock in the afternoon that we came near
the south-easterly point. The weather being fine and the water
quite smooth we were able to sail with the light easterly breeze
within about two hundred yards of the beach, where we saw
numerous natives lined up on the shore and apparently waiting
for us to make a landing. Being near enough, we could plainly distinguish men, women and children, all of a dark colour and wear-
ing very little clothing, some of them having no garments at all.
As the looks of the natives at close range did not serve to increase
our trust in them, we abstained from attempting a landing and
proceeded along the coast to the northward. When they noticed
that we, evidently contrary to their expectations, did not land,
they came running along the beach, shouting, halloaing and making signs to us to come ashore. We could see beautiful cocoanut
and other fruit trees and, tempted further by the inviting gestures
of those on the beach, we were seriously considering a landing,
and finally altered our course for the shore.

An old saying is: 'Tell the truth and shame the devil!' and that
I will do now. When we came near enough to see the white in
the black fellows' eyes we got the shivers and thought it a better

policy not to try our luck here! So we headed seaward again and when well clear of the land we shaped our course towards the next island, Tanna, situated about forty miles to the north-west of Aneityum. At nightfall a fresh breeze came in from the south-east, and at one o'clock the following morning we hove to three miles off the east coast of Tanna and just about due east of an active volcano, whose fire we had seen all night. The latter is about eight miles west of Port Resolution, a pretty little harbour, so named by Cook after his ship, at the time of the discovery of these islands.

At dawn we prepared to sail into the harbour where we hoped to find a missionary, but the wind died out and a current setting to the southward carried us a long way from the land. The day was most beautiful and calm, and in drifting about we amused ourselves by tackling several large sharks. We dispatched these tigers of the sea to the other world by sending a bullet through their heads. At three o'clock a moderate breeze started blowing from the south-east, and with it we sailed up to the entrance of Port Resolution. It was just about sunset when we approached the harbour, and the wind fell very light. We were not able to make out anything but cocoanut and other trees, besides an old house of apparently native build near the water. So we headed seaward again with the intention to stand off for the night and look for a mission house next morning. Some of my readers might think that we acted timidly in not sailing into the harbour to anchor there for the night. To these I wish to point out that the inhabitants of the New Hebrides in former days had a very bad reputation for cannibalism and treacherous manners in their intercourse with whites. Being only two in a little vessel, and neither my mate nor myself disposed to be slaughtered and eaten or to become involved in trouble, we took this precaution. We had just swung the boat round and pointed to the open ocean when we noticed a boat passing the head of the harbour. I took a quick glance through my glasses and distinguished eight fellows, who pulled straight towards us. By that time the wind had completely died out, and it was impossible for us to keep clear of the approaching boat; we therefore at once made our firearms ready for instant use.

The natives drew steadily nearer, and when they were within about four hundred feet we put our rifles to shoulder and taking aim shouted 'Hands up!' At this the steersman immediately swung the boat round and all hands stopped pulling. Thereupon, the former stood up in the stern, and I must confess that I felt somewhat cheap when he called out in fairly good English, 'Are you afraid of us, Captain?'

'Not exactly that,' I answered, 'but we want to know what you are after!'

The man then explained that a missionary had sent them out to tow us into the harbour.

'A missionary,' I said; 'where is the mission house?'

He then pointed to a small opening in the tops of some high trees, just large enough to allow a glimpse of the steeple of the mission church. By that I knew that the man had told us the truth, we laid down our rifles and invited the black strangers to come alongside, which they did. To be friendly with the darkies, I presented each with a small plug of tobacco, and as there was no wind the natives towed us into harbour.

On arrival at the anchorage near the mission house three Europeans came off in a small boat to meet us. When on board one of the gentlemen introduced himself as Mr Watt, missionary of Tanna, and one of his companions as Mr Wilson, a trader, while the third was a young assistant missionary. When the anchor was down, we gave a short explanation as to our visit and cruise. Following Mr Watt's invitation we accompanied the party ashore, where we enjoyed a very nice dinner with him and his wife.

In the course of the ensuing conversation I asked Mr Watt about the habits and customs of the natives, and especially whether cannibalism was still practised. This question was immediately answered by the trader who assured me that they ate a native man there only a few days previously. And Mr Watt added that it was very difficult to stop this horrible custom. Mr Wilson further explained that on the last occasion the younger missionary had gone to the place where the feast had occurred in order to reason with the natives. But instead of taking his advice they had picked up some of the bones and throwing them at the missionary gave him to understand that he had better mind his own business.

On my enquiry regarding the enormous quantities of pumice stone we had met with, and of which we saw much had also drifted on to the beach of Tanna, Mr Watt stated that it was first noticed three months previously, but he had no clue as to its origin.

The next day we had a look at the village and its surroundings. The chief missionary was living in a nice cottage with a clean little church beside it. The only fault I could find with the station lay in the circumstance that it was hidden by trees and therefore could not be seen from the beach, at least very little of it. This should always be considered as a most important point on an island where the inhabitants are reputed to be cannibals and not to be trusted. For it may not only prove a place of rest for seafaring men, as in our case, but the outward sign of a European habitation will always indicate a safe refuge for vessels in distress and shipwrecked sailors. Strange to say that little heed seems to have been paid hitherto to this simple fact, as I have found the same 'invisibility' of the outposts of European civilisation in other solitary spots of the Pacific.

It may be appropriate here to say a word or two regarding missionaries and traders in the Pacific. Both have been subject to adverse criticism by travellers as well as from those who have spent longer periods in these regions. As far as I have come in touch with them my impression has been a most favourable one. And this holds true also with native missionaries, who far exceed others in number. Missionary and trader have shown me kindness and genuine hospitality throughout, and though they do not always agree between themselves, which seems natural, the difference being rooted in their callings, they always did their best to entertain the stranger, whom it must be remembered, they had little reason to believe they would ever see again. Some of the traders even went so far as to supply me with provisions and material without accepting anything in return.

A native village clustering near the mission was composed of the shabbiest dwellings I have seen on my travels: little huts consisting of rough posts leaning at an angle against a ridge pole and covered with palm leaf fibre or coarse grass. The whole resembles a large dog kennel, with an opening at one end. To effect an entrance one has to crawl on his hands and knees. The inner floor is bare earth, and no furniture of any description is provided, except, perhaps, some mats to sleep on.

The natives of the New Hebrides belong to the Melanesian race. The colour of their skin is very dark and they are rather strongly built. At Tanna, round the village, they were dressed in calico garments. But some men who had come in for the day from a longer distance, and were called 'bushmen' by the Europeans, appeared quite nude. The natives were hospitable towards us new-comers in general and presented us with fruit. Nevertheless, in conformity with my above explanations, I should not care to land from a small boat on any part of these islands where there is no European settlement near at hand.

Tanna is a most fertile island and produces an abundance of excellent fruit and vegetables. Erromango is another island of the group, and two men from there had arrived at Tanna some time previously in an occasional steamer. They now were desirous of returning and asked me to afford them a passage, having heard that my course lay their way. I would have taken them back home with pleasure, but Mr Watt, who had spent many years on these islands and knew the treacherous habits of the people, advised me not to do so. It was just on Erromango that a Mr Williams, the author of missionary enterprise in the South Seas, met with the fate of so many brave men, and, like several who succeeded him, was murdered.

Our second and last evening on Tanna we spent with Mr Wilson in his nice little European-style house. Both missionaries and the trader made things so pleasant for us during our short stay, and the natives of the island were so interesting, that we should have liked to remain longer. But as my cruise in the Pacific had already exceeded by far the time provided for this part of the voyage and there was still a long way to go, we tore ourselves away that night at ten o'clock to make ready for the start next morning.

The *Tilikum* was anchored about fifty yards from the shore and we went off in a small boat belonging to Mr Watt. Coming on board we found to our surprise three bushmen in Adam's costume sitting in the cockpit.

'What do you fellows want?' I demanded, not forgetting at the same time to reach into my back pocket.

'Whisky, tobacco,' one of the darkies replied, evidently the only two words they knew of English.

Having explained that there was no chance for whisky, I gave a stick of tobacco to each, for which in return they gave us several large oranges. Then the three uncalled-for guests transferred themselves into a small canoe in which they had arrived and, apparently much satisfied, paddled back to land. My mate said he did not like the look of the chaps and they needed watching. However, we remained at our anchorage, and nothing unusual happened during the night.

On September 5th at ten o'clock we again went ashore to bid good-bye to our hosts, and many native men, women and children crowded round us to have a handshake with the foreign visitors, likewise. Then we returned on board and, accompanied by the three Europeans in their boat and by several canoes filled with natives, we headed for the sea again. The harbour entrance was soon reached, and, after a final good-bye to the friends we left behind, with a moderate south-easterly breeze we made a course for the gate of the Pacific, Thursday Island, in the Torres Strait, about two thousand miles distant!

Tilikum *and "curios" on display in Hoopers Furniture Warehouse,
Dunedin, New Zealand, March 1903.* (ALEXANDER TURNBULL LIBRARY,
NATIONAL LIBRARY OF NEW ZEALAND/TE PUNA MĀTAURANGA O AOTEAROA #F168495½)

TOP: Tilikum *at Forbury Park Floral Fête and Gymkhana, Dunedin, New Zealand, March 1903.* (DeMaus Collection, Alexander Turnbull Library, National Library of New Zealand/Te Puna Mātauranga o Aotearoa #G244G½)

BOTTOM: *The* Moesang *with the* Tilikum *in tow leaving Otago Harbor, New Zealand, March 1903.* (OTAGO WITNESS, Courtesy Maritime Museum of British Columbia)

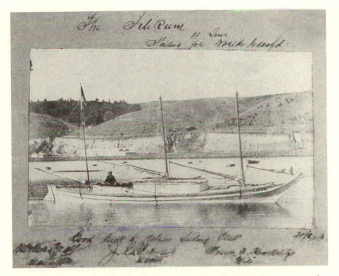

TOP: *A photo of* Tilikum *under sail, 1903, inscribed by the crew to the Nelson (New Zealand) Sail Club.* (MARITIME MUSEUM OF BRITISH COLUMBIA)
BOTTOM: Tilikum *at Table Bay, Capetown, South Africa, 1903.* (BC ARCHIVES B-09352)

TOP: *Captain John Claus Voss, taken in South Africa.* (BC Archives A-00855)
BOTTOM: Tilikum *on display at the Navy and Marine Exhibition, Earl's Court, Margate Harbor, London, 1905.* (Maritime Museum of British Columbia)

At some point after his voyage ended, Voss either gave away or sold Tilikum. The new owners cruised the eastern coast of England for several years, but in 1926 she was found abandoned on the Thames (top photo, MARITIME MUSEUM OF BRITISH COLUMBIA) by a naval officer who contacted officials in Victoria, B.C. These officials arranged to have Tilikum shipped back to Victoria, where the boat was displayed for some years under a shelter built—at their own expense—by several lumber companies. After some restoration efforts undertaken by members of the Thermopylae Club, Tilikum was moved to Thunderbird Park (bottom photo, BC ARCHIVES I-26982).

Finally, in 1965, Tilikum *was moved to the Maritime Museum of British Columbia where she remains today. Captain Voss's daughter and Norman Luxton's daughter paid the costs of restoring* Tilikum *and repairing the neglect that years of outdoor exposure had caused (*BC ARCHIVES I-26838*).*

TWENTY-FOUR

*THE GREAT BARRIER REEF—THE PEARL
AND BÊCHE-DE-MER FISHING INDUSTRIES
OF THURSDAY ISLAND—A 'CURE OR KILL'
REMEDY—MARINE LIFE EXTRAORDINARY*

ON THE FOLLOWING morning we had lost sight of the New Hebrides and were sailing over the Coral Sea towards Rain Island Passage in the Great Barrier Reef. The Coral Sea is considered the most dangerous portion of the Pacific to navigation, owing to numerous small islands, shoals, reefs, and the strong currents prevailing there. However, by carefully manoeuvring our boat and keeping a sharp lookout we got across without a hitch and safely arrived at the 'Barrier.' This great reef is unequalled for its vast extent, and is a formidable obstruction to sea traffic. It runs for about a thousand miles along the north-east coast of the Australian continent and extends still farther to New Guinea. At low tide the reef is nearly level with the water, and numerous small black coral rocks appear here and there in the heavy surf, which ceaselessly breaks all along the great barrier. It is so low that it can be seen only within a distance of about four miles from a vessel's deck, and owing to the strong current setting through from the east, the passage is extremely dangerous after dark. Rain Island Passage forms one of several gaps which ships going east or west may use. The width of the channel is about five miles, and Rain Island, which is marked by a beacon, is almost in the centre.

Shortly after clearing the passage we sighted a schooner lying at anchor near a small low island. The wind being light and the water smooth we sailed alongside, and on invitation from the captain went on board. The latter was a Japanese from Thursday

Island, the schooner's home port, and was engaged in fishing for 'bêche de mer,' the edible sea-cucumber so highly valued as an article of diet by the Chinese. All the crew were absent plying their trade, and as the boats were at no great distance from the schooner we could plainly see how these men went about their work. Each boat was manned by two naked native divers, one rowing, while the other would frequently dive and bring up some slugs.

We stopped there for about two hours, watching the divers and talking to the captain who was himself busy spreading and drying the slugs in the sun. I noticed several large sharks hovering round the vessel, and with regard to them asked the captain whether it was not dangerous for his men to dive whilst they were about. He assured me that he had never lost a man through the medium of a shark although he had followed this business for years. This statement is in accord with my own observations. The surrounding water was infested with sharks, but, as in many other localities, where there is every opportunity to feed on human flesh the so-called man-eater never even attempts to attack a man. No doubt there are species more ferocious than others, but I have come to the conclusion that the average shark is not so bad as his reputation.

After bidding farewell to the captain of the schooner we shaped our course for Cape York, the northernmost point of the Australian continent, which narrows the Torres Strait to a width of about a hundred miles. The weather was perfect and the wind moderate, and as we sailed along we passed numerous islets, some very low and without vegetation while others were covered with cocoanut and other trees. Small schooners were anchored here and there, fishing for pearl or bêche de mer. The ever-changing scenery made the cruise across the Great Barrier Reef a most delightful one.

At dark we anchored near one of the islets and stopped there till next morning when we resumed our journey. At ten o'clock Cape York was rounded and at four o'clock the same afternoon, September 22nd, we arrived at Thursday Island. Here we were warmly welcomed by the Honourable Mr Douglas, the resident magistrate, and the people, amongst whom were many Europeans. In the evening we delivered a lecture on our cruise and illustrated it with the aid of lantern slides.

At Thursday Island is stationed a large fleet of pearling schooners, small vessels of about twenty tons manned with a diver and four sailors. Some of the leading business men told me that pearling was a very profitable business. But sometimes heavy losses are sustained, for the weather is not always as pleasant as that we chanced to meet with at the pearling grounds, which extend all over the reef and the Torres Strait. A few years previous to that time a typhoon had swept down upon the pearling fleet and nearly a hundred vessels and four hundred lives were lost in a few hours.

While in port I received a letter from Auckland informing me that Buckridge had started for Europe in a boat called *Keora*, accompanied by a mate. On the first day out he had drifted ashore, but the boat was taken off and repaired, after which he had again sailed.

On September 26th we took our departure from Thursday Island. A fine breeze blew from the south-east, and the weather was splendid; so we stood in for the Arafura Sea and shaped a course towards the Cocos Keeling Islands in the Indian Ocean, the destination of the New Zealand fruit cake which still lingered in our hold to fulfil its destiny. The distance to be covered approximated two thousand five hundred miles, and as the breeze stayed with us we crossed the mouth of the Gulf of Carpentaria, a distance of about three hundred miles, in fairly good time.

It was on the third day out, and we were sailing near Wessel Island on the west side of the gulf, that I felt a sudden attack of painful cramp in my stomach. There was a fair medicine chest on board, and I resorted to various kinds of medicine which I deemed appropriate. But all salts, castor oil and similar strong remedies failed to bring relief. We had plenty of tinned fish on board, of which I had frequently eaten. Some of it must have been

bad and thus became the source of my indispostion. I suffered terrible pain, and as I was unable to secure relief we steered in for
Wessel Island, which we reached in a few hours. Luckily, we struck
a good landing-place, with smooth water and a fine sandy beach
clothed with bushy trees and green grass patches. We secured the
Tilikum, and with the assistance of Mac I managed to get ashore.
Under a shady tree I dropped down on the grass. Added to the
painful cramp, I now developed a very bad headache, and as by
that time I was so weak that I felt sure my end was near at hand, I
asked Mac to bring writing materials from the boat, as I wished to
leave a testimonial to exonerate my mate from any blame in case I
should die. Mac was squatting at my side, and on looking at him I
could see that he felt nearly as bad as I did myself.

'I think I know of a remedy that will do you good,' he said.

'Then let me have it by all means, whatever it may be,' I
replied hopefully.

'It will either cure or kill you,' Mac added.

'Then you had better get me the writing materials first,' I
retorted, somewhat abashed.

'I will not,' he replied, 'but will run the risk and administer the
medicine first!' and with that he went off to the boat.

Meantime I lay there, rolling about in convulsions, and thinking of the past, the present and the future. The awful pain racked
my body, and I yelled for Mac to hurry with his medicine, for it
seemed to me an hour since he had gone. On his return he said
that it had taken him ten minutes to provide his 'kill or cure'
remedy, which consisted of a cupful of hot water and a table-
spoonful of Colman's mustard. These he mixed and ordered me
to swallow immediately, and every drop of it!

Now, a little mustard with meat is all very well, and a little too
much of it—we all know what that means. But when Mac told
me to swallow this concoction I thought it would be impossible.
Nevertheless, under the circumstances, and with Mac insisting
that it must be taken at all costs, I raised the cup to my lips and
drank the nauseous mixture! When half of it was down it endeavoured to return immediately. However, I was determined it

should not, and in this matter I was victorious. But the feelings that stormed within me it is impossible to describe. Mac was kneeling by my side and had reverted to his former calling, as I faintly noticed. My inside felt afire, and it seemed as if an explosion would take place in my stomach. I was just about to accuse Mac of killing me when suddenly I became very busy. I could hear Father Mae praying that I might be helped out of my misery, then 'Colman' got to work and before two minutes had elapsed nothing could possibly have been left in my stomach! I felt a wonderful relief, and after a short rest was myself again.

Well done, Doctor Mac! But the forced vomiting had made me very weak; so Mac went to work and made me a plateful of Quaker oats. This helped me to my feet again, and I soon began to feel as well as ever.

It was nearing evening, and we had been ashore for two hours. The wind was very light and the weather beautiful, and as this was splendid camping ground we decided to stay there for the night. The favourable weather continued next morning, and therefore, after having enjoyed a hearty breakfast, we each took a gun to do a little hunting; but the interior appeared to be sandy and barren and we could detect no signs of habitation. Nothing worth shooting was to be seen, and as the day promised to be very warm we did not proceed farther, but retraced our steps towards our little floating home and were glad to be back although without any game.

At ten o'clock the *Tilikum* resumed her westward voyage under all sail and with a light breeze. During the following two days we accomplished a hundred miles of our course, and were then becalmed for three days. During this time we experienced the hottest weather on the whole cruise. If it had not been for the awning spread over the after-end of the boat in all probability we would have melted into grease spots. But by occasionally soaking the canvas roof we managed to weather this trying time with comparative comfort.

The sky was clear during the three days of calm, and with the aid of my sea telescope we could see plainly to a considerable depth into the waters beneath us. It was here that I saw the greatest variety of sea life I ever have witnessed during my travels at sea. Some big, grey sharks lay motionless quite near our boat, while others could be seen moving lazily to and fro further down. Each of the monsters was accompanied by a herd of pilot fish. The latter are small and striped greyish black. About a dozen of them would busily ply round the head of a shark, sometimes entering his mouth, but soon came out again. On one occasion I noticed a shark, twenty feet in length, apparently asleep within five feet of the bottom of the boat. Through my telescope I could distinctly see that his eyes were shut; the only part of his long body that moved was the tail, which slowly swung from side to side. His pilots, however, seemed to be on the alert; they kept swimming around the big fellow as if on the lookout for danger. It was a real piece of life in the briny deep, and when we had watched it for some time, I took an oar to give our friend a call. But quick as I was, the shark got out of danger before I could reach him.

Besides the sharks and their pilots there was a great variety of fish of different size and colour. These were either motionless or sluggishly moved about as if also affected by the heat of the day. I observed a yellow sea snake, from three to four feet in length, pass through the school of fish in a great hurry. There were many more of these venomous reptiles twisting and turning in all directions below or whipping along almost on the surface of the sea. But one and all, wherever they were bound, showed the same haste, in contradistinction to the finny philosophers near by. The appearance of these strange creatures was sufficient to give one the 'creeps.' With the exception of the mermaid and the mysterious sea serpent, this representation of marine life seemed to be complete.

Light variable winds, alternating with more calms and most beautiful weather, followed. These conditions lasted for nearly a month. One evening I was sitting in the cockpit, smoking my pipe and waiting for a breeze to take us into the Indian Ocean. Suddenly I felt a tremor through the boat similar to an earthquake.

'What is that?' Mac shouted out of the cabin where he lay in his bunk.

'An earthquake,' I volunteered, wondering myself what it could be.

'It must be a seaquake then,' my mate responded.

Just then we received another shock and it dawned upon me that some large fish must be rubbing or bumping himself against the *Tilikum*'s bottom, which caused her to shiver from end to end, so immediately I seized an oar and gave our unwelcome visitor, whoever it may have been, a good and hard dig in the ribs which induced him to make a speedy retreat.

Near Bathurst Island, on the south side of the Arafura Sea, is an expanse of shallow water called the Mermaid Shoals. I had been told by seamen that the famous mermaids there had their abode. Others connect the name with the simple report that a ship of that name had been wrecked on the shoals. Be it as it may, we decided to visit the place, and altered our course to that direction.

On approaching the home of the sea beauties we parted our hair in the middle and made ourselves look respectable, as if going to a Sunday afternoon church meeting. When we reached the shoals the wind became light and the water smooth. So we again brought our water telescope in position and kept a sharp lookout for the ladies. We saw many fish loafing about, but whether they were 'mashers' or not it was difficult to conclude. As in other places, these waters teemed with life, but the mermaids were evidently out on a picnic, for we could not discover their whereabouts. Of course, it was the old story; my usual luck with the ladies!

TWENTY-FIVE

*IN SIGHT OF THE COCOS KEELING
ISLANDS—A MISCALCULATION AND ITS
CONSEQUENCES—TROPICAL RAINS—THE
NEW ZEALAND FRUIT CAKE ARRIVES, BUT
AT THE WRONG DESTINATION*

IN SUCH MANNER we had spent a month on the Arafura Sea, drifting about and only occasionally helped by light winds which gradually transferred us into the Indian Ocean. Then the south-easterly trade winds took us in charge and made the *Tilikum* again spin along at her best. The steady cool breeze came as a great delight after the hot time we had experienced in the tropical Arafura Sea, and we made from a hundred and thirty to a hundred and fifty miles daily towards the west. In the morning of November 8th we sighted the Cocos Keeling Islands. When within four miles of the south-eastern end of the group the wind died out and once again we were becalmed.

'Just as the doctor ordered it,' I said. 'Now we have a few hours in which to clean things up and get dressed, and when the breeze comes in this afternoon we shall sail into port in style and deliver our mail!'

But sailing vessels will always be victims to uncertainty, and no one can rely upon the time of their arrival. So it was in our case; I had made a mistake in the calculation. If we had known what lay before us we could easily have pulled in to land, but we did not, expecting the wind to come up every minute. However, we drifted all afternoon, and to kill time put everything on board in order. The following morning we found to our great surprise and consternation that a strong current had carried us nearly out of sight of the islands. During the forenoon a light breeze com-

menced blowing from the east and we tried to beat back to
Cocos Keeling. But despite all our efforts the current forced us to
the west and the islands finally disappeared below the horizon. It
was not only for the promise I had made the old lady at Nelson
to faithfully deliver the parcel to her son, and which could not
now be fulfilled, but still worse, we had only eight gallons of
fresh water left in our tanks, and the next land on our course was
Rodriguez, a small island about two thousand miles to the
west-south-west of the Cocos Keelings. Calling to mind the good
old lady who brought the cake on board I felt sure that she would
forgive me under the circumstances, but to start a two-
thousand-mile trip across the ocean with only four gallons of
water per head aboard was somewhat disheartening!

The weather was fine, but the light easterly breeze and current
setting to the west made it absolutely impossible for us to return
to the islands. I was fully aware of the fact that whatever happens
on a sea voyage, be the vessel large or small, the master is responsible. And accidents will happen sometimes, but nine out of ten
so-called accidents are due to carelessness or ignorance. When we
sailed from Thursday Island we had our tanks full, enough water
to last us for seventy days. We were now forty-three days out and
having only eight gallons left I could not help accusing myself of
carelessness, and the weight of the thought lay heavy on my mind.
The *Tilikum* was a poor vessel to sail by the wind, and to take a
course for Rodriguez with the light breeze then prevailing and
eight gallons of water in the tank meant almost certain death from
thirst. However, in going on we had two chances in our favour.
One, that we could be benefited by a strong trade wind which
would enable us to make the run in about sixteen days, and by
being economical the water supply would just last for the voyage.
The second chance was the possibility of our meeting with rain on
the passage. Consequently we decided to reduce our daily
allowance to one pint of water each, and set off for the west.

One pint of water per day is very little in warm weather, but
circumstances compelled us to follow the lines we had laid down
and use the little we had in a way that would give the best satis-

faction for quenching our thirst. To begin with, we ate all our food cooled and without adding salt. Potatoes were boiled in salt water and eaten after cooling. Instead of consuming our pint neat, which would have been an unsatisfactory and therefore uneconomical way, we mixed half with a little oatmeal and used the remainder in making coffee. Both beverages proved to be greater thirst-quenchers, and we drank sparingly. We also took frequent salt-water baths, and kept the deck and cockpit wet. Neither of us was in the habit of chewing tobacco, but at times, when our daily allowance was exhausted, and we felt dry, we found that great relief was obtained by keeping a small piece of tobacco in the mouth. By adhering to these rules we trusted that we would be able to keep alive for from sixteen to twenty days, and in such condition as to be capable of sailing our boat to Rodriguez.

The first and second days passed, and on the third the weather was still warm and the wind light. Mac said he would give ten pounds for a good drink of water. I would have given that myself, as water under the circumstances was much more precious than money. And if the *Tilikum* had been loaded down with gold and diamonds it would not have made an iota of difference: we had to get along as best we could on our allowance!

Our suffering from lack of water reminded me of Captain E. Reynolds, with whom I sailed as first mate when still quite a young man in the American ship *Prussia*. Captain Reynolds was at that time over seventy years of age, and had been a master of sailing vessels for over forty years. The old gentleman used to tell me, with a look of pride in his eyes, that during all those long years he never lost a vessel nor met with a serious accident. When I joined the *Prussia* I was, as already stated, very young and had had little experience in first mate's duties. And the old salt instructed me in what way he wanted to have things done in general. In particular he dwelt on the water tanks as we were going on a long voyage. 'Be sure and see that our water tanks are in good order, properly cleaned and filled to the top with pure water. After our departure a certain quantity is to be given out daily and no more.' He was the same captain who made me a seaman, and though he has been dead for many years I never forgot his teaching, and to him I owe thanks for having roamed the seas for many years in the same way as he did: without losing a vessel. Had I followed his instruction on the water question, there would have been no occasion for us to suffer.

On November 13th four days had passed since we kept off to the west. During this time we ran off two hundred miles of our course; indeed very slow progress. There were no signs of rain or of the light wind improving, so we did what people in Australia do during a long drought—prayed for rain. It seems strange, but nevertheless true, the same night the breeze increased rapidly and the sky became cloudy. On the following morning we had all the wind our boat could stand under all sail, and to make things still more hopeful heavy clouds darkened the sky in the south-east, a sure indication of approaching rain. Mac opined that our prayers were about to be answered. At noon the clouds hung over our head, but as so far there was no rain our midday meal consisted of cold unsalted food and a little cold coffee, as before. Meanwhile the heavy clouds accumulated, and an hour later it began sprinkling. Not heeding the favourable and strong wind which sent the *Tilikum* along at her best, we lowered all sail and spread them over the deck to catch the precious fluid. We had hardly done this when the rain came down in torrents. While this lasted we employed ourselves with buckets, and by three o'clock our water tanks were filled to the top!

The wind kept fresh and fair, but with our tanks full we were not in a hurry to get under sail again. First of all, we lit the stove to prepare a good drink. While thus engaged, I said to my mate: 'I say, Mac, try to reef yourself through the after-hatch, and right at the end of the boat you will find a square tin box; fetch it up and bring it into the cabin.' Mac, no doubt, had a faint idea that there was something good in the box, for without a word he disappeared, and in a few minutes I saw the box coming through the hatch and Mac's face behind it.

'What's in this?' he enquired, on entering the cabin.

'Open it and see,' I replied, and he certainly lost no time. There before us was a fruit cake, to all appearance as good and as new as on the day it was made. Mac looked at it in astonishment and believed it was God-sent. 'Not exactly that, Mac,' I assured him, 'the rain was God-sent, perhaps, but this cake was sent on board by a kind old lady of Nelson, New Zealand, to be taken to her son who is in the British cable service on the Cocos Keeling Islands; therefore, it is not my property; but under the circumstances, what do you think we ought to do?'

The coffee was ready by that time, and Mac asked me to pass him a knife and he would tell me what he thought of the New Zealand lady and her cake; and eventually we were agreed that it was one of the very best we had ever tasted, and as we had been without such luxuries for so long a time, and being now provided with plenty of water, I am sure neither Mac nor myself will ever forget how we appreciated the coffee and cake aboard our little vessel that afternoon on the bosom of the great Indian Ocean. And I sincerely hope, as there had been no possibility of my delivering the parcel, that the good lady and mother, on receiving my letter of explanation from Durban, South Africa, has forgiven me!

The wind kept up its force, the rain continued pouring down, and after finishing our coffee we enjoyed a smoke and a sociable chat, congratulating ourselves on our good luck. Then we hoisted sail and with the strong trade wind—the heavy rain preventing the seas from breaking—the *Tilikum* went flying to the westward again.

The rain had been the most welcome occurrence that could befall us, and we therefore did not register any complaints when its ceaseless downpour made things rather uncomfortable for us. We simply kept a-going and looked pleasant. It rained all the afternoon, night and next day, and when it did not stop on the third day we thought that another great flood was descending, and we might be doomed to sail for ever. The wind stirred up a small gale, and only the heavy rain, by keeping the high seas from breaking, enabled us to keep our course. These conditions lasted a whole week, for eight days, during which time we saw neither sun, moon, nor stars, and we were thankful when the rain ceased and the weather cleared up. Then the wind died out and we found ourselves becalmed once more in the finest weather imaginable. For the first time since the rain had begun we took our position and ascertained that we had made a little over twelve hundred miles during the deluge.

TWENTY-SIX

*EXCITING FISHING EXPERIENCES—THE
DEVIL IN THE COCKPIT!—A LUXURIOUS
BREAKFAST—RODRIGUEZ ISLAND—THE
EFFECTS OF A CYCLONE*

CALMS, AS A RULE, are considered unwelcome visitors to sailing vessels, but as almost everything on board had become wet we appreciated the change of weather which afforded us an opportunity to dry things. On that warm sunny day we lowered all sail and hung our wet garments about the deck and rigging, which made the *Tilikum* look more like a floating Chinese laundry than a sailing vessel. Thereupon we spread an awning over the cockpit and, devoting our energies to a comfortable smoke, took the world easy.

While thus resting, stretched out on the seats of the cockpit, we observed a flying-fish crossing over our heads. Getting up we found ourselves surrounded by a school of these fish chased by dolphins. The latter showed great skill in pursuit, taking long reaches, they were right on the spot to seize their prey whenever one was compelled to drop into the water, its wings becoming dry after an extended flight. Flying-fish had become very common on our daily bill of fare, but dolphins had so far never entered the galley of the *Tilikum*. So many leaping about tempted us to get out our fishing gear to secure one for home consumption. Dolphins are caught in much the same way as salmon or bonito. In either case the boat sails through the water while a long line with a hook and a white rag attached to the end is kept trawling over the stern, when the dolphin will mistake the rag for a fish. On large vessels I have also on different occasions caught dolphins as well as bonitos by means of a line similarly prepared but attended from the jibboom while the ship was travelling at a good speed. On this occasion, with the *Tilikum* lying motionless, but for a lazy roll caused by the ocean swell, the dolphins devoted their attentions to the flying-fish and ignored our fishing gear.

It was shortly after sunset, and the beautiful tropical stars twinkled overhead. The dolphins had abandoned the chase and were indolently swimming around the boat. Now and then one would roll over on its side as if to turn in for the night. While sitting in the cockpit I noticed a fat fellow in that attitude within easy reach and, thinking that I could master him, I grabbed his tail to pull him aboard. In this, however, I was much mistaken. No sooner did I touch him than he dealt me such a blow with his tail that it reminded me of an electric shock. I was only too willing to let go, and off he went like a shot. About eight o'clock, when I had retired to the cabin and Mac was still flirting with a dolphin, I suddenly heard heavy splashes followed by a tremendous noise in the cockpit. My mate sang out, 'What is this? What is this? I have caught the very devil himself!' Out on deck I went like a flash, and there found Mac scared to the top of the cabin deck, keeping well out of the way of something struggling in the cockpit, nearly smashing in the floor in an attempt to escape. Owing to the darkness I was unable to identify the noisy stranger, but on getting a light I quickly recognised a young shark, about three feet and a half in length, making desperate use of his tail. In accordance with seamen's etiquette the world over we despatched him and threw the body overboard.

The incident had resuscitated our hunting spirit. Dolphins were still hovering about, and as all other means had failed we decided to rig a spear. For this purpose we employed a combination of a boathook, a knife and a spike, and Father Mac, who claimed to be an expert spearsman, took the matter in hand. When the next dolphin turned over within reach he succeeded in sending the spear through his body and pulled him aboard. We hung up the prize in the mizzen rigging for the night and the following morning our bill of fare consisted of cream of wheat with cream, fresh fried dolphin, hot biscuits with New Zealand butter and coffee (Quality No. 1). Such was our breakfast after being fifty-eight days at sea. Now, you landlubbers, do you think you can beat it?

On that day we had dolphin for breakfast, dinner and supper, and still there was a good piece left for consumption the next morning. During the day a light breeze came up from the south-east, and we proceeded on our course. The following morning the remainder of the fish, though it felt somewhat flabby, smelt and looked quite good and, as our boat was going at a good speed and the chances of catching another dolphin were small, we cooked what was left and thoroughly enjoyed it. Soon after, however, I was taken bad with pains in my stomach and also felt a slight headache. My mate complained of a similar indisposition which with both of us rapidly increased. My head throbbed terribly and felt as if it were likely to split. There was little doubt that the fish had turned without our noticing it; we had made a good meal and now were suffering from the effects of fish poison. In such a case, if quick action be not taken, death may be the consequence. Remembering well the excellent service the mustard had done in a similar case on Wessel Island, without delay we hove the boat to and lit the stove. The mixture was soon ready, and each swallowed his share, which promptly relieved us of all pain. However, feeling still weak, we remained hove to all forenoon and at midday partook of a light meal only, consisting of cream of wheat and a cup of tea. This made us feel better and enabled us to resume our voyage an hour later. The same night we had a substantial supper, after which we felt fully recovered.

By that time we were within four hundred miles of Rodriguez. The south-easter kept blowing fresh, and on the morning of November 28th we sighted the island. In the afternoon, when approaching the south-eastern end, seeing quite a number of fishing craft going in towards the land, we followed them. By and by we entered the coral reefs by which part of Rodriguez is surrounded and soon dropped anchor among the fishing boats which had arrived just beforehand.

When our anchor was down several negro fishermen boarded us. They spoke French, and Mac, who had a good knowledge of that language, soon talked some fine living fish out of the darkies, which we cooked for supper. Having finished our meal we were invited ashore by the fishermen, who numbered about forty in all. They had a camp, consisting of a few roughly-built houses along the beach, where they slept whenever time did not admit of the walk to their homes which were some distance away in the town on the northern end of the island. To the latter place we sailed the following morning, and on arrival made fast to a small wharf. A little later the magistrate of Rodriguez came aboard to acquaint himself with the particulars of our voyage. On invitation I accompanied him to his house, Mac staying aboard, and with him and his family spent a pleasant day. In the course of the afternoon, while we were sitting on the spacious veranda talking on various subjects, a gentleman stepped up to me and said: 'Are you Captain Voss of the *Tilikum*?' I affirmed the question, when the stranger introduced himself as the manager of the British cable station, at the same time handing me a cablegram which read:

'TELL CAPTAIN VOSS TO SEND THAT CAKE.'

'What is the meaning of this, sir?' I enquired. The manager explained that he had been on board the *Tilikum*, where my mate, amongst other things, had recited him the history of the New Zealand fruit cake and its unforeseen though glorious end. In possession of this news he had at once cabled to his colleague on the Cocos Keeling Islands, with the result that the indignant consignee sent back the above stern demand. The gentleman evidently found it difficult to suppress a smile when adding that he had further received instructions to immediately take steps for recovering the cake. 'Now, what are you going to do about it?' he asked.

To reproduce a cake which had been consumed head and tail a fortnight previously, was certainly impossible. So I gave a short explanation why we did not reach the Cocos Keeling Islands despite all our efforts, and of the troubles encountered in the Indian Ocean—not forgetting, in conclusion, to praise the high quality of the subject under discussion—and finally I asked the manager to express my regret to the consignee and transmit him my apology. Both gentlemen had a hearty laugh, and we all agreed that the matter was settled.

A short time previous to our arrival a cyclone had visited the island, leaving considerable devastation in its track. My host said it had been the worst on record on Rodriguez. A flagstaff had been erected near the magistrate's residence, made of hard wood, nine inches in diameter and measuring thirty feet from the ground to the cross-trees where it was stayed with four strong wires. But the force of the hurricane had snapped it at the middle like a piece of glass. On my enquiring about the velocity of the wind the manager of the cable station informed me that he had no record, as his anemometer, together with the building in which it was mounted near the station, had been blown to pieces and scattered so thoroughly that he was unable afterwards to recover any of the fragments. Iron pillars that supported the roof of the veranda at the cable station were broken and houses razed to the ground; much damage had been done all over the island. 'If the cyclone had struck you in your little vessel,' the manager added, 'you would never have lived to tell the tale!' 'I am not so sure about that,' I replied. 'I think our risks on the open sea would not have been any greater than yours on the island here, with broken flagstaff, pieces of iron pillars, houses, trees and other heavy material flying about your ears.'

On the second and last day before our departure I went on an exploring excursion. Rodriguez is a high and not too fertile island, extending about twelve miles from east to west and six from north to south. The population aggregated about three thousand, and consisted chiefly of African negroes intermingled with settlers of French origin and some mixed descendants.

Cattle, beans, salt fish and goats form the principal articles of export. My mate and myself were honoured with a dinner at the cable station, and on the next morning a mass was read in the Catholic church, out of regard to my mate, for a successful voyage. Thereafter, we set sail for Durban.

TWENTY-SEVEN

*ANOTHER MISCALCULATION AND A
MEAGRE XMAS DINNER—SAD NEWS
RECEIVED AT DURBAN—UNEXPECTED
VINDICATION AND MEETING OF AN OLD
FRIEND—THE* TILIKUM *AS A MOUNTAIN
CLIMBER*

WE MADE A GOOD start with a fresh south-easterly breeze, and in fifty-two hours were near the south end of the island of Mauritius. We sailed close enough to the shore to obtain a good view of some of the great sugar plantations for which Mauritius is famous. Cane fields of a beautiful green hue came almost down to the shore, being planted on a gradually inclining sweep of land which extended to a considerable height. Here and there comfortable homesteads, surrounded by trees and gardens with an occasional windmill were interspersed, which lent a prosperous aspect to the landscape. There is a splendid harbour on the north-western coast; the population numbers nearly four hundred thousand. I felt a strong inclination to call here, but being short of time, kept on our course for Durban.

The south-easterly trade wind stayed with us until we reached a position fifty miles south of Madagascar, when it became very light and gradually hauled into the south-west. The following two days we drifted about and at times were becalmed in sight of the great French island. There is a saying that a lull precedes a storm, but on this occasion we obtained a moderate north-easterly breeze instead, with which we approached the South African coast in fine weather. It was only a few days before Christmas, and the wind being fresh and fair, while the distance to Durban was not more than a hundred and fifty miles, we wanted to make sure of spending the approaching festival on terra firma.

On December 22nd we had the coast of Natal in sight and at noon Durban was yet seventy-five miles away. The north-easter sent the *Tilikum* along almost at top speed and we got things ready for entering the port. An hour later the wind increased to such an extent that we were compelled to take in some of our sail. The sky looked clear, and the land seemed to grow in proportion to our hopes.

'Roast beef and plum pudding and a small or perhaps a large bottle of wine will be my Christmas dinner,' said Mac in jubilation. Just then I noticed a small dark cloud rising in the southwest, and promptly advised him not to count his chickens before they were hatched. The cloud quickly grew larger and assumed a threatening appearance. Its evolution left little room for doubt that there was a strong wind behind it, and as another strong wind blew from the opposite direction the two were bound to clash, and we hoped and prayed that the north-easter would get the better of the battle. About two miles ahead we could distinctly see the spray and foam flying into the air. This was a sure sign that the two winds had met and now were fighting for supremacy. To our sorrow we noticed that the south-wester gained ground and developed into a heavy storm, and as a precautionary step we lowered all sail.

In a few minutes we were caught between the two air currents. As both were of nearly equal strength, heavy whirlwinds were formed, but gradually the north-easter retreated before its opponent. The resulting whirls caused the *Tilikum* to swing round three times in rapid succession and thereupon the south-wester enveloped us, and heavy spray drenched the boat from end to end. The strong blow lasted for nearly two days and during this time our boat laid nicely to sea anchor and riding sail. This gave my mate occasion to make different plans for his Christmas dinner. December 25th proved a beautifully calm day. Our position at noon was a little over a hundred miles from Durban, and we had drifted out of sight of land.

The unforeseen lengthy passage across the Indian Ocean had worked havoc among our provisions, some of which had run short. Of flour, rice, biscuits, butter and the like we had ample, but on the other hand, there was little meat left, and instead of roast beef, plum pudding and a bottle of champagne which Mac had promised himself, our last half-pound of corned beef had to be shared for dinner, supplemented by Mac's celebrated New Zealand pancake biscuits and butter, and a cup of Lipton's Ceylon tea.

On the succeeding two days we experienced light variable winds and fine weather. On the 28th we got becalmed about three miles outside Durban Harbour. A large tug-boat came out and on approaching us slowed down her engine. When within hailing distance, the captain on the bridge bade us good morning, and asked where we were from. 'Victoria, BC, Canada,' I said.

'By Jove, you have got a nerve!' he ejaculated.

'Absolutely necessary to get along in this world,' I assured him.

'Going into Durban?' was his next query.

'Yes,' I answered. 'What is your charge for towing deepwater vessels into port?'

'Sixpence a ton,' was the reply.

'Give me your towline, then,' I said, 'I'll take you at that.'

'What is your tonnage?' he enquired.

'About three tons,' I replied.

'That would hardly be sufficient to pay for a long whisky-and-soda,' the master of the tug-boat calculated, and this ended our conversation. Thereupon the tug steamed out to sea to look for more profitable business. However, we did not have to wait long, when a small launch came up and towed us in.

Durban, or Port Natal as it is sometimes called, was full of vessels of all nations, being very busy at that time. We had difficulty in finding sufficient wharf room to tie even the *Tilikum* up. Having looked around for a while we succeeded in squeezing in between two large vessels and made fast to the pier. Owing to the smallness of our boat the customs had taken no notice of her on coming in; when I reported our arrival at headquarters the *Tilikum* was freed from all obligations pertaining to deep-water vessels.

While on my cruise I had been kindly admitted as an honorary member to many yacht clubs. I took about a dozen of these membership cards and introduced myself to some of the leading Durban yachtsmen. These at once took matters in hand and were good enough to attend to all our needs. A spacious drill hall was placed at my disposal for exhibiting the *Tilikum*. On the same afternoon the boat was lifted out of the water and transported there.

Soon after our arrival at Durban I received very sad news from Auckland. My former mate, Mr Buckridge, had lost his life in the renewed attempt to sail his yawl *Keora* to England. His companion experienced a very bad time and hard struggles, but he had contrived to regain the coast of New Zealand. Thus what I had foreseen had happened. Buckridge had undertaken too great a task. He was a genial and jolly good fellow. May his unlucky fate be a warning to all to thoroughly test their abilities before undertaking a similar venture on the high seas!

As it was my first visit to South Africa I did not think that anybody knew me there, in which, however, I was mistaken. Whenever the boat was to be taken out of the water, I had made it a point to employ the services of a good man to lead the work. My reason was that onlookers, of whom there always were many, would ask me all sorts of questions which made it impossible for me to devote proper attention to the transportation. But I was always present incognito among the spectators to keep an eye on the boat. On this occasion, as in other places, I enjoyed immensely listening to arguments and surmises brought forward with regard to my own person.

'Where is the captain of this little thing?' somebody asked. 'He has come all the way from British Columbia in her; I should like to see him.'

'Rubbish,' a sceptic replied. 'Came from British Columbia in this nutshell! Never! This man, I tell you, is a fraud!'

'Yes,' another one affirmed, 'you know where British Columbia is, he is a liar if he says so!'

These and similar remarks naturally amused me. Then my attention was drawn to a gentleman, a short distance off, who assured the crowd that these remarks were unjust.

'Gentlemen,' he said, 'I have heard here various observations about this boat and the man who has sailed her. May I tell you that Victoria, BC, has been my home for many years and I personally was there when this vessel started on a cruise round the world, and furthermore, the captain is a personal friend of mine, although I have not seen him here as yet. You may safely believe that he has done the voyage in this boat, which is in reality an Indian canoe. Anybody with eyes in his head may convince himself of the fact!'

The speaker evidently was annoyed by these utterances in a much greater degree than myself. Stepping up closer, I recognised him and said, 'Thank you, Mr Ervin Ray, for taking a poor orphan's part.' Mr Ray and I had been intimate friends in Victoria for several years, and it certainly was a surprise to both of us to meet again under such circumstances.

I remained a fortnight at Durban and was honoured by splendid receptions from clubs and individuals of prominence. Unfortunately, Father Mac contracted the gold and diamond fever and left me to become a millionaire. My old Victoria friend, Mr Ray, held a position with the South African Railway at Pretoria. He had come to Durban only to spend the Christmas and New Year festivals and was now anxious that I should accompany him home. I agreed, having an inclination myself to see something of the interior. So the *Tilikum* was entrained, and made the journey via Pietermaritzburg across the high Drakens Mountains to Johannesburg and Pretoria, dropping anchor there for some time.

At Pietermaritzburg, the capital of Natal, I stopped over for a few days, and thereafter proceeded to Johannesburg. The war had come to a close only a comparatively short time since, and many places along the railway in Natal and in the Transvaal still bore traces of the devastation it had left in its track. The first impression I received was at Colenso, near the Tugela River, where a burial ground was fenced in and beautifully decorated with flowers. Amidst many graves, where British officers and soldiers had found their last resting-place, there was a stone erected to the memory of a young officer, the son of Field-Marshal Lord Roberts, whose bravery will be remembered for many generations to come. A little later the train crossed the Tugela River and stopped for a few minutes at Colenso. Thereafter, we passed through Ladysmith and across the border into the Transvaal. Here and there other burial grounds were visible; farmsteads and guard-houses in ruins, and fencing wires, covered with all sorts of tin cans, which had served to give alarm of the approaching enemy.

Arriving at Johannesburg the *Tilikum* was placed on exhibition in the 'Wanderers' grounds. My boat was the first deep-sea vessel that had ever come to that city, and therefore she attracted large crowds. A visitor told me that he had followed the call of the sea for some time in his younger years, but had then quit and was now the proprietor of a gold mine. He congratulated me on having established a world's record.

'I beg your pardon, sir,' I said, 'my record has not been completed yet, and it will not be until I have crossed the Atlantic.'

'Quite so,' the visitor assented, 'but it is a different record I am referring to. We are here about six thousand feet above sea level, and I feel pretty sure that no other deep-sea vessel has ever reached such an altitude.'

TWENTY-EIGHT

JOHANNESBURG—'MAC THE
BOAR-HUNTER', ANOTHER SURPRISE—
SUCCESS IN LIFE AND HOW IT WAS
GAINED

AT JOHANNESBURG there was a great surprise in store for me.
One day, when I had just finished a short explanation to a large
audience, one of the members addressed me, saying, 'What
about that big boar on Cocos Island?' This took me unawares,
but a pleasant explanation followed when, looking at the
speaker, I recognised the face of my old shipmate Mac who the
reader will remember was a partner in the *Xora* treasure cruise.*
At a glance I could tell that Mac had met with success in life.
'Come up and dine with me to-night,' he said, and of course I
accepted the invitation.

When arriving at Mac's residence I found a most beautiful
home. He was seated in an easy chair, smoking a big cigar. His
wife, a handsome lady, was also present, and two sweet little
children played on the floor. After an exchange of words of a
more general nature I said to Mac, 'It seems to me, old boy, that
you have struck oil.'

'Yes,' was his reply, 'I have, for there is more gold and diamonds in this country than on Cocos Island, and if you stop
here, I will see that you also will strike a well.'

'I appreciate your kindness, Mac,' I said, 'but Johannesburg is
six hundred miles away from salt water, and if I took up a lands-

---

*Editor's Note: Voss's story of the *Xora* cruise, included in his *Venturesome
Voyages of Captain Voss*, is the least remarkable of his tales and has been excluded
from this edition of his work.

man's calling, it may prove injurious to my health and perhaps mean early death to me!'

At my request Mac then gave me an outline of his experiences since we parted at Callao, and related how he reached South Africa without money. I shall state here a few particulars of what I learned that afternoon. This is going off my course, but I trust that my readers will pardon me, for the yarn is interesting enough, showing as it does what a man can accomplish by sheer force of will once he has made up his mind.

In 1898, when we had reached Peru on board the *Xora*, we received the first news of the South African war having begun, when Mac proclaimed emphatically, 'South Africa for me, it is there that I will shine.'

'How will you get to South Africa without a dollar in your pocket?' Jack asked him.

'Where there is a will there is a way,' was the laconic reply.

Owing to his distressed financial circumstances Mac was unable to secure a passage to the country of his dreams. So he sailed north again in the *Xora* and safely reached San Diego, in California. Here his tale commences, and for convenience' sake I shall relate it in his own words,

'When I arrived at San Diego,' Mac said, 'I had just enough money left to buy a railway ticket to within about two hundred miles of San Francisco, and to get over this distance I was compelled to ride brake beams, walk railway ties and do the best I could. On one occasion I hung on for dear life to a cross-beam under a freight car while the train went along at about forty miles an hour. My strength was giving out and every minute I thought I would have to let go and be cut up by the wheels. However, I managed to hang on until the train halted between two stations, when a brakeman passed along to examine the axles and discovered me. He at once notified the fireman by calling out that there was a tramp stealing a ride. Thinking that the two most likely would be too much for me I made myself scarce. The train soon restarted, and I was obliged to foot it over the sleepers for the next four hours. Finally I reached a small town, hungry and dead tired. I asked a good-natured-looking policeman whether he could direct me to a place where I might obtain food and a night's lodging. The gentleman in Uncle Sam's clothes looked at me severely and said, "Move on, move on, we don't allow tramps here." "But," I commenced to entreat—"Never mind the but," the preserver of the law cut me short, "move on as I have told you, or I'll put ye in jail and supply ye with fourteen days of hard labour." It was the fortnight of hard labour that I respected, otherwise, if it was for one night only, I would have gladly availed myself of the opportunity to obtain lodging, even in jail. Walking over railway ties when tired out and hungry is hard luck, but that big policeman again put me on the march. My progress was slow, and soon after I had left the town I saw two covered freight cars standing on a siding. The door of one of them was open, so I crawled in and laid down, and was soon fast asleep. When I woke up the door had been closed, the car evidently had been attached to a train and was travelling at a good speed. I wondered whether I was retracing my steps or whether I thus approached my destination. Finally the train stopped. Looking through a crack in the door I could see that it was daylight, and a signboard just opposite reading "Restaurant" reminded me, if that were necessary, that I must get something to eat at any cost. I called the attention of a man who happened to pass by and the door immediately was thrown open. "What are you doing in here? Every one of you d—tramps should be in jail and break stones," was the gentleman's morning greeting. Getting away from that cheerful stranger, who threatened to "put a head on me" if he caught me in a car again, I made a straight course for the restaurant.

'On entering I said, "Good morning, madam," to the woman behind the counter. Turning round she at once sized me up and said, "If you want something to eat go in the backyard and split firewood for an hour, then I will give you a good breakfast." I accepted the job and after an hour's hard work the good woman proved true to her word and provided me with a first-class meal. This made me feel much better, and when ready to leave I thanked her for her kindness and enquired the name of the town and the distance to San Francisco. "This is Berkeley," she replied, "and it will cost you fifteen cents to get to San Francisco."

"Madam," I said, "I will split wood for another hour or two if you will oblige me with the fifteen cents." To my surprise she handed me my fare and said that she was well satisfied with what I had done, and added, "You have accomplished more in one hour than other tramps will do in a day," and I scarcely knew whether to feel flattered or angry.

'The same morning I arrived at San Francisco and took up lodgings at a sailors' boarding-house, the proprietor of which directed me to the shipping office he had business relations with. At eleven o'clock I signed on as an AB in a large sailing ship bound for Liverpool, for twenty-five dollars a month.'

Here I interrupted my old friend saying, 'Excuse me, Mac, how could you sign on as an AB, for you were not an able seaman.'

'Quite right,' was his reply, 'and that is how I got into trouble.'

Then he proceeded with his narrative.

'The proprietor of the boarding-house looked also after some other fellows who were to sail with me in the same ship. He handed us five dollars each, out of one month's advance, and at the same time gave sharp instruction to everyone to be on hand the next morning at seven o'clock to go aboard. All were ready at the appointed hour, and accompanied by the boarding-house keeper and his "runner" (a hard case) we went on board.

'On reaching the vessel's deck I asked my host about my advance. "It is in that bundle there," he answered, pointing to a parcel of considerable dimensions. "Take it forward," his runner added, "and get ready for work." We had hardly been ten minutes in the forecastle when the first mate appeared in the door and shouted, "Get out of this now, you fellers, heave anchor!"

'I had just time enough to discover that the contents of the parcel sent on board by the honourable boarding-house keeper were not worth five dollars; but the gentleman had left the ship and we were ordered to heave up. Anchor up, we were taken in tow, and when outside the Golden Gate the tug blew two whistles. Then the first mate roared out like a lion, "Loose all sail! Hurry up, now, and get the canvas on her. You young feller over there," pointing at me, "get a move on you quick and loosen the main royal and skysail!"'

'Did you get up?' I again interrupted Mac. 'Go up; how could I? I had no intention of breaking my neck!' Then he continued:

'I was going to give an explanation by commencing: "Please excuse me, Mr —," when the mate harshly attacked me. "Excuse nothing, get up there, I tell you, and no more of your confounded back talk to me!" At the same time he rushed at me in a most threatening attitude and like a shot I made for the rigging, just in time to keep out of his clutches. I managed to climb up as high as the mainyard, and not for all the gold and diamonds in the Transvaal would I have ventured any higher. The first mate was a big, raw-boned Irishman and meantime was busy chasing others round the deck and up the rigging.

'I had been hanging on to some ropes for dear life, and hardly five minutes had passed when the big mate spotted me again. The vibration of the shout he let out almost caused me to let go. "Come down, come down, you—" he roared in a great rage. Talk about a man between the devil and the deep sea, he was I! I had no alternative but to face the brute, so I clambered down. No sooner did I touch the deck when I received such a kick, that I was lifted clean into the air. He then told me to help pulling on ropes, and that he would speak to me later on.

'By noon we were going along under full sail, and with the exception of one man at the wheel all hands were gathered in the forecastle for dinner, and ship and officers were discussed. One old sailor, who had shipped many years before the mast, said that if he had not been drunk he would never have gone aboard this red-hot Nova Scotia packet. "Yes," another one remarked, sending a stealthy glance sideways at me, "the mates are regular floating devils, and anybody who does not properly understand his business will have a hot time of it!" "Quite right he should," a third one declared; "a man has no right to sign on to a ship as an AB who doesn't even know how to go up and loosen a sail!"

'At eight o'clock we were ordered to line up on deck, when the mates would pick their watches. To my distress, I was included in with the first mate's watch. This over, we were addressed by the first mate as follows:

"'Now, boys, do as you are told, for if you don't I will make yer do it. The port watch takes the first watch on deck, the star-board watch goes below. You, young feller," pointing at me, "come over here, I want to speak to you." With trembling knees and a fast-beating heart I walked over to where the mate stood, expecting more trouble. It was a clear moonlit night and when I came near that big man who had more power on the ship than any king has in his country, he put his right hand on my left shoulder, looked me straight in the face and said in a serious man-ner: "How did you dare to board this vessel as an able seaman?"

'Thereupon I told my hard-luck story, and when I had fin-ished the mate said, in a more friendly tone, "Well, you are here, and I guess we have to take you along. But, mind you, be quick and obedient at all times!"

'I strictly followed the chief officer's instructions, and experi-enced little further trouble on the voyage. Four months later I was paid off with fifteen pounds at Liverpool. I bought some clothes, and a few days later shipped on board a steamer bound for Cape Town, as a steward. When we arrived at the Cape, orders were given to the crew that no one was allowed to go ashore. However, I succeeded in effecting my escape. Having put on my best suit I left the ship in the company of some pas-sengers and walked up to the dock gate. Here I showed my card, on which was written "Reporter," to the guard, and I had no difficulty in getting past. Thus I reached the goal, and though I was still poor I entered Cape Town with the gait of a million-aire. I soon found employment and gradually worked my way up. And as you can see with your own eyes,' Mac concluded, 'I am now well off and in happy circumstances.'

'You certainly are, Mac,' I assented, 'and a good man will always come up in the end; but tell me, was that big boar which you shot on Cocos Island really as large as you claimed it was?'

'Oh, yes,' his pretty wife here chimed in, 'what a great time you people must have had on Cocos Island. I would have given anything to have been there. And what about the goat my husband was fight-ing on some other island? He tells me that the animal had horns as large as bent table legs and a beard longer than Uncle Sam's!'

'That is so,' I affirmed; 'I saw it myself.'

TWENTY-NINE

WHAT HAPPENED TO THE TILIKUM *IN LANDLOCKED PRETORIA—ENGAGING A MATE AGAIN—GENUINE 'CAPE HOPERS'— LEAVING CAPE TOWN*

A FEW DAYS LATER I put the *Tilikum* on the train and travelled to Pretoria. Arriving there I found that my old friend Mr Ray had made all arrangements for my lodging and the exhibition of the boat. The next morning I went to the station to see whether she had arrived. It was quite early and the office not yet open. I enquired from a young man, who apparently belonged to the railway staff, whether he had seen a boat come in on a train. 'Yes,' was the reply, 'she arrived last night, and after we 'ad taken 'er off the car an 'orse came along and kicked 'er 'ead off.'

'A horse kicked what head off?' I demanded anxiously.

'The 'ead of the boat you are speaking about. You know, that figure-'ead.'

We then walked to where the boat lay, and, sure enough, the *Tilikum*'s figure-head had been smashed and the pieces placed on the deck. The young man closely examined the broken parts, and then said, 'You know, Captain, the 'ead on this 'ooker of yours was an awful-looking thing. A man who had a drop or two too much and 'appening to be confronted with it was likely to get it bad. No wonder that 'orse was scared. But I am quite sure, when the incident has been reported to the office, your boat will be refitted with a respectable-looking figure-'ead free of charge.'

The figure-head had been a genuine Indian carving, and, therefore, could not be replaced in Pretoria. However, the railway company placed a carpenter at my disposal with orders to do anything I wanted to have done with regard to my boat. So it came about that the original figure-head was replaced by one that looked a little more civilised. As to other repairs, almost nothing was required; nevertheless, I wish to acknowledge the generosity of the railway officials in Pretoria.

I met several old friends from Victoria, BC, who had come here during the war and stayed. This induced me to stop at Pretoria a good deal longer than my programme allowed. There I also had the pleasure of shaking hands with General Botha, who told me that he would rather go through another South African war than attempt to cross the Atlantic in the *Tilikum*.

Mr Ray introduced to me a young man of about twenty-two years of age, by name E. Harrison, who was employed in the same office as himself. He asked me to take his young friend along as a mate to England. Mr Harrison was a native of Gippsland, Australia. He had left Melbourne about a year previously as passenger on a steamer for South Africa.

He had had very little experience, I discovered; however, my general impression was a favourable one, and I accepted his services as a mate. As he could not leave his office then, it was arranged that he should meet me in Cape Town.

The day fixed for my departure came and the *Tilikum* was lifted on to the train, and in company of Mr Ray, who had arranged for a furlough of ten days, I journeyed down to East London. Here I secured a temporary mate for the run to Cape Town, and sailed for Port Elizabeth, a distance of about a hundred and thirty miles, arriving there after a journey of twenty-three hours' duration.

Port Elizabeth does not possess a harbour proper, but only a roadstead, formed by a wide bay open to the south-east. There I witnessed a sight the like of which I have never seen before or since. More than two dozen large square-rigged sailing vessels lay stranded high and dry on a sand beach near the city! I was informed that all these doomed vessels had been lying at anchor in the roadstead, some loading, some discharging cargo, while others had been ready for sea and just awaited orders from their owner. Suddenly a heavy south-easterly gale had sprung up, accompanied by large breaking seas, and all these unfortunate ships were torn from their moorings and driven ashore to meet their fate. When the vessels had parted with their moorings they had come in contact with each other; parts of their masts and yards were carried away, while some of them were almost entirely dismantled. Others were apparently left in a fairly good condition; but one and all had abandoned the blue waters of the ocean for ever, destined to be broken up on shore or to suffer slow decay.

Mr Ray had followed me by train to Port Elizabeth, and when I sailed from there I said good-bye to this faithful friend, who had a railway ticket already in his pocket to return to his home in Pretoria. He asked me once more to take good care of young Harrison, and added, 'I think he has got a touch of consumption, but the cruise in the *Tilikum* will do him good.'

'Consumption,' I said; 'in that case I cannot take him along.'

Mr Ray, however, pleaded so strongly for his protégé that I finally agreed to take him on the voyage to London, saying, 'All right; the *Tilikum* has driven all sorts of troubles out of my former mates, and at times has put even myself in proper condition. She may perhaps succeed in taking the small touch of consumption, as you call it, out of him.' With this my friend was greatly pleased, and we parted after a final handshake.

The distance to Cape Town is approximately four hundred and fifty miles. The weather showed good behaviour when, with a fresh north-easterly breeze, we sailed out of Algoa Bay and shaped a course towards the Cape of Good Hope. The wind kept fresh till we had Mossel Bay bearing north, and then at first became light, but soon hauled into the west and started to blow. It was the first time I had rounded the Cape, but I knew its reputation, and therefore did not care to get mixed up with one of its famous westerly gales and bad seas, so I steered in for Mossel Bay. The wind was increasing fast, but by sailing under small sail and with the lee rail constantly under water we managed to evade the gale and anchored in Mossel Bay, which is perfectly safe from westerly blows. The next morning the weather had resumed its normal condition, and, the wind coming in from the east, we proceeded on our course. This lasted until we had reached the neighbourhood of Danger Point, about forty-five miles from the Cape. Then the wind again hauled into the west and commenced blowing. Not knowing of any suitable place to run into for shelter, I therefore steered the boat off the land, and, when we had obtained sufficient sea room, we hove to, to ride out the gale.

After sunset, when we were below in the cabin, I asked my mate, who had sailed the ocean for many years and rounded the Cape more often than he counted fingers and toes, whether he ever saw the Flying Dutchman which is said to haunt these waters in preference. 'I have,' he replied, 'on several occasions, after drinking bad whisky, but as long as you stick to a good brand you will never see him!'

During the night the wind developed into an extremely heavy gale and, owing to a strong current setting through in the opposite direction, we experienced a bad hollow sea. At midnight gale and seas were at their worst. Now and then a high sea would break under the bow of our little vessel, making her shiver from stem to stern. From time to time I took a turn on deck to see whether our riding light was burning and everything in order. On one occasion, when glancing up through the scuttle, I saw the little vessel working her way apparently with great difficulty over the roaring combers. 'Well, *Tilikum*,' I said, 'how do you like the Cape Hopers?' And through the howling wind and the noise of the breakers it seemed to me an answer came, 'Be at ease; I'm not afraid of them; they are not half as bad as the hind hoof of a certain horse in Pretoria.'

The *Tilikum* mastered the Cape Hope gale about as well as all previous storms. A few days later we arrived at Cape Town, where the first man I met on landing was Mr Harrison, who shortly before had come down from Pretoria to report himself ready to join me. A large circus building controlled by the city authorities was placed at my disposal for exhibiting the *Tilikum*. Here I kept her for three weeks, and during this time nearly all the people of Cape Town came to inspect what some styled 'the little Vancouver Island ship.'

Shortly before our departure the *Tilikum* was treated to a new coat of paint, and when in the water again made ready to cross the Atlantic to Pernambuco, Brazil.

On April 14th, equipped with full provisions, water, and quite a quantity of mail for Europe on board, she lay to anchor near a small wharf a little outside of the docks. Our start had been fixed for three in the afternoon. A little beforehand, the embankments began to throng with crowds who had come to witness our departure. Tug-boats and other small steamers moved round us, now and then one would come alongside, and passengers would pass on board various presents. All these parcels were piled up in the cabin as they came along, we being very busy then hand-shaking and saying good-bye.

The weather was calm and beautiful. Sharp to time one of the small steamers took us in tow, and, accompanied by a fleet of about a dozen others, each loaded with passengers, we pro-ceeded seaward. It was a real pleasure being thus towed out, the steamers cruising round us and their passengers waving hats and handkerchiefs. When we were just outside Table Bay a light breeze sprang up from the south, and we set sail. The steamers whistled for the last time, and from the cheering crowds on their decks handkerchiefs, hats and caps again went up into the air. Then all steered round to return to the harbour, while we headed for the north.

THIRTY

I THEN BEGAN examining the presents. The first parcel contained what looked to me like roasted turkey.

'Have a little turkey, Harry?' I called out through the scuttle. 'No, thank you,' the answer came.

The second parcel was a duplicate of the first, and putting the two aside I opened the next. This contained another fine bird, evidently goose.

'Have a little roasted goose, Harry?'

'Don't care about any.'

'How about some chicken?'

'Chicken I don't like,' he replied.

'Now, then, here is something you are bound to like.'

'What is it?'

'It looks to me like roasted ostrich.'

'I don't think I'll have any,' was the languid reply.

'You don't seem to be hungry. Here are some bottled goods. Perhaps you would prefer a drink?'

There was beer, fine old whisky, three-star Hennessey, and a variety of wines. The label on the bottle read, 'Mumm, twenty years old.'

'Harry,' I said, 'this old wine must be consumed at once, else it might get spoiled on our hands.' I at once got busy, and no sooner had I cut the wires than the cork went off like a cannon ball. I thought sure that it had pierced the cabin deck.

In sampling the Mumm I found that despite its old age it was of the best quality. I passed a glass out to my mate, who sat there with one hand on the tiller and the other on his stomach, and shook his head. The *Tilikum* had begun to feel the swell of the Atlantic Ocean—and so had my mate. I advised him to take a drink of salt water in order to quickly get over the trouble and help me to do honour to some of the presents.

We were nearly up to Robben Island, about ten miles to the north-west of Cape Town. The wind fell very light. Therefore, we dropped anchor under the east side of the island, in smooth water, near the beach. By that time my mate had mastered the spell of sea-sickness and both of us did justice to the provisions. The following morning, after a substantial breakfast, we proceeded on our voyage. A moderate wind blew from the south and soon we dropped the little island and the coast of Africa below the horizon. However, my mate was ill again as soon as we entered the ocean swell.

The weather continued fine, and with a steady moderate breeze from the south, day after day, it was a most pleasant sail. But my poor mate remained sea-sick and was unable to get over his trouble; even the salt-water cure did not bring him relief. In this he somewhat resembled the Australian bush pilot who accompanied me from Newcastle to Melbourne, sea-sick day after day, eating very little and with a strong inclination to discard. In fact, in either case, it was a mystery to me how they managed to keep alive. As Mr Harrison suffered so much, I shaped a course for St Helena. When we had entered the region of the south-easterly trade wind the weather still kept fine, and seventeen days after leaving Cape Town we dropped anchor in St James' Bay on the north-west coast of St Helena, the best known of all the solitary islands in the world.

No sooner had my mate stepped on shore than he felt well and was able to eat a hearty meal, which, after his prolonged indisposition, was remarkable indeed. We remained for two days on the island, and visited the residence of Napoleon Bonaparte, in which he died on May 5th, 1821. Although the building was unoccupied, everything was kept in good order. The white-painted exterior of the house, and a well-trimmed flower garden surrounding it, gave the whole a neat appearance; but in the interior about the only thing worth noticing was a marble bust of the great soldier. A short distance off, between low green hills and near a small fresh-water spring that gushed out from the hillside, Napoleon's tomb is preserved, though the remains have been transferred to Paris. A small building near by contained a book in which were written the autographs of visitors from all over the world. I added my signature to their number.

We spent a very enjoyable night in the company of some gentlemen of the cable station and other residents. The following day we took our departure, shaping a direct course for Pernambuco. The moderate trade wind and the splendid weather continued, but no sooner had our little vessel begun to enter the ocean swell than my mate fell sick again. However, he was not of the kind that gives way to the feeling, but regularly took his turn on the rudder. The trade wind sent us along at a rate of about a hundred miles a day, which enabled us to accomplish the passage from St Helena to Pernambuco in eighteen days. Shortly before dark on May 20th we obtained our first glimpse of the South American coast.

The following morning, at four o'clock, we dropped anchor in the roadstead of Pernambuco, which made it three years, almost to the hour, since I started from Victoria, BC. Thus the *Tilikum* had succeeded in crossing the three oceans and the contract I had entered upon with Mr Luxton was fulfilled.

A long time had elapsed since I first arrived at this port. It was in 1877, on my first voyage to sea in a three-hundred-ton sailing vessel from Hamburg, bound for Guayaquil, Ecuador. The captain was taken ill at sea, and we put in at Pernambuco to secure medical assistance. At that time the roadstead was full of sailing vessels of all nations. But on this particular morning, instead of the beautiful sailing ships enlivening the picture, one smoky old steamer was the sole ornament. I thought to myself, if I could be almighty only for a short while, the first thing I would undertake would be the wiping of all those old smoke-pots off the seas and replacing them by fine, fast, square-rigged sailing ships, a delight to every seaman's eye.

At seven o'clock the customs launch came off, and after I had made the necessary reports the captain was kind enough to give us a tow into the harbour. On the way we passed the Pernambuco lighthouse, which is built on the northern end of the most remarkable natural breakwater that can be found anywhere. Along the right side, on going in, extends a fine stone quay with an avenue of shady trees running along it, backed by a row of business houses. The left side of the harbour, which forms an oblong about one hundred yards in width, runs parallel to the stone quay opposite the breakwater. It consists of dark coral, and its uniform shape makes it hard to believe that this is the work of nature. All along the breakwater were moored vessels from distant countries. And while large waves restlessly broke and worked on the outside of this wonderful structure, the inside, with the exception of occasional spray, was quite calm. I moored the *Tilikum* near a boat-landing and reported our arrival to the British Consul, Mr Williams. This gentleman showed much interest in my cruise and accompanied me to the harbour to inspect my boat. 'Well done,' he said, when stepping aboard; 'crossing the three great oceans in this vessel certainly constitutes a world's record!'

The following day, while I was in the Consul's office, Mr Williams said, 'Yesterday, when on board of your vessel, I noticed that you are flying the Canadian flag. I must tell you that this is against the law. I am, therefore, obliged to ask you to replace it by the British ensign.'

I had sailed the *Tilikum* for three years under the Canadian flag, and therefore I did not altogether appreciate the Consul's order. However, orders from the Government representative given to shipmasters in foreign countries must be complied with, so from that day I flew the British flag.

We remained a fortnight in Pernambuco, during which time Mr Williams entertained us splendidly and looked after our wants in every way. He also secured for us free railway passports, thus affording us an opportunity to see something of the rich level country so abundantly wooded. Sugar cane, tropical fruits, palm nuts and many other useful plants are raised in this stretch of Brazil. Here and there, nestled amidst trees and gardens, small villas appeared, and naked little negro children were playing about in the sun. Through the influence of the Consul we furthermore received several invitations to dinners, and the night before our departure a banquet was given to us at the British cable station, at which many people were present.

Although Mr Harrison had been sick all the way across the South Atlantic, he insisted upon completing the voyage to London. On the afternoon of June 4th, at three o'clock, we were taken in tow by a launch, and, accompanied by a steamer loaded with passengers, including the British Consul, we proceeded seaward. When five miles outside the breakwater we set sail and let go. We then bade farewell to our hosts, and giving three dips with our new British ensign we shaped a course towards our final destination, London. Owing to the north-east trade wind we were obliged to follow different courses. Thus it came about that the total distance amounted to about six thousand miles.

THIRTY-ONE

*BOUND FOR LONDON—THE ATLANTIC
CALM BELT—WHAT THE* TILIKUM *DID
FOR MY MATE—WHEN SHIPS MEET ON
THE HIGH SEAS —SHORT OF PROVISIONS
—BOAT AND CREW IN QUARANTINE*

A NEW COAT OF PAINT had been presented to the *Tilikum* by the captain of a Norwegian ship, and, under all her canvas, with a fresh trade wind, she went along as proud as ever. Who will wonder that the little vessel by that time had become to me something more than inanimate wood, constructed to be run down and then replaced without difficulty by another? No, she was worth more to me, having proved a trustworthy friend on many occasions, as her name implied. I never felt this more than on that day, when, starting out for a final run, and, patting her side, I said, '*Tilikum*, after all the ups and downs you have experienced in surveying the three oceans you have taken it cheerfully, and it was to you like a picnic. You have weathered heavy gales; seas have broken over you; every bone in your body was crushed at Melbourne, and at one time even your head was knocked off. Still, here you are, looking as well as ever, and working diligently your way over the salt waves towards your final destination. Sure enough, it is quite a long way yet, six thousand miles across the ocean; but if we look after each other as we have done in the past we are bound to make it! We shall then, on our arrival at London, have the satisfaction of laughing at all those "didn't-I-tell-you" people and other sceptics who prophesied at our outset from Victoria, BC, that we would perhaps get to sea but never return to land again!'

We had not gone very far when my poor mate hung his head

over the rail again. However, as before, he faithfully attended to business. The trade wind kept fresh, and on June 4th the *Tilikum* crossed the equator and passed into the northern hemisphere. My mate crossed the line for the first time, but, as he still was sick, Neptune had pity and did not trouble him.

A few days later the trade wind became light, and on a beautifully bright morning we found ourselves becalmed. We had entered the Atlantic equatorial calm belt. This was the first morning, indeed, the first occasion, since our departure from Cape Town that my mate displayed signs of an appetite. 'That is a different proposition,' I said: 'what would you like? Ham and eggs?' Just the thing,' he answered. I prepared a large dish of the favourite breakfast food, and it was a real pleasure to see Harry diving into it. Up to that day he had been very quiet and poor company to me, but from that time onward he seemed to be a changed man and said that he felt quite sure that if he ever had a touch of that deadly disease Mr Ray spoke to me about the *Tilikum* had shaken it out of him.

The North Atlantic calm belt did not turn out as troublesome as its counterpart in the Pacific three years previously. After two days of variable weather, spells of calms interspersed with puffs of air from different directions and accompanied by rain showers, we passed into the influence of the north-east trade winds. I trimmed the sails by the wind, and during the following three weeks we covered a distance of two thousand miles, the boat going along without steering.

After we had lost the trade wind we followed a northerly course in order to reach the region of the North Atlantic westerly winds. In this we were successful, and made good time until we arrived at a position about one thousand miles west of the Azores, where we again got becalmed. After having made a fairly good run we did not mind a day or two of calm, but to my sorrow the matter did not end here. Day after day we drifted about, and when at times we made a few miles on our course with light, variable puffs we would invariably drift back again, and consequently, when a fortnight had gone by in this manner, we had covered only twenty miles in all!

Anyone recovering from a long period of sea-sickness generally will make up for what he has missed in eating in a short time, and most likely he will even do more than that. At least, I received such an impression from my mate. He could eat at almost any hour. The colour which, so he said, he had lost in Pretoria, returned to his cheeks, and he put on flesh every day. On the other hand my provision locker was losing flesh fast and the voyage becoming protracted, I began to fear that my mate would have me eaten out of house and home before we reached England. These circumstances induced me to change our course for the Azores Islands.

We had drifted about in calm weather for about fifteen days when, on July 24th, at daybreak, we sighted a sail about seven miles to the north-eastward. We at once completed our breakfast, and then started rowing towards the stranger, hoping that he could possibly provide us with enough provisions to take us through to England. The *Tilikum* was only a small vessel, but we found that rowing her at sea meant hard work, and not until almost noon did we arrive alongside. A side ladder was immediately lowered and I went on board.

The vessel turned out to be the British barque *Port Sonachan*, one hundred and forty-two days out from the west coast of Costa Rica with a cargo of dye wood, and bound for Dunkirk. On comparing the logs I found that we had crossed the equator on the same day, but the *Port Sonachan* had been becalmed for three weeks and, like ourselves, was short of provisions. The captain told me that flour and salted beef were the only foodstuffs left on board, and of these, he said, they had sufficient to last them to their destination. The calm continued for two more days, during which we remained on board the barque and spent an enjoyable time with the captain and his officers.

When the wind freshened we parted company, the *Port Sonachan* sailing northward while we went to the east, and we soon lost sight of each other. We experienced moderate and at times fresh westerly winds, and on the morning of August 3rd, when near the south point of San Miguel Island, we were compelled to shorten down. While running under mainsail only, the strong wind blowing split the sail from top to bottom! This was the first and only sail split on the whole cruise. At half-past five we sailed into the harbour of Ponta Delgada and dropped anchor near the water front among some pleasure yachts. A few minutes later a doctor came alongside in a launch and asked me, through an interpreter, for a bill of health from our last port of departure.

The Consul at Pernambuco had assured me that I did not require a bill of health, so I had sailed without one. When I informed our interviewers of the fact, it was funny to see how the crew of the launch, who had their hands on our boat to keep her alongside, let go, as if the *Tilikum* was a hot brick. We then were ordered to immediately move to the quarantine station. This was very much against our liking. I therefore asked the interpreter whether it could be arranged that we might receive the provisions which we were badly in need of. After that we would not trouble them longer but proceed on our voyage. We were then informed that they would tow us out to the quarantine station, after which arrangements would be made to meet our wants. About half an hour later we were swinging to our anchor just outside the harbour, left to ourselves.

We then both went below to survey our remaining stock of provisions. We discovered that in spite of our long passage from Pernambuco, ample flour, rice, lard, butter, hard bread, and a few other things remained. In view of this fact we had just decided to get up anchor and proceed on our voyage when we heard a voice outside. 'Somebody is coming,' I said, and looking out of the cabin I saw a boat with several men in it lying about fifteen feet away. One of the occupants then passed a basket to us, attached to the end of a long pole. The basket contained beef-steak, mutton chops, eggs, vegetables, and fresh bread-and-butter. After having delivered it, and without accepting payment, the boat was rowed back to shore.

We had just got our breakfast ready, and what a breakfast it was! It did one good to look at it. Then another small boat came alongside, and the operation was repeated. This basket contained several bottles of wine, and the label on one read, 'Ready-Mixed Cocktail.'

Well, now, after a sixty days' ocean voyage in the *Tilikum*, if anyone thinks that we did not know what to do with that ready-mixed cocktail he would be mistaken, and with the above-mentioned breakfast on top of it we came to the conclusion that we would stay a little longer with the Portuguese to see what else they would do for us.

At nine o'clock the interpreter came and enquired whether we were willing to have our boat and our persons fumigated. 'Quite all right,' I replied. He then left, but at ten o'clock returned with the news that a cablegram had been sent to Lisbon, the capital, to ask permission for us to land without being fumigated.

Two hours later the interpreter returned with the welcome message that a dinner would be prepared and sent to us at noon. This promise was duly redeemed.

THIRTY-TWO

THE AZORES—A ROYAL RECEPTION—
TWO EXCURSIONS—A MULE AS
DISTURBER OF THE PEACE—LEAVING
THE HOSPITABLE SHORES

DURING THE AFTERNOON we had many callers, but one and all kept at a distance, until at about five o'clock, when a launch came right alongside our boat. Our friend the interpreter was again in evidence and a well-dressed gentleman in his company stepped over into our boat. Then the interpreter introduced his companion as the Mayor of Ponta Delgada and commodore of the yacht club. After supplying the gentlemen with a few particulars of our voyage and showing them at the same time a few of my honorary membership cards from various yacht clubs, we were towed back again to harbour. On landing we both were ushered into a carriage, and accompanied by the mayor and the interpreter, drove into the city, where we were taken to an hotel.

In the evening we were entertained by many ladies and gentlemen, and the interpreter being the only one speaking English, he gave to the audience a short explanation of our cruise. After he had finished we were embraced by the gentlemen present, but I considered myself very much out of luck again when the beautiful Portuguese ladies, in their snowy-white attire and their dark hair decorated with flowers, only shook hands,

The following morning the mayor in his carriage drove up to the hotel, accompanied by the interpreter, to take me down to the harbour. On the preceding night I had asked the interpreter whether there were facilities for hauling my boat up for general cleaning and eventual repairs, to which he assured me he would attend. On stepping out of the carriage it was, therefore, not a small surprise to me to see my little vessel lying high and dry and men engaged cleaning her, inside and outside, scraping spars and repairing the split main-sail.

In the afternoon we were shown round the city and suburbs. Ponta Delgada is the capital of the Azores, and has a population of about twenty thousand. It is a fine city, and the climate is perfect. Its latitude is about the same as that of Washington. Tropical fruits of the best quality grow here, notably pineapples, which are raised in large glass-houses and thus mature all the year round. I was told by a fruit merchant that some of the pineapples will fetch as much as a pound each in England about Christmas time.

It was a fine Sunday morning, just five days after our arrival, and Mr Harrison and myself were looking out of the window when we were attracted by the music of a brass band marching towards our hotel, and which halted at the entrance. 'They must be playing a salute to some high personage stopping at this hotel,' I said to my mate. With that we saw the mayor and the interpreter alighting from a carriage which had followed the band. A few minutes later both entered our room and informed us that they had come to take us along for a ride. We accepted the kind invitation, and with the brass band at the head and many people following we proceeded through the main street down to the harbour. Without my knowledge the *Tilikum* had been launched again, and with everything cleaned and shining, freshly painted, and with flags flying on all three tops, she looked a pretty sight. Two passenger steamers, decorated with flags and loaded with people, were lying near by, and flags flew from all the yachts and other vessels.

'What is up to-day?' I enquired. 'Is the King of Portugal expected?'

'Not that,' was the reply, 'but a grand excursion has been arranged in your honour!'

The mayor, with the interpreter, my mate and myself, then went aboard the *Tilikum*, and a few minutes later were taken in tow by one of the excursion steamers. With the band playing on the other one we left the harbour and followed the coast eastward, a fleet of yachts under sail following in the rear. After an hour we anchored at Alagoa, a small city, the population of which afforded us a splendid reception. Large fire rockets were sent up into the air, although it was midday and bright sunshine. Basketfuls of beautiful flowers were showered over us as we marched through a long narrow street which led up to the city square. On our arrival there the people were addressed in a speech which gave an explanation of our cruise. In short, everything with regard to the excursion and our reception had been carried out in a most complete and successful way. The only disappointment lay in the circumstance that the embracing following the public speech was again exclusively confined to the sterner sex.

Two days after another excursion was undertaken. Accompanied by eight gentlemen, we left the city at six in the morning in two carriages. The road which we followed at first ran along the coast, affording fine views of the ocean on the left, while on the right rich cultivated land extended, divided into small patches by fences. Here and there farmhouses could be seen partly hidden amongst fruit trees and flower gardens. After a drive of an hour and a half we turned to the right, and a steep incline necessitated our changing the comfortable carriage for a mule. In another place I have already stated that I am a poor rider, and mules I consider still worse than horses, and, naturally, I did not feel much inclined to avail myself of this means of locomotion. However, being assured that the animal was very quiet, I mounted and followed the rest up the long, sloping hillside. We had been riding for about an hour and a half when, near the road, a circular pool appeared, about two hundred feet in diameter, and fed by a small stream which rushed down from the mountain. Large boulders projected here and there from the basin and pieces of washing lay piled up on some. About a score of women with double-reefed petticoats were wading in the water, the latter reaching above their knees. They stood scattered all over the pool washing clothes. Our mules evidently had become thirsty, for they made a straight course for the water and carried us in a few minutes near the women. The animal I rode, apparently being older and therefore more experienced than the others, passed all of them, and despite my efforts to hold him back rounded the margin of the pool till he came near the place where the mountain stream emptied itself. He then entered the water to obtain a good drink of the clear liquid. In doing this he naturally stirred up a good deal of mud and gravel, and when the dirty water reached the washerwomen they became angry, and several of the sturdier specimens approached me in a threatening manner. I saw trouble coming and tried my best to persuade the beast to retire. But as anybody knows, a mule is a stubborn animal, and will always be so, and no earthly power can change his disposition. I pulled with all my might on the bridle, kicked him in the ribs, and shouted at him, but in spite of all the mule remained as immovable as one of the boulders and took his time in taking a long draught. In a short time I found myself surrounded by the washerwomen, and judging by their expression and gesticulations with wet garments in their hands I knew that they meant business.

One of the militants struck my mule over the head, while another belaboured him with a wet garment at the other end. Two or three carrying similar weapons aimed at me, but before the first swing got home my companions came to the rescue. By this time the troublesome quadruped seemed to have quenched his thirst, and quietly retired from the protesting amazons, and it was left to my hosts to finish the battle. Experienced men know that whenever an argument arises with the other sex the latter should be permitted the last word; and it is also a fact that if it is not conceded she will take it nevertheless. This little trouble ended in the same manner: some of my companions received a good soaking with wet clothes, and the tongues of the indignant women were wagging rapidly when we rode over a small eminence near by and lost sight of them.

About an hour later we all had reached the top of the mountain. After dismounting, Mr Harrison and myself were blindfolded and then each led by two of the gentlemen a short distance. Soon we halted and the bandage was removed from our eyes. Then the most wonderful panorama I have ever seen stretched before me. We found ourselves standing on the brink of a lofty and steep mountain; one step farther and we would have dropped into a lake about a thousand feet below. Apparently we were on the edge of an old crater, the bottom of which formed the lake. The latter measured about three miles in length and had an average width of half a mile. A peculiarity was that the water showed two distinct colours, being a muddy grey at one end and at the other a beautiful dark blue, resembling ocean water. The dividing line of the two colours ran straight across the lake about one mile distant from the west end. Mountain peaks and smaller crags, clothed with vegetation, surrounded the lake on all sides, and below, to the left, half hidden in green foliage, and almost level with the water, a little village nestled near the shore, along which a few boats lay.

San Miguel is a most beautiful spot, and owing to its lovely climate, rich tropical vegetation, and excellent harbour is destined to become one day a great holiday resort, the more so as it may be reached in a few days from the English Channel. With regard to ourselves the inhabitants' genuine hospitality and obliging kindnesses were carried to the extreme. Mr Harrison or myself could go into any store or hotel and be served with anything we cared to ask for, but payment was never accepted. When I requested my bill for cleaning and painting the boat and the fresh stores which had been provided I was politely informed that everything, including our hotel bill, had been settled! As a matter of fact, neither Mr Harrison nor myself ever had a chance of spending one cent during our stay.

But the day came when we had to bid good-bye to the amiable people of San Miguel. On August 13th, at two o'clock, escorted by a fleet of yachts, we sailed out of the harbour. About an hour later all the yachts dipped their flags which we answered from our mizzen. They then returned to port while we proceeded on our course to London, a distance of about eighteen hundred miles. The wind kept blowing fresh from the south. During the succeeding five days we covered seven hundred miles of our course, attaining a position about three hundred miles west of Cape Ortegal, on the Spanish coast. The wind then hauled into the south-west and for thirty-six hours blew a heavy gale.

THIRTY-THREE

THE COLONIAL EMPIRE—ARRIVAL IN ENGLAND AND A HEARTY WELCOME!

THE GALE WAS SUCCEEDED by a fresh westerly breeze, which lasted until August 25th and then moderated. At nine o'clock that morning we sighted a sail on our starboard bow. The vessel was going to the south, therefore we changed our course to meet the stranger. At half-past eleven we were within hailing distance. She was a large four-masted British barque, the *Colonial Empire*, and as seen from the cockpit of the *Tilikum* looked like a huge floating island. All the crew stretched their necks over the rail to watch our approach.

'Good morning,' I shouted to a group of men standing on the after-end; 'what is your longitude?'

'Come on board and I'll tell you,' a man answered from the quarter-deck.

Next we heard the order 'Back the main-yard,' followed by the loud command, 'Starboard main-braces.' The big yards and sails swung round, the ship stopped headway, and I sailed the *Tilikum* alongside and tied her up to the *Colonial Empire*. She was from Antwerp and with a general cargo bound for San Francisco. Captain Simson, the master, proved an hospitable fellow. He invited us to dinner and tried hard to keep us on board until dark. But as he went to the south and the wind freshened up, which would have taken us away from our destination, we were obliged to part company.

On the following day we experienced another westerly gale, in which the *Tilikum* proved that she was able to cope with the Atlantic combers as well as with the 'Cape Hopers' and others. When the gale had died out easterly winds commenced blowing which headed us away from our course. On August 29th, at three in the afternoon, we were tacking within a mile of the Scilly lighthouse. On the next day the wind hauled into the west; at midnight we passed the Cape Lizard light and the following forenoon sailed within a stone's throw of the Eddystone light.

The westerly breeze kept fresh and the *Tilikum* sailed through the English Channel, passing one lighthouse after the other until on September 2nd, at four o'clock, with a very light breeze we rounded the jetty at Margate, where thousands of people crowded to watch our approach. When we were within speaking distance a voice from the jetty called out, 'Where are you from?'

'Victoria, British Columbia,' was my reply.

'How long have you been on the voyage?' the questioner enquired.

'Three years three months and twelve days!'

A loud applause followed. When we were inside we tied the *Tilikum* up to a fishing vessel called the *Sunbeam*. Thereupon I stepped on the jetty and at once became very busy shaking hands. While this was going on I suddenly felt myself lifted from the ground. Some gentlemen had got hold of me from behind and carried me over the heads of the cheering crowds, finally dropping me into a carriage. We soon arrived at an hotel, where our successful arrival from the long voyage was celebrated with champagne.

The British Consul at Pernambuco had provided me with a letter of introduction to Sir Alfred Harmsworth, proprietor of the *Daily Mail*. At ten o'clock the next morning I entered the offices of this newspaper, and when I presented the letter to the gentleman in charge he looked at me in surprise.

'Where do you come from?' he asked. 'Arrived here yesterday,' I answered.

'Did you not meet our representative off Dover? We had a steamer cruising round there for the last two days with orders to look for you.'

Unfortunately, we passed Dover at night, which easily explains that the *Daily Mail's* representative overlooked the tiny *Tilikum*.

The *Tilikum* had come to a well-deserved rest. During the Navy and Marine Exhibition in 1905 she was exhibited in Earl's Court western garden.

While in England, shortly after my arrival, I again met with Lieutenant Shackleton, who then held a post as secretary of the Scotch Royal Geographical Society. It was through his influence that I was able to lecture on my cruise in the *Tilikum* before large audiences at Edinburgh and Glasgow, and at various places in England, and later on was honoured by being elected a Fellow of the Royal Geographical Society in London.

SEA
QUEEN

The crew of the Sea Queen.

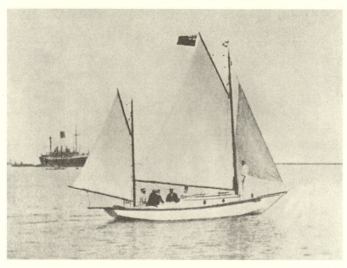

Sea Queen *under sail.*

ONE

ONE FINE SUNNY day in the month of October, 1911, I was sitting quietly in the cabin of the sealing schooner, *Chichijima Maru*, which was at anchor in Yokohama Harbour after her voyage to the Siberian coast. I was thinking over the law which had just been passed prohibiting sealing, and what to take up next, when two young men came on board, and after introducing themselves said, 'Are you the same Captain Voss that made the voyage round the world in the *Tilikum*?'

'Yes,' I replied, 'I am.'

From that time I had a good many visitors to the schooner, all more or less interested in my past experiences. Sealing, however, was prohibited for fifteen years, so on the 1st of November I left the vessel and took lodgings ashore.

In 1911 a treaty was made between the United States, Canada, Japan and Russia to prohibit sealing for fifteen years. A sum of money was set aside to compensate all sealers, and as I came from Victoria, British Columbia, to take charge of a Japanese sealing vessel, and had sailed out of Yokohama for three years, my share of the compensation should have been paid by the Japanese Government. But they were very slow about paying out.

In the month of June, 1912, while I was busy waiting for this money, the two young Yokohama yachtsmen who had first called on me, came and enquired if it was quite safe to make a voyage across the ocean in a small vessel. My reply was precisely what it has always been to questions of this kind since I made the cruise in the *Xora*, that a small vessel is as safe at sea as a large one. At times, when making statements of this kind, people would look askance at me as if to say, 'Oh, tell that to somebody else.' On such occasions I have put my foot down and retorted, 'Yes, and a good deal safer than some of them,' a statement which has surely been proved by the cruise of the *Sea Queen.*

The two young men who spoke to me about making a long voyage were Messrs F. Stone and S. A. Vincent, and in the course of that day's conversation we three agreed to attempt a cruise round the world in the yawl *Sea Queen*, which was then being built by Mr Stone and about half finished. The *Sea Queen* was built on the lines of the *Sea Bird*, in which Mr T. F. Day, editor of the *Rudder*, made his famous voyage from New York to Rome. Her dimensions were: length over all, twenty-five feet eight inches; water-line, nineteen feet; breadth, eight feet three inches; and draught, three feet six inches; sail area, four hundred square feet.

In the beginning of July the little vessel was launched, and on the 26th we put on board a hundred and thirty gallons of fresh water, three months' provisions, two rifles, one revolver and ammunition, one kodak, one gramophone, navigation instruments and our personal effects. The vessel was then ready for sea. All three of the crew being members of the Yokohama Yacht Club, we were honoured with a farewell dinner by the members of that organisation.

At two o'clock on the afternoon of July 27th, 1912, accompanied by all the boats of the club, we started on our voyage. There was a light wind blowing from the south, and our progress was slow, so the *Sea Queen* was caught up by a steam launch and taken down Tokyo Bay at a seven-knot clip. When the launch cast off the cable with which it had been towing us, I accidentally let the flag drop overboard while endeavouring to unfasten it, and it drifted away and disappeared from sight. The launch was filled with passengers who had come to see us off, and we heard one of them say 'Down goes the British flag.' Vincent, who was still dressed in his shore-going clothes, said 'Never!' and dived into the sea, coming to the surface after a few moments with our ensign safe and sound. On reaching the yacht, he was loudly cheered by the onlookers.

After the launch had given us three blasts of her whistle, our friends turned back towards Yokohama, and we with our wet flag on the mizzen-mast gave three dips as a farewell salutation. We then proceeded under all sail towards the south. The light south-westerly breeze took us within about three miles from Uraga, which is about fourteen miles from Yokohama. All the yachts had been keeping close under the land, where they had a nice off-shore breeze and soon came up with us.

It was understood that we would anchor that night in Uraga Harbour. On account of the light wind, it was rather late before we dropped anchor. All hands went ashore, and to our great surprise the crew of the *Sea Queen* were honoured by the yachtsmen to a geisha dance, which was kept up till the early hours of the morning. It was a most enjoyable night.

The following morning at eight o'clock all the yachts set sail, and after wishing us a final farewell they departed for Yokohama, while we were obliged to remain at anchor to repack our stores. During the last few days we received numerous gifts from our friends, chiefly in the way of provisions, and the cabin and cockpit were filled with all kinds of things which had to be stowed away before we could go to sea. This repacking and various other minor details kept us busy all day, and it was not until six o'clock on the 29th July that we sailed out of Uraga Harbour.

The little *Sea Queen* sailed away from Uraga with a light northerly breeze, which increased in force somewhat as we rounded Sunosaki, the last point of land, after which we directed our course to the eastward, and the blue bosom of the great Pacific Ocean appeared before us. The wind was then hauling gradually to the east-north-east; and with a light breeze and quite a large easterly swell the *Sea Queen* made slow progress to the south-eastward. This of course was not according to our wishes, our plan being to sail some thousand miles east before going south for the Marshall Islands. However, we had to take the wind as it came, so let our ship go full and by, and after a good meal of soup, fish, tinned meat and stewed fruit, and while enjoying our after-tiffin smoke, we set to work and fixed up our rules and regulations as follows:

1. Three watches of four hours each shall be kept, with the exception of from four to eight p.m., when the four-hour watch is divided in two, these two-hour watches being known at sea as 'dog watches.'
2. Meal hours to be as follows: breakfast at seven o'clock, lunch at noon, and dinner at half-past five.
3. There is on board the good ship *Sea Queen* a place for everything, and everything must be kept in its place.
4. The man at the helm is responsible for keeping the boat either full and by or on her given course, and is prohibited from falling asleep under pain of a bucket of sea water thrown over his head by the man who catches him. He shall not leave the deck when on duty, but must wait till relieved at the end of his watch.

Rules and regulations being duly approved, we sailed to the south-eastward full and by, every now and again passing a Japanese fishing junk. We were now lowering the peaks of the mountains on the horizon, and by the evening we were almost out of sight of land. At daybreak next morning the *Sea Queen* and her crew of three were well out on the broad expanse of the Pacific Ocean, where mosquitoes, flies and gnats are unknown, and smiling income-tax and bill collectors do not pursue the luckless human, fleeing from pecuniary embarrassments.

The 30th July opened out with a gentle south-easterly breeze, which remained the same all day. We sighted two whales, which appeared to us to be fighting, as they were leaping out of the water together and making a tremendous fuss. The next day we had a moderate easterly breeze in latitude thirty-five degrees forty-four minutes north, longitude one forty-two degrees ten minutes east, with a strong current setting to the north-eastward. During the afternoon, the wind hauled more towards the south, enabling us for the first time since we took our departure to lay our course, but later freshened considerably, and we were compelled to tie one reef in the main-sail. The boat then went along for about twenty-five hours at a speed averaging five knots an hour.

The wind lightening early on the morning of the 1st August we shook out our reef, but this only proved to be the calm before an approaching storm, as within a few hours the weather became very threatening, commencing to blow hard at about nine o'clock. The main-sail was immediately reefed, but the weather getting worse, the yacht was laid to under jib and mizzen, when she rode over the large seas in fine style. As the gale showed signs of still increasing, we hove to under a sea anchor. The *Sea Queen*, under a sea anchor alone, acted in the same way as the *Xora* and *Tilikum*, as without a riding sail she laid sideways to the sea, but no sooner was the little mizzen hoisted, and the sheet hauled in flat, than the vessel swung head to sea and rode every sea that came along so beautifully that in the cabin one would not have imagined that the vessel was really at sea, so steady was her motion. It was very fascinating to my two young shipmates, who had never had a like experience, to watch the way our little vessel rose up on the crests of large seas, and then gently sank again into the hollows ready for the next. I expected to see them get sea-sick for a few days, which of course would have been hard luck on them, but it would have saved the provisions, and a man on a voyage of this kind has to figure out everything, but there was no such luck. They were always ready to do their duty at meal hours, and sometimes between meal hours too. I was soon convinced that my hopes were vain, and it made me think very seriously as to how I could manage to reduce their appetites by about two-thirds.

That same night, while the *Sea Queen* was hove to, our dinner consisted of four fried eggs each, four large slices of bacon, apples, bread, butter, cheese, tea and stewed fruit. We passed the evening away smoking, chatting and listening to our gramophone. We were hove to all night with a full moon and a beautiful evening, but blowing hard.

The following morning the wind moderated, and we got under way again under a single-reefed main-sail. That day and part of the next we experienced fairly good weather, and with a moderate westerly breeze were making an average of about four miles an hour. Toward night the wind increased rapidly, and by ten o'clock it was blowing hard, which compelled us to heave to under reefed sails. The blow, however, did not last very long, and an hour after midnight we were going along before it again.

On August 5th the wind hauled into the north-east, with increasing force, but as the seas did not appear to be dangerous we kept the yacht going under small sails to the south till about two o'clock in the afternoon, when we had a warning from nature to heave to. A large breaking sea struck the *Sea Queen* on the port quarter, which almost turned us on our beam ends. Stone and I were on deck at the time, and it was as much as we could do to hang on. Vincent was thrown clear of his bunk against the opposite side of the cabin. A considerable amount of damage was done below in the way of broken crockery, and a box of eggs overturned, precipitating its contents into Stone's new helmet, giving one an impression of a saucepan in preparation for frying eggs. This seemed to amuse the crew, with the exception of the worthy owner, who did not appreciate the point of the joke himself. Rifles, ammunition, camera and outfit all got their share of sea water. We then hove to under a sea anchor and riding sail. About a dozen eggs got broken in the helmet. Vincent said they were too good to be thrown away, and as Stone refused to keep them in his helmet, the broken eggs were transferred to the frying-pan, and disappeared with our afternoon coffee.

At four o'clock I went out into the cockpit to see how the vessel was getting along with the breaking seas, when I noticed that she was still laying head to sea and riding the huge mountains most gracefully, but the speed of her stern drift had increased to about double. Something wrong with the sea anchor, I thought. Looking towards the bow, I noticed that the sea-anchor float was still in the same position. I was in the act of going forward to find out if there was still a strain on the rope, when I saw a great shark right under the anchor float. It struck me at once that the big brute had been playing with our drag.

'Bring a rifle on deck!' I shouted.

The beast swam round the boat some two hundred yards away. Now and then he would appear on top of a sea and look at us, as if to say, 'I have done my work; the seas will do the rest and you three will be my victims,' but I think he soon discovered that the crew of the *Sea Queen* and a rifle were a little too much for him, and decamped. An hour later it was blowing a heavy gale, accompanied by a large breaking sea, and to show my two friends the effects of oil on breaking seas, I did a little experimenting with different kinds of oil which we carried for the purpose. Our first experiment was with kerosene. Now, kerosene, being very thin, takes quite a lot to do any good, but by using heavy oil, such as fish oil, just a small drop will smooth the top of a large breaker. It is certainly astonishing to see the effect of a small drop of oil on large breaking seas. As soon as the oil strikes the water it will spread itself over quite a large surface, and as soon as a breaking sea strikes that part, it appears to crawl under the oil, and loses its breaking top.

As the *Sea Queen*, like the *Tilikum* and *Xora*, weathered all seas without the aid of oil, we saved it for some future occasion. Vincent, after being knocked off his perch several times, managed to get some photographs of the breaking seas. The boat was drifting astern at an unusually fast rate, but as she lay very comfortable we let her drift for the night. The next morning we noticed for the first time that our yacht had sprung a leak. During the forenoon the gale moderated, and hauling the sea anchor aboard, we found it very much torn. This, no doubt, was what caused the fast drift the previous night. The damage had undoubtedly been done by the shark. The wind moderated, and as it kept in the north-east we let her go to the south-east. The leak became worse, and it being dead against my principles to go on a long voyage with a leaky boat, whether large or small, I proposed to put back to the Japanese coast to overhaul her. My two mates were very much against my proposition, and offered to bale night and day if I would only keep on going to the east, so I consented, provided matters got no worse. However, the leak increased from time to time, and I was afraid that the weight on the keel was too heavy for the boat and was gradually loosening the fastening in the frames. We had then about two thousand miles to cover before sighting the nearest island of the Marshall group, and only about five hundred miles to the Japanese coast. I therefore again made the proposition to turn back, and after explaining the danger of proceeding in a leaky boat on a long ocean voyage, my friends both agreed to my suggestion. We then declared to make for the Bonin Islands.

On August 6th the wind hauled into the south-east, the weather clearing, and for the first time in three days we had a look at the sun and got our position, finding the vessel in latitude thirty-seven degrees fifty-three minutes north and longitude fifty-one degrees forty-five minutes east. The northeasterly current had carried us a hundred and twenty miles more to the north than I had expected, and owing to our leak increasing, we altered our course for Aikawa, a whaling station near Sendai, which, according to my reckoning, was about five hundred miles distant. Never before in my life have I been obliged to turn back with a leaky vessel, and I therefore felt bad about our luck. To make matters worse it was my birthday; I was fifty-four years of age, but it had to be done. We shaped our course to the westward, and with a fresh south-easterly wind the leaky *Sea Queen* under all sails stood in for the land. On the morning of August 7th the wind increased to a moderate gale, and once again we were obliged to reef the main-sail.

At three o'clock the following morning, while the boat was going it pretty strong, a small sea came over the stern, which I took to be a warning from nature to shorten sail. After that we took in the mizzen-sail and kept running before a strong easterly wind and quite a large sea under the stay-sail only; the boat went along that way very comfortably till on the morning of August 8th things got a little too wet round the cockpit, so we hove to under a reefed mizzen and storm stay-sail with the sheet to windward. In that condition, in spite of the strong wind and large seas, she lay very comfortably. At ten o'clock the wind moderated, and at noon the little vessel under all sail went along again towards the coast of Japan like a scared dog. The afternoon turned out beautiful.

From the day we left the Japanese coast we had experienced nothing but bad rainy weather, so the change in the elements was very welcome. The night was fine too, and it was really a pleasant change to find oneself lying peacefully in one's bunk, without the howling of the wind and the noise of breaking seas, the little *Sea Queen* sailing peacefully along with a light breeze and smooth water. After our evening meal, owing to the beauty of the night, we all three sat in the cockpit talking over our experiences since we had left Japan, and about our misfortune in having sprung a leak. At nine o'clock Vincent and I turned in, leaving the mate to keep watch till midnight, after which it was Vincent's turn till four o'clock the following morning.

When I went below, I said, 'Now look here, I'm going to have a good sleep, so don't you people start shouting again "All hands on deck, shorten sails."' I had hardly touched the bunk when I was off to sleep, and I slumbered till I heard those familiar words which I had spoken so often myself during the last ten days, 'Reef the main-sail!' but this time it was Stone who spoke just before his watch finished. In a second I was on deck. There was the *Sea Queen* going along like a racehorse, with her lee rail under water. We put one reef in the main-sail and took the mizzen in, after which the yacht went along quite comfortably. At midnight Vincent took the rudder, and Stone and I turned in. I then slept soundly till I heard Vincent's gentle voice coming down the companion-way: 'Down below there, Captain, it is four o'clock; your watch on deck.'

'All right,' I said; 'how is the weather?'

'Fine,' came the answer. I then went on deck, and, sure enough, the wind had moderated, and the sky was clear. After setting all sail again I took the rudder and Vincent lit the stove to make a cup of coffee. Within half an hour the coffee was ready, and as the morning was so beautiful we all three had our coffee in the cockpit.

At about nine o'clock we sighted smoke to the northeastward, and by looking through our glasses we could see two masts and the top of a smokestack rising gradually out of the water. It was apparently a large steamer steering to the south-west, and an hour later, when the steamer was about a mile and a half ahead of us, she turned and stood towards us, and coming alongside proved to be the Japanese steamship *Chicago Maru* from Seattle, bound for Yokohama.

'What are you people doing round here in that boat? Have you been blown away from the land? Are you lost?' the Japanese captain shouted. 'Come alongside, and I will hoist you on my davits and you can go with me to Yokohama.'

We thanked the captain for the trouble he had taken for us, and for his kind offer to take us on board, and after a short explanation of our doings, the captain gave us his longitude, and we parted the best of friends. In less than an hour the steamer was out of sight and we were left to ourselves again.

At about noon we got amongst a lot of fish, in fact, the water was just alive with them. Hurrying through tiffin, we got our fishing gear on deck. My two mates were well satisfied that I should take the rudder while they did the fishing, and so was I, because I knew from former experience that fish in that part of the ocean were very hard to get. While they were almost breaking their necks to catch a fish, I told them that I would eat raw all the fish they caught during the day. About four o'clock in the afternoon a school of porpoises came gambolling along, and both fishermen made a dive down into the cabin for rifles. In less than a minute they were standing on deck with loaded rifles waiting for the porpoises to come near our boat. No sooner were they within range than my mates opened fire, and one of the big fish turned belly upwards.

'Tack ship!' 'Wear ship!' 'Put her round!' 'Quick, hurry up, he is sinking!'

I received about a dozen orders in one second, and getting so rattled with all the orders, I got the boat between two winds. At least I could not do anything with her to get near the fish.

'Hoist the main-sail,' Vinny said. 'Hurry up; if we lose that fish there will be trouble in the family.'

'The main-sail is up; what are you talking about?' I asked. However, after all kinds of shouting and manoeuvring we got alongside the dead fish.

'What are you going to do with it?' I queried. 'You can't get that fish on board, it weighs about five hundred pounds.'

'If the weight is a thousand pounds he has to come on board,' Vincent replied.

The main-sail was then lowered, and by hooking the main throat halliard on to the tail of the fish, we gradually managed to get the monster on board.

Having the fish laying across the forward deck—the weight of the same almost putting the bow of our little vessel under water—Vincent looked at me and said, 'I heard you say that you are a man of your word.'

'Every time,' I replied.

'Eat that fish raw then.'

'Eat what?' I asked indignantly. 'I am afraid you will have to excuse me this time, Mr Vincent, because you will doubtless remember that a porpoise is not a fish but is classified by zoologists as a mammal.' Thus I managed to escape the penalty for a hasty assertion. However, the incident served as a lesson to me, and I made up my mind to refrain in the future from rash promises.

The weather continued fine, and on Saturday, the 10th August, at half-past four in the afternoon we sighted land. However, the wind died out, and we were becalmed until the following morning, when a light breeze came up from the south-east, and at eleven o'clock we dropped anchor in the snug little harbour of Aikawa, a whaling station situated on the mainland and about four miles west of Kinkasan Island.

Aikawa is only a small place, and there is no accommodation for repairing vessels; but with the assistance of Mr Kurogane, the manager of a whaling company, we got the *Sea Queen* out on the beach, and found the cause of the leak was bad caulking, otherwise the vessel was in first-class condition. We had her recaulked, and after putting her in the water again she was as tight as a bottle.

During our stay at Aikawa, we made a trip on a small coasting steamer to Kinkasan Island. This island is a resort for pilgrims, being dedicated to religious purposes. Deer are numerous there and are considered sacred. On our arrival the steamer was anchored about a hundred yards from the west coast of the island, where we landed with much difficulty owing to the heavy surf breakers. After following a trail which led towards the summit of the island, we came to a large Japanese temple, where we were invited by one of the priests to inspect the great temple, which the Emperor of Japan, I was told, visits once a year for the purpose of worshipping. Entering the temple, we were shown into a large Japanese room and treated to Japanese tea and fancy cake. 'How kind this old priest is,' I thought; but my opinion of the old gentleman changed when he told us that it was the custom, among foreigners visiting the island, to give about a hundred yen towards the upkeep of the temple.

'Pretty expensive afternoon for distressed sailors,' Stone said.

'I think so, too,' I replied. 'I haven't even got a hundred yen in my pocket.' However, after we explained our circumstances, he was satisfied by our paying for the tea and cake only.

The island is covered with different kinds of large and small trees and splendid grazing lands for the deer, which can be seen in herds all over the island, and are as tame as sheep. On the east side of the island stands a lighthouse, which shows a fixed bright light and can be seen at a distance of nineteen miles.

TWO

THE SEA QUEEN, after completing repairs, and with everything ready for sea again, left Aikawa on August 22nd at half-past three in the afternoon, and proceeded on her course toward the Marshall Islands. When outside the harbour we steered south-east by east. The weather was dull, with a heavy swell setting from the north-east. The wind being light, our progress was slow, and at midnight Kinkasan light was bearing north by west, distant nineteen miles. On the following two days we experienced light and variable winds accompanied by spells of calm. August 25th the *Sea Queen*'s usual head wind arrived, starting to blow from the east and accompanied by a choppy sea. Similar conditions were experienced on the 26th and 27th, the wind blowing from the east with increasing seas and heavy rain squalls. The boat was kept going to the southeast.

On August 28th our position at noon was latitude thirty-two degrees forty minutes north and longitude one forty-five degrees five minutes east. This day came in with a strong southeasterly breeze, accompanied by heavy rain squalls, and a very large swell set in from the same direction. Towards noon the weather cleared and the wind moderated, but the swell kept on increasing. According to the state of the weather and the swell setting in from the south-east I said to myself, 'I should not be at all surprised if we get a change, and that it will be from bad to worse,' as according to indications a typhoon was approaching. I, however, kept my thoughts to myself till the following day, August 29th, which was ushered in with a moderate easterly breeze and clear weather. Apparently Father Neptune was trying to make things a little easier for the crew of the *Sea Queen*, but the large south-easterly swell continued, and at about nine o'clock a large heavy-looking ring of varied fiery colours formed round the sun. The atmosphere became very sultry, and the appearance of a dense bank of clouds of threatening appearance on the horizon convinced me that the dread visitor was close at hand, and that I would be called upon to prove the statement I had so often made, i.e., that a small vessel is as safe at sea in a gale as a large one.

It was then that I spoke to my two shipmates about the approaching typhoon. The large circle and the similar appearance of the sky followed the sun round till about four in the afternoon, after which the sun disappeared behind the cloud-bank on the horizon. Between sunset and dark the clouds which covered the sky became a fiery hue. The weather during the night was warm and pleasant, and anyone who does not understand the indications of a typhoon would not have thought that, inside of thirty hours, the *Sea Queen* would lay in the centre of one of the worst typhoons that has ever blown in the North Pacific. When darkness set in and the angry clouds had disappeared, the only indication of the approaching typhoon was the south-easterly swell and the barometer, which, however, was not a low glass by any means. At eight o'clock it stood at twenty-nine eighty, but was going down steadily, and between this and the increase in size of the tremendous swell, which almost began to break, I was sure that the approaching hurricane was not far off.

August 30th came in with a light, baffling wind, flying about between east and south, and accompanied by a dark, cloudy sky. At six o'clock the wind settled in the south-east with increasing force and occasional heavy rain squalls. At noon Port Lloyd of the Bonin group bore south by west-half-west two hundred and forty-five miles. An hour later, as the wind was still increasing and the squalls getting heavier, we laid the boat to under a reefed mizzen and storm stay-sail, but at two o'clock we were obliged to put the little vessel under sea anchor and riding sail. The barometer registered twenty-nine forty-five and was falling steadily.

During the afternoon and night the wind continued to increase in force, accompanied by heavy rain squalls and breaking seas, and by two o'clock the following morning the force of the wind was that of a heavy gale, and as the seas were breaking badly we hung two oil bags over the side, which we changed every hour. The proud little *Sea Queen* rode the large seas as they came along; now and then a sea would break near us, and she would give an extra little roll. At eight o'clock it was blowing so hard that I did not think it possible for the wind and sea to increase, and seeing that the boat was laying head to wind, with her drag ahead and a reefed mizzen over her stern, and in spite of the large seas lying quite comfortably, I told my shipmates that the little vessel would weather the typhoon without much trouble; and I am certain she would have done so had our storm gear been stronger.

After making the cruises in the *Xora* and *Tilikum*, I thought I surely knew all about the sea and what was required to manage a small vessel through a heavy gale. As far as heavy gales are concerned, I am quite sure I did understand the management of a boat, but was convinced that morning that I still had to learn something about typhoons. At nine the wind blew with such force that it was impossible to stand on deck, and we were obliged to lie flat down in the cockpit and hang on for dear life. Still the gallant little boat kept facing the gale, and it was most wonderful how she got over the top of the tremendous seas. Up to an hour previously the oil bags did quite a lot of good in keeping the break off the large seas, but now the oil seemed to have little effect, and no trace could be detected on the water. Nevertheless my two mates were employed in the cabin getting the bags ready, while I looked after them outside, thinking that if the oil did no good it would not be harmful. The water was then flying over the boat like a heavy snowdrift, and it was impossible to look up against it, but fortunately no heavy seas came aboard, and there was therefore no danger of the vessel foundering. Vincent and Stone every now and then would open the cabin scuttle a little to enquire how we were getting along. My reply was always the same—'All right.'

Shortly after nine, when I noticed the boat fell sideways into the sea, the mizzen sheet parted. 'All hands on deck!' I yelled. In a second my two mates were alongside me. All three of us were crawling about the deck on all fours on the after-end of the vessel, and with the seas washing over us we managed to take in the mizzen and save the sail. We then found that our sea anchor was lost. Stone managed to get forward and pull the anchor rope on board, and Vincent and I got busy and made a temporary sea anchor by tying together the cabin ladder and one of our anchors. All this had to be done while lying flat upon deck. After fastening the anchor line to the temporary sea anchor we dropped it overboard, and as it was impossible to set the mizzen again we were obliged to let the vessel lay to this temporary arrangement alone. Owing to the fact that this sea anchor was not much of a drag, and being without the aid of the storm sail, it did not do much good. Shortly before eleven o'clock we lost the temporary sea anchor also, and the boat then lay sideways to the sea. The rudder up to this time had been lashed amidships, but as the boat was lying sideways to the sea, I took the rudder lashings off to allow it to swing about and give her a better chance to drift sideways with the seas.

My two mates were down in the cabin again and I was lying in the cockpit holding on with one hand and with the other keeping the oil bags in the water when a huge sea struck the boat and put her on her beam ends, in which position she remained for just a second or two. I wondered what would happen next; whether she would recover or turn turtle. I was not left long in doubt, for I then felt a little jerk which told me that the boat was turning bottom up, and to save myself from getting under her I let go my hold. The next moment I was in the water, and felt certain that it was all up with us; in fact, I took two big mouthfuls of water, thinking to go down quickly and be done with it. When a man gets into a fix of that kind, however, many thoughts will run through his mind, and after I had said good-bye to the World and taken in the water ballast I thought of my two young shipmates who were inside the boat and unable to get out, and wished just to see them once more to say good-bye. By that time I had been under water long enough to be dead, but wasn't. I popped up again behind the stern of the boat and saw the *Sea*

Queen in front of me, with her keel pointing to the sky. I made one kick and grabbed hold of her stern, and then made up my mind to get on her bottom and do something towards righting her again.

I have heard it said that 'While there's life there's hope,' and 'Where there's a will there's a way.' At that time I was still alive and had a little will left, but I thought it was going hard with the hopes and ways. Anyway, I made use of the little determination that remained and climbed over the stern of the boat. Just as I got on the bottom I saw an enormous breaking sea coming towards us, so I dug my nails into the keel to avoid getting washed off again. In a second the sea struck the boat along the keel, but I managed to hang on. The same sea caused the boat to heel over, and the weight of the iron on the keel slowly but surely brought her right side up again, and as she turned over I scrambled over the gunwale, and by the time the little vessel was floating on her bottom again I was in the cockpit. The next thing I saw the scuttle open, and heard Vincent shouting at the top of his voice, 'Are you there, Captain?' And then my two shipmates leaped out of the cabin.

No doubt some of my readers have seen two porpoises jumping out of the water at sea, one after the other. Well, it looked just like that to me. In spite of being on a small craft which was broadside on to the worst storm and largest sea that I ever experienced in all my years at sea, and all three of us lying down in the cockpit and hanging on for dear life, our meeting after the incident was quite joyous, and if the boat got smashed up in the typhoon, it would have given us a chance to say good-bye to each other.

The storm was then at its worst, and the force of the wind was that of several concentrated heavy gales. Large seas were washing over us in rapid succession. Owing to the wind, the heavy rain and salt-water spray, we were absolutely unable to open our eyes when facing windward, and could only see about a hundred feet to leeward. Every few minutes the little vessel was heeled over with the mast in the water. The vessel and gear up to that time were still in good order, and nothing had been lost or broken, but in turning upside down a tremendous amount of water got into her. We were lying with our starboard side to the sea and wind, and as our cabin scuttle was on the port side it was taken under water every time the boat was thrown on her beam ends, and consequently much water got into the cabin. It was impossible to open the cabin door while the boat was lying on the starboard tack, and we were therefore unable to bale her out. At the same time I was certain that if she kept in the same position for another twenty minutes she would have filled with water and foundered; so the only thing that could possibly be done was to put the boat on the port tack, and owing to the condition we were in it had to be done quickly. Consequently, I told my mates to hold on tight so that none of us would get washed overboard during the operation. I then put the helm up to get headway on the boat, and to make her steer I slacked the mainboom off. No sooner was that done than the little vessel started to go ahead, and in a few seconds we were round on the other tack. Everything had gone wonderfully well until the boat came sideways to the sea, and as she was still going ahead a sea broke over the top of us and smashed the mainboom. This was the first thing, apart from the sea anchor, that had got broken until then.

The next thing to be done was to bale some of the water out of the boat. Stone and Vincent both knew what it was like to be in the cabin when she turned bottom up, and both being good swimmers elected to take their chance on deck. I myself, being a very poor swimmer, stood a better chance inside; so it was therefore agreed that Vincent and Stone would tend the scuttle, keeping it open when there was a chance, and I went below to bale her out. It was also agreed that in the event of the boat turning bottom up again my two faithful, athletic shipmates would get on the lee side of her bottom and help the large seas to right her again.

The scuttle of the cabin door was then opened and I made a dive into the cabin. No sooner was I inside than the scuttle was closed over my head and the boat thrown on her beam. I felt sure that she would turn bottom up again, and with all the water that was already inside I thought it must be the last of us. To my surprise, however, she righted herself to an angle of about forty-five degrees, which of course raised the scuttle out of the water, and it was at once slightly opened by my mates on deck. I shall never forget the sight that met my eyes in the cabin. Apart from having a good opinion of my ability to handle boats at sea, I also thought I had learnt all there was to know about stowing stores and cargo so that they could not shift in any weather. In this I was rudely disillusioned, and consequently I came to the conclusion that I was adding to my experiences during that typhoon in more than one sense.

The boat was just about one-third full of water, in which were floating pieces of our gramophone and many records, amongst them 'Life on the Ocean Wave.' Our photographic outfit, tinned goods of various descriptions, bedding, blankets, books, clothing, silver watches, gold chains and navigation instruments were washing about in a mixture of fish oil, kept for use against stormy seas, which had got upset amongst the lot. Now the smell of fish oil is about the least dainty perfume I can possibly think of. The smell and the rolling of the boat, with everything washing from one side of the cabin to the other, and myself amongst it, almost turned me sea-sick. But I gave my stomach to understand that I could not afford to be particular just then, but was obliged to set to work to get some of the water out. For a baler I used a five-pound sugar tin, and whenever my mates outside had an opportunity to open the scuttle far enough I threw some water out. It was certainly baling under difficulties, for nearly every minute the boat was thrown on her beam ends and the scuttle had to be closed till she righted again; then, instantly the scuttle would be opened, and I emptied the tin as fast as I possibly could.

We had kept up the performance for about an hour, and as I had made very little impression on the water in the cabin I thought that the little vessel must have sprung a leak, but as it was a matter of life or death we kept at it. A little later Vincent opened the scuttle just enough to shout through the opening, 'Stone is overboard!' and then quickly closed it to keep the water from pouring into the cabin, for again the boat was put on her beam ends. Next time she righted the scuttle was opened and Vincent shouted, 'He is on board again.' Of course I was quite certain that neither of my shipmates would get away from the boat as long as she kept afloat.

We had been working hard for three hours, and in spite of the boat being thrown on her beam ends time after time she never turned turtle again, and the water was then pretty well out of her. Vincent opened the scuttle again and said, 'Captain, I think we are in the centre of the typhoon.' 'No, not in the centre yet,' I answered, 'but I think we will be shortly, and the sooner we get there the better.' I knew by that time that in spite of the tremendous size of the breaking seas they could not harm our little vessel, but that it was the terrible strength of the wind that forced her bottom upwards, and put her on her beam ends time after time. I knew also that in the centre of the typhoon there would be no wind, and we should be all right.

Stone got washed overboard a second time, and the nerve-racking experiences were now beginning to tell upon both my companions, so, as the cabin was free of water and nothing further could be done on deck, I advised them to come down into the cabin. We then shut the door up as tightly as we could and waited for further developments.

Our timepieces being out of action, we did not know the exact hour, but I think it was between two and three in the afternoon that the barometer registered twenty-eight twenty-five, and after the three of us had been sitting down some time expecting the boat to turn turtle again any second, we were surprised at her righting herself on an even keel. I at once opened the scuttle, and found that we were in a dead calm, and that both masts and all the gear were overboard. All three of us lost no time in getting the broken spars, gear and sails on board again. We were then in the centre of the typhoon.

I have heard ship captains say that once a vessel gets into the centre of the typhoon she will never get out again. After my experience, I can quite agree where a large vessel is concerned, as with such tremendous seas and without a breath of wind she would roll herself to pieces. But the *Sea Queen* did not mind it in the least; she just simply bobbed up and down as the seas came along. I never had a better chance to prove my statement, both while the typhoon was blowing and after we got into the centre of it, that in a heavy gale, be they large or small, as long as their headway is stopped and they are allowed to take a natural drift with the sea and wind, a sea has no power on vessels, and if it does roll on board a large vessel there is no force behind it.

After we got all our gear aboard and well secured on deck we cleared up the cabin; and of course everything was soaked with salt water and fish oil. You may talk of the odour of bad eggs; it isn't in it with the smell of fish oil. All our bedding was saturated, and consequently we were obliged to transfer it to the deck and manage without for the time being. We only had one thing dry in the boat: that was our matches, which we kept in sealed bottles. Our stove was similar to the one I used on the *Tilikum*, which, like my sea anchor, never failed me. On this occasion, however, the sea anchor had failed to do its duty, but the stove, in spite of being tumbled about in the cabin, was there ready when wanted, and in a very short time we had water boiling and made a good cup of coffee, which put us all three in good humour again. This was the first time in all my experiences in small vessels at sea that I was obliged, owing to the weather, to go without my regular meals.

As the barometer remained stationary, we were certain that the second half of the typhoon was near at hand. We were not mistaken, for in about half an hour's time we entered the second stage. It then blew very hard for about four hours from the west, but with the spars out of her it was a picnic for the little vessel. Shortly after the wind changed the barometer started to rise, and by midnight showed twenty-eight fifty-five. During the following twenty-four hours the weather gradually cleared, but as there was still a large sea and strong wind from the west we were unable to do anything towards repairing the damage.

September 2nd came in with a moderate breeze and a large westerly swell, and as the boat was still tumbling about quite a lot we were unable to do anything to our main-mast, but managed to lash together a piece of the broken mizzen-mast and spinnaker-boom, and after some difficulty we managed to step the same in place of the main-mast. Owing to the flimsiness of our temporary jury-mast, all it would carry was the storm stay-sail. During that day and night we experienced fresh south-west breezes, and with our stay-sail made a mile and a half an hour to the north-north-west. The distance from Yokohama was about three hundred and fifty miles.

September 3rd came in with a moderate south-westerly breeze. At daybreak the wind became very light, and as the sea was quite smooth we went to work brightly and early to look over the damage that had been done, and to repair it as best we could. In our survey we found that the main-mast had been broken just above the deck and about three feet below the eyes of the rigging, the main-boom about four feet from the inner end, and the mizzen-mast, like the main-mast, just above the deck, about five feet higher up and again just below the eyes of the rigging. The rigging and chain-plates were in good order, so the two masts had simply buckled up and by the force of the wind blown out of the boat in pieces. The rudder post was broken in the top part of the rudder blade. The hull of the boat was as good as ever.

The dimensions of the main-mast were: Length from deck to eyes of shrouds, twenty-one feet nine inches. Diameter at the lower break, five inches. Diameter at upper break, four and a half inches. Length of mizzen-mast from deck to eyes of shrouds, fifteen feet. Diameter at lower break, four inches; at next break, four inches; and at the eyes of the rigging, three inches.

Both masts were made of Japanese pine, and at the time they blew out of the boat she was lying sideways to the sea and wind at an angle of about forty-five degrees away from the wind. Now, I should like to know what was the speed of the wind when the masts were broken!

Having cleared the rigging, ropes, sails, etc., from the deck, we laid the two broken ends of the fore-mast together, after which we took half-inch pine boards, which had served until then as inside planking along the side of the boat. These boards we cut into narrow strips three feet long and nailed them side by side around the mast. We then put five lashings over the nailed-on strips of wood at an equal distance apart. This is called 'fishing a spar' and if properly done the spar will be as strong as ever, which was the case with us. Owing to the lower break being near the deck, it could not be 'fished' very well without enlarging the mast hole through the deck, and as we did not wish to do that, we cut a step on the mast at the lower break, which of course made it that much shorter. It was then about eleven o'clock and the main-mast was ready to be stepped again.

Ever since the typhoon the talk in the *Sea Queen* had been in connection with getting the main-mast into the vessel again, and as we had such difficulty in stepping the first jury-mast, my two young mates had almost given it up for a bad job, and when I repeatedly told them that to men like us, with good hands, it was nothing, they replied that I was blowing my whistle again, as I had done about eating raw fish.

The main-mast was lying on the deck with all rigging, blocks and gear attached, ready to be stepped, and we proceeded as follows. We took the small jury-mast down, and used the spinnaker-boom for one sheer leg and part of the main-boom for the other. We then put on the sheer lashing, fore- and aft-guys and a tackle to raise the mast with. The sheerlegs being in place, we set up the fore-guy to the end of the bowsprit, and the after-guy to the end of the boom-kin. The lower ends of the sheerlegs we lashed solidly to the chain-plates. The sheerlegs were thus so secured that not even a typhoon could have blown then overboard. The lower block of the tackle was then fastened about eight feet from the lower end of the mast, and when everything was ready to hoist, and as things then looked very prosperous for the *Sea Queen* and her crew to get back to mother earth, I said to the mate, 'By the way, Mr Stone, just before we put in this mast we must have a little understanding about the promise you made the other day. You remember when we were in the centre of the typhoon and just after the masts blew out, you said something about if we got safely back to land you would treat the crew to a champagne dinner. Now I would like to know if that promise is still good.'

'I shall certainly keep my word,' he replied.

'Mr Vincent,' I said, 'you heard that?'

'I did,' said Vincent, 'and shall see that he carries it out.'

'Hoist away on the mast halliard,' I said, and up went the mast.

Owing to the sheerlegs being too short to sling the mast in her balance, we were obliged to fasten the tackle in such a position that the lower end of the spar would just clear the deck when it was hauled down to be stepped. Consequently, when the mast was hoisted up the top was lying on the after end of the deck, and the lower end was sticking up over the bow. Just then the vessel got broadside to the swell and started rolling about, which certainly made it very difficult to step the mast, so by means of our oars we brought the boat head to sea, and then, by pulling the lower end of the mast down by means of a rope it was stepped almost as quickly as I can write it. It was a great relief for the crew of the little boat to see a mast in her again. Of course, it was about three feet shorter than originally, and the splice below the eyes of the rigging gave it the appearance of a horse's leg in splints. Still, it was a mast; and we were well satisfied, since it was large and strong enough to take us back to land. Our medicine chest still contained some brandy, and we would have celebrated the occasion but for the fact that there was a lot of other work to be done before we were able to set sail again; so we had a little tiffin instead.

We then shortened and reset the rigging as before, after which we 'fished' the main-boom, repaired the main-sail, which had been badly torn, and also the jib. To repair the rudder, we fastened two ropes to the after part of the rudder blade, carrying one up either side of the vessel and fastening them to the tiller. The mizzen-mast, being in four pieces and therefore beyond repair, our work was completed at half-past four, and the *Sea Queen* was ready to sail again. Vincent, who had been attending to the cooking during the day, giving us a hand when called upon, sang out, 'Come down here, you sailormen, and have a number one and a half cup of coffee,' and as the weather was calm we joined the cook in the cabin and over a nice cup of coffee and a smoke decided to sail back to Yokohama, a distance of about three hundred and twenty miles.

Half an hour later a light breeze sprang up from the south-west accompanied by light drizzling rain, so we set our reefed main-sail and jib. Under these two sails, and with a moderate breeze, the little *Sea Queen* sailed along again almost as if nothing had happened. The rudder also worked as well as ever. The only trouble then remaining was the ever-present perfume of fish in our bedding and most of our clothes, which were saturated with the horrible oil, and since there was no prospect of eliminating the smell, we cast them all overboard. Two blankets were all that remained on board for the accommodation of the crew and they also smelt so bad that we gave them a wide berth. In an endeavour to remedy this, we tied them to a rope and dragged them through the sea. In the evening, the weather being quite cool, Stone lay down on the bare bunk boards to have a sleep, saying that he would be quite satisfied to sleep on the boards if he only had something to cover himself with. 'There is the frying-pan lying near the stove,' Vincent suggested; 'you might use that.'

The blankets we towed for about twenty-four hours, but as the smell was as bad as ever, we gave them up for a bad job and cut the rope.

September 4th came in with a moderate south-westerly breeze, accompanied by thick and rainy weather. During the forenoon the weather cleared, and at midday, by an observation of the sun, I found that we were about two hundred and forty miles south of Yokohama. Owing to our chronometer being put out of action in the typhoon, and the strong current setting to the north-east, we were not sure of our longitude, and as the wind had hauled into the south-west we kept steering by the wind to the north-west to get the land aboard. The two following days the weather continued much the same, so we kept the boat under small sails, making a northerly course, and prayed for better weather.

During the first and middle part of the next day the strong south-westerly wind was accompanied by large seas and heavy rain squalls. The boat was hove to under a double-reefed main-sail, and storm stay-sail to windward, under which our little vessel rode the large seas like a duck. In the afternoon the wind moderated and the weather cleared up. It was about three o'clock, shortly after having shaken the reef out of the main-sail, that, with the little vessel in a fresh westerly breeze making in for the land, I was sitting in the cockpit steering, and on turning my face to windward I fancied I could smell land.

'Land ho!' I shouted, and my two mates, who were at the time resting on the bunk boards, came bundling into the cockpit and demanded, somewhat excitedly, 'Where is it?'

'Can't see it just yet, but I can smell it,' I assured them.

Neither of my friends having stood in the background when those organs were passed round, pointed their smellers up against the wind. After they had been sniffing for a few minutes Vincent, with more than an element of disappointment in his voice, said, 'I can't smell anything.'

'Neither can I,' agreed Stone.

'Yes,' observed the former, 'I'll eat my hat if anybody can smell land from here'; and with that they both dived back again into the cabin.

The weather was quite clear, and as no land was visible I became a little doubtful of my own sense of smell. About twenty minutes later, however, I saw a dragon-fly circle the boat looking for a resting-place. When these flies can be seen it is a sure sign that land is not far away; and if this was not a sufficient reassurance I later saw a land bird, and this completely satisfied me.

Not having seen anything of the sun since September 4th, it was a difficult matter to ascertain our position within a hundred miles. According to our dead reckoning we should have been in the neighbourhood of Oshima Island. This is very high land, and is visible for a distance of fifty miles. However, while the weather was clear no land was in sight, and I was not a little puzzled, having made sure of seeing land by sunset. Nevertheless, we continued in a north-westerly direction.

Shortly after sunset, the west wind increased to a strong breeze and the weather became threatening, so, as the night was very dark, we hove to till the morning. The threatening appearance of the weather prepared us for another storm, and at midnight the wind increased and was accompanied by heavy rain, but half an hour later the weather calmed down and the sky cleared. At one o'clock it was a dead calm, and with the exception of a thick haze round the horizon the weather was clear. During my watch on deck I thought I heard a light rumbling noise. I was listening for the sound again, but owing to the slatting of the sails, caused by the rolling of the yacht in the calm, I was unable to distinguish the sound or its direction. I immediately lowered all sails, and then, by putting my ear to the deck, I could hear plainly that the rumbling noise was the sound of surf breakers, and that we were not more than five miles from land.

The remainder of the night kept calm and fine, and at four Stone commenced his watch. It was about five o'clock when daylight made its appearance, and almost immediately afterwards, in tones which almost made the little vessel shiver from stem to stern, he yelled 'Land ho!' Coming on deck, I saw to the west the summit of a high mountain over a dense fog. It was only a small piece of land, but after all our vicissitudes it was a welcome sight, and to show our appreciation we all three made a bow, saying, 'Good morning, Mother Earth, we are very glad to see you.'

The calm continued until seven o'clock, when a light breeze sprang up from the south and the fog round the land lifted, and on seeing the outlines we put it down to be Oshima Island, which is sixty miles from Yokohama. We then shaped our course for Tokyo Bay, and as the light wind soon increased made certain of being in Yokohama the same night. The weather was much the same as on the previous afternoon, fine and clear, and one would have thought that on such a day high land such as we saw would be visible at a distance of fifty miles, but we were not more than twelve miles away when the island was enveloped in the same kind of mist as we experienced the previous afternoon. At the time when we saw the dragon-fly and land bird, we could not have been more than fifteen miles from the island. Sailing along with a fresh southerly breeze we should, at noon, have been near the Boshu coast, when to our surprise high land loomed up out of the fog about six miles away on our port beam, which proved to be Oshima; that we had sighted in the morning was Miyake Island. However, we were right then, and as the wind was from the south, we would most likely be in Yokohama some time during the night. At three o'clock, when Oshima Island was about twelve miles distant on our port quarter and the coast of Boshu looming up on our starboard bow, the wind fell light and hauled into the north-east, which was very much against the wishes of the crew of the *Sea Queen*. Later in the afternoon the weather commenced to look threatening, with a fast increasing wind, and we kept off for Habu Harbour, Oshima Island. The entrance of this harbour is very narrow, and darkness setting in before we fell in with the land we hove to under sails for the night. The following morning, at daybreak, with a strong north-easterly wind, we steered in for Habu Harbour. On nearing the land the wind became light, and a strong current setting to the south-west we drifted to Toshima Island, about ten miles south-west of Habu. During that day and the following night we experienced squally, rainy and misty weather. It was weather that you read about, but seldom see. The current was now against us, but by taking advantage of the heavy squalls which struck us at different times, from all points of the compass, we managed to get near the mouth of Habu Harbour by ten the following morning, September 10th, and in an hour were snugly moored. We found the village wrecked by the typhoon through which we had passed, and were told by the oldest inhabitants that it had been the worst on record. Besides wrecking their town it had torn up trees by their roots, and sunk a two-thousand-three-hundred-ton steamship, with her crew of forty men, but the *Sea Queen* had passed through the centre of the typhoon and brought her crew safely back to land.

With regard to our health, after the hardships we went through Vincent was in excellent health. I myself during the typhoon received a bad cut on my left leg, and not being able to treat the wound properly, I had a pretty bad leg on our arrival at Habu. After that it soon got well. Stone was still worse off, as at the time when the vessel turned turtle he happened to be in the forward end of the cabin where our gramophone and a heavy box containing our photographic outfit was placed, and as the boat turned bottom up these two articles got mixed up with Stone on the round journey. Stone said when the *Queen* turned bottom up it became pitch dark in the cabin, and as the gramophone and box were flying in all directions and made an attack upon him in the dark, he being helpless, the two articles with their sharp edges and corners dug holes into his unfortunate ribs and other parts of his anatomy. The wounds, like my own, not receiving proper attention, had got worse instead of better by the time we arrived at Habu. We had almost given Stone up for a bad job, and it came therefore as welcome news to the crew when we were told by a Japanese doctor at Habu that he was still worth repairing.

After remaining a few days at Habu we sailed under our jury rig to Yokohama, where we arrived safe and sound. And as Stone was true to his word, we celebrated the cruise of the *Sea Queen* with a champagne dinner.

IN CONCLUSION

IN THE APPENDIX I have said much about sea anchors, riding sail and oil. My readers will, no doubt, agree with me that they are useful things, but no one can appreciate their value in a higher degree than he who had to rely on these friends at the time when death stared into his face. Sea anchor, riding sail, and oil bag, despite their great importance, are apparatus by no means found aboard every vessel and lifeboat, and deserve to be much better known than they have been hitherto.

The cruises which I have made in small vessels not infrequently have been denounced as foolhardy undertakings. However, when I had given a short explanation such doubters would become silent. They soon understood that there is still much to be learned about breaking waves, and that there is no better way to study the safety of ocean travel than these solitary cruises on which all kinds of weather and sea dangers are met with and fought.

Then, I ask, why should not a seaman like myself who loves the ocean and likes to sail on it, devote his time to this study? The more so as I for one feel perfectly convinced in my own mind that I am safe in my small vessel of which I have complete control, far safer indeed than thousands who race across the briny deep in big greyhounds and have to entrust their lives to the care of others!

Captain Slocum, who made a trip round the world in the *Spray*, a twelve-ton yawl, was lost when attempting another long cruise in the same boat. The *Pandora*, a ten-ton yawl, left Australia on a cruise round the world, and after arriving in New York and having departed again, met with the same fate. Both these boats were considerably larger than mine, the *Tilikum*, and the two cases have been cited frequently as a sure proof that small vessels were not safe at sea.

Captain Slocum sailed single-handed and, therefore, was unable to watch his vessel night and day. The two men constituting the crew of the *Pandora* have stated that both of them on repeated occasions went below, and like Captain Slocum left the vessel to look out for herself. A practice of this kind may pass for a long time, but sooner or later it will revenge itself, for the dangers are many if a vessel is not properly navigated and watched. Both small boats, through accomplishing long cruises previous to their disappearance, had certainly proved their seaworthiness. The ill fate they met with was not due to size or faulty construction but rooted in quite a different cause. Nobody will ever exactly know what happened to them. Therefore it would be unjust to blame those who perished and are unable to defend themselves; but I wish to emphasise that human weakness is common the world over, on land and sea, on vessels large and small; and wherever poor management is met with it originates in such weakness or, as an English philosopher has aptly put it, 'the intelligent human mind, face to face with something it downright ought to do, does something else.' But for a great many it is much easier to find fault with others or with the dead material than with themselves.

The call of the sea is a strong one. The blue waves and whistling breezes have a never-ending charm to him who spent a life in their company. And though it had been much toil and little gain it does not make an iota of difference. As I have already stated, I am advanced in years but still feel confident and strong to venture out on another cruise. I have a longing to visit old places and shake hands with old friends once more. If fortune favours me and this desire be fulfilled I shall be ready to conclude my life as a sea-faring man. And to all those to whom the ocean is not a barren desert but a source of life and wholesome joy I bid a hearty GOOD LUCK AND A FAIR WIND!

APPENDIX

DURING MY TRAVELS, principally in small vessels, I have, perhaps, met and exchanged views with more yachtsmen than the average man afloat. I have found that the majority, although fully capable of sailing a small boat on an inland lagoon or other land-locked waters, also like to know something about the peculiarities of the high seas and how to overcome the danger of breaking wind waves. As stated in my narrative, I have sailed in and managed sailing vessels of different sizes, from the tiny *Tilikum* up to a ship carrying nearly three thousand tons of cargo. This has offered me an excellent opportunity to study breaking seas under all weather conditions, of which I have tried to take the best advantage. The knowledge thus obtained in my long sea-faring career has condensed into certain rules which, I have reason to hope, may prove of practical value to a wider circle. And I trust that these explanations and instructions will not alone be interesting and useful to yachtsmen, but also may serve as hints to young officers and even masters of ships, when danger looms ahead.

I have provided twenty paragraphs in all which follow under their respective headings. The subsequent remarks and reflections on loading, ballasting, and the management of steamships in heavy gales are a further attempt on my part to contribute to the interests and the safety of practical navigation.

I. THE SPEED, HEIGHT, AND DANGER OF BREAKING WIND WAVES.

The speed of waves I have estimated in the open ocean during various gales when they had attained full growth, as follows: When hove to under a sea anchor with a hundred and fifty feet of anchor rope out and when just on the top of a large wave, the sea-anchor float which was fastened with fifteen feet of line would appear at a distance a little less than half-way to the top of the next wave. By allowing for the angle in which the anchor rope inclined I ascertained an approximate total distance from crest to crest of three hundred feet. Under the same conditions I have measured the speed of the waves by marking the difference of time between two succeeding seas when their crests passed the boat. The interval was seven seconds on the average. In basing the calculation on the above figures an average speed of twenty-five and one-third nautical miles per hour is obtained.

The height of waves I have ascertained on large vessels. I chose a position in the rigging just high enough so that the tops of the large waves would appear a little below a line between my eyes and the horizon. The exact distance from the water-line of the ship to the level of my eyes was known to me. While hove to in the ship *Prussia* during a heavy gale in the South Pacific I found in this way the height of the waves from trough to crest to amount to nearly forty feet. In this connection I may mention that in books and newspaper reports from time to time statements appear recording the height of waves encountered at sixty and even seventy feet!

Breaking wind waves in the open ocean where no obstacle is met are caused by strong winds the speeds of which are much faster than the velocity of a wave. As the wave culminates in a crest the wind behind forces it over, transforming that part of the wave into a forward-moving body of water, spray and foam. A wave in this condition is termed by seamen a 'breaking sea.'

Breaking seas have washed countless numbers of seamen off vessels' decks and provided them a watery grave. Their irresistible force has smashed in bulwarks of ships, buckling and bending iron stanchions, and tearing away steel plates; and many cases are on record where breaking seas have sent to the bottom new and strong ships with every man on board. There seems to be no limit to the destruction wrought by the overwhelming power of breaking seas. But are these breaking seas so formidable in themselves, or is there not many an instance where those responsible for the management must be blamed for the damage suffered by their vessels during heavy storms? I take the liberty of stating certain facts, and making certain inference.

When sailing in large sailing vessels I have noticed that they will lie perfectly comfortable and dry, provided they are properly loaded and hove to. Even when storm sails are carried away, there is no imminent danger: the vessel will roll about and in doing so ship seas, but the water in this case is harmless.

For five years I have been master of sealing vessels averaging in size seventy-five tons. In these I have sailed from Victoria, BC, and from Yokohama in the depth of winter, when they were loaded down to the scuppers with sealing outfit. From six to nine sealing boats, each from eighteen to twenty feet in length, were lashed on deck. These latter were built of so light a material that their planking could have been knocked in with a stroke of the fist. In those vessels I have ridden out the worst of gales in which other ships were smashed to pieces. But through properly heaving to, on no occasion did I ever have a boat smashed in, nor have I sustained the slightest damage to vessel or outfit.

Thus it becomes evident that the action of heaving to in time and in the right way is of the utmost importance in order to avoid damage or, eventually, total loss. I may say that I believe in oil to calm breaking seas. I have always used it freely when in sealing vessels during heavy storms for the protection of the boats. For if our boats had been broken we would have been robbed of the means of carrying out our enterprise. It is advisable, however, not to attribute too much efficacy to oil, as the following incident goes to show. On March 19th, 1911, while three hundred miles to the south-south-west of Cape Lopatka in the seventy-five-ton schooner *Chichijima Maru*, from Yokohama, we were hove to in a heavy gale. When oil was administered it froze as soon as it came in touch with the water. Notwithstanding this, and despite the vessel being loaded down to the scuppers, we did not sustain the slightest damage to ship, boats or outfit. But we were readily hove to and thus safe from shipping seas, which proved to be a sufficient safeguard.

I will go a little further, claiming—and I have absolute confidence in doing so—that on no occasion while in charge of a vessel which was hove to under storm sail in a violent gale, have I shipped a sea that caused any damage to ship or outfit, even though the storm sails had been carried away by the force of the wind. And the same applies to the small boats I have sailed on long cruises when they were hove to under sea anchor and riding sail.

These results I have obtained by observing the following: The storm sails were trimmed in such a way that the vessel's head lay near the wind, her headway was stopped and she made a nearly square drift. The wake then, instead of being under the stern, as is the case in sailing, will appear along the vessel's weather side, which has a most wonderful effect in smoothing down breaking seas on their approach.

To sum up, I have found that breaking wind waves in the open ocean become dangerous only when the vessel is driven through the water, and the faster she is travelling the more damage a sea is likely to inflict. Pooping seas, i.e., seas breaking over the stern when running, are the worst of all.

2. In What Size of Vessel is it Safe to Heave to Under Sail in Bad Weather?

The smallest vessel in which I hove to under storm sail only, i.e., without using a sea anchor, was the *Ella G.* from Victoria, BC, an eighteen-ton schooner, forty-nine feet over all, fourteen feet beam, and eight feet draught. In her I weathered four heavy gales in the North Pacific while under a storm try-sail hoisted on the main-mast. With this she swung about, sideways to the sea and wind, as much as eight points. However, a square drift with the wind was maintained throughout and never a sea was shipped. I used oil in addition. From this experience I conclude that a vessel of at least fifty feet in length is quite safe to heave to, with the exclusive use of storm sails.

3. The Proper Time to Heave To When Running Before a Strong Wind and Sea.

With regard to this, I may say that even a large ship, when deeply loaded, is liable to be smashed up by a single bad pooping sea. Consequently, to be on the safe side she should heave to right at the beginning of a gale. But the greatest care and precaution are necessary when small vessels are concerned. Therefore, my recommendation is, at the approach of a gale, when waves commence breaking and the vessel becomes heavy on the rudder, heave to. Always remember that things are quite different in running from when you are sailing with a beam or by the wind. In the latter case a vessel will ship spray, which serves as a warning to you. This happens more often and gets worse as the wind and sea increase, until you are obliged to shorten sails and heave to. But in running before it your vessel may go along quite comfortably and dry for a time, and then, with dreadful suddenness, a sea may come over the stern and put you and your ship out of business. So, once more, I repeat my advice: be most careful in running, and heave to rather a little earlier than might be deemed necessary by others.

4. How to Heave To When Running Under Sail.

If a vessel is about to heave to before the seas have started breaking heavily, all that is required is to put the helm down and let her come to the wind with the sails she is running under. But if it be blowing hard and bad seas are appearing already, care must be taken in bringing the vessel's head to sea. For if a bad sea is met with in coming round while the vessel is still retaining headway, disastrous results may ensue. To avoid this the man in charge should be on the lookout for a chance when the seas are running fairly smooth, which will occur from time to time even in the height of a gale. Then put your helm down and let the vessel come up with a stay-sail sheet to windward. The latter will help to stop the ship's forward motion when she swings head to wind, which is the principal factor in the manoeuvre.

While sailing in sealing vessels I have on various occasions when running before a bad sea lowered all sail and let her come up to the wind under bare poles, setting storm sails afterwards. And I have found it to be an excellent plan.

5. What Storm Sails Should be Carried in a Gale, and How to Set Them.

It depends entirely upon the build, lines and rig of a vessel, as to which sails she will lay under to the best advantage. To find out this early, one must study her weak points, and it is the duty of every shipmaster to make trials with regard to this matter at the beginning of the first gale he encounters. I shall cite an instance here.

The schooner *Jessy* from Victoria, BC, length over all seventy-five feet, beam twenty-two feet, draught aft eleven feet, forward nine feet, was built on the lines of a yacht and was a very fast sailor. With this vessel, deeply loaded to the scuppers, I sailed from Victoria on December 1st, 1907, and a few days later met with an exceedingly heavy gale off the Columbia River. At the beginning of the storm I went through a variety of storm-sail drills, and by doing so found that she lay to splendidly under three-reefed fore-sail with the sheet well hauled in, double-reefed fore-stay-sail with the sheet nearly at midships, and the wheel a little down. Under these sails the vessel reached ahead a little and lay to very comfortably. Gradually, as the wind and seas increased, I put the wheel down more and more and hauled the stay-sail sheet more to windward. When the gale was at its worst she lay comfortable and dry with a double-reefed fore-stay-sail sheet to windward, three-reefed fore-sail sheet well in and the wheel half-way down, and made seven points leeway.

Another example is the previously mentioned schooner *Chichijima Maru*, length over all seventy-five feet, beam twenty feet, draught aft eight feet, forward six feet six inches, full built but fairly fast. This vessel lay to excellently under a three-reefed fore-sail sheet well in and a close-reefed try-sail, the sheet flat at midships, and also made seven points leeway.

Other vessels will lay to under close-reefed fore-stay-sail, fore-sail and try-sail, and so on, according to their peculiarities.

6. What Signs Assure The Master that His Ship is Properly Hove To in a Gale, and Thus Safe from Shipping Seas.

If your vessel lies four to five points from the wind and makes nearly a square drift she is safe.

For example: if a vessel lays to on the port tack in a north-westerly gale she should be heading about north to north by east and make an approximately easterly drift. However, she may fall off at times a point or two, but as long as the vessel does not range ahead there will be no seas coming over to do any harm.

7. The Drift of a Vessel When Hove To Under Storm Sails.

This depends upon the draught. A vessel with a deep keel or great draught respectively will drift from a mile to a mile and a quarter per hour in a heavy gale, while shallow, round-bottom craft will be borne away at the rate of nearly two miles per hour under like conditions.

8. How to Heave To Small Vessels of About Twenty-Five to Fifty Feet in Length, Under Storm Sails in a Moderate Gale.

The sloop *Xora* behaved surprisingly well under a small storm-stay-sail-tack set up over the stem with the sheet to windward and closely-reefed main-sail with the sheet well in, the helm being half down.

The yawl *Sea Queen* went through a moderate gale under a storm-jib with the sheet to windward, single-reefed mizzen, and the helm a little down. On another occasion she lay to even better than in the former case under the storm-stay-sail with the sheet to windward and a close-reefed main-sail, the helm half-way down.

When trimmed in this manner vessels will range ahead a little and make about four points leeway. But it is surprising to see how nicely they will ride over large combers, at the same time remaining comfortable and dry.

9. WHY SMALL VESSELS SHOULD HEAVE TO UNDER SEA ANCHOR AND RIDING SAIL IN A HEAVY GALE.

A small vessel hove to under a sea anchor and riding sail is comfortable and dry. She is out of danger from shipping seas and needs little watching. This will give the captain the chance of a night's rest.

10. THE BEST KINDS AND DIMENSIONS OF SEA ANCHOR SUITED TO DIFFERENT SIZES OF VESSELS.

In the *Tilikum*, owing to her light draught, I used a sea anchor made of an iron ring twenty-two inches in diameter and a bag four feet in length. Riding to this the little vessel weathered sixteen heavy gales without shipping as much as a bucket of water at one time. The same sea anchor I employed for crossing the dangerous bar near Melbourne and also in the demonstration at the Sumno Bar, New Zealand.

In the *Sea Queen*, which had greater draught, I increased the dimension of the ring to twenty-six inches, while the length of the bag was not altered. To this sea anchor she lay splendidly in heavy gales, and even rode the tremendous waves of the typhoon in style until the bridles broke. I am quite sure that, had the gear been stronger, the tiny craft would have weathered the typhoon without a hitch!

I should, therefore, recommend for boats and yachts up to thirty feet in length sea anchors made of a conical bag with a round mouth, and for vessels from thirty to fifty feet in length a square mouth. It makes, of course, no difference in principle whether the mouth be round or square as long as the bag is fairly deep and the diameter of the mouth large enough to suit the size of the respective vessels. My only reason for choosing a sea anchor with a round opening in the case of a small vessel is the consideration that there is less room to work. The iron-ring style is ever ready, besides involving less trouble when put out.

There is still another style of sea anchor, which is especially useful when surf breakers are crossed in a small boat. This type I claim to be my own invention, having constructed the same and experimented with it for the first time when on the *Tilikum* voyage. Instead of the iron ring, one made of strong, flat wood is employed, weighted at one side with a piece of lead just heavy enough to cause the ring to tilt up when put into the water. The canvas bag will then quickly fill with water and the whole sink to the required depth.

This style avoids the necessity of using a float and line, and facilitates readier handling; besides which, the wooden-weighted ring will skim over the water when hauled in by the tripping line without the danger of the latter becoming entangled with the anchor rope. The iron ring, on the other hand, is liable to sink too deep and get foul of rocks or other obstacles hidden in the shallow surf.

However, for long voyages and in deep water I recommend the iron ring and float type, as it is stronger and stands more wear and tear.

The dimensions of sea anchor for a deep keel boat of about twenty feet water-line should be as follows: Diameter of mouth, twenty inches; length of bag, thirty inches; opening at point, two inches. For larger boats, add for every foot more of water-line one inch to the diameter of mouth and an inch and a half to the length of bag. Increase the width of opening at point in proportion. A sea anchor with a thirty-inch ring should have a point opening of four inches.

A square-mouthed sea anchor of say thirty inches in width is constructed as follows: Two flat, wooden or iron bars, each forty-eight inches in length, are fastened to each other in the middle with a pin swivel. The mouth of the canvas bag in this case is shaped square and rope is sewn all round, leaving a small loop at the four corners in order to haul the bag out taut and secure it to the ends of the bars. If wooden bars are used, put a weight on the sea anchor to sink it to the required depth. When not in use the bag may be taken off, and after being dried, wrapped round the bars, which are brought together on the swivel pin, and the whole stored away in a dry place.

The dimensions of sea anchor for a deep keel boat of thirty feet water-line are: Mouth, twenty-eight inches square; length of bag, forty-two inches; opening at point, four inches. For larger boats add proportionately, as before.

A small strop, by which it is hauled on board, should be placed over the point opening in both styles of sea anchor. Two bridle ropes, to which the anchor mouth is fastened, must be of the same length as the bag, and should continue along and be sewn to the latter down to its point. With the square type they run over the corners and edges. A cork float of sufficient size to keep the anchor suspended at a depth of fifteen feet completes the outfit. All iron parts should be galvanised, and everything must be made of the best material.

11. THE BEST KIND OF CABLE FOR THE SEA ANCHOR, WITH REGARD TO MATERIAL AND LENGTH, AND HOW TO FASTEN THE SAME.

Manilla rope of a good white quality serves the purpose well. The size varies according to the length of the boat. Thus, with vessels of twenty feet water-line, two and a half inches circumference; thirty feet, three inches; forty feet, four inches; fifty feet, five inches, should be employed. Length of the rope from vessel to sea anchor, one hundred and fifty feet.

In long, lasting gales the rope is liable to get chafed on bow or headgear; therefore a chain should be spliced to its upper end, and should be sufficiently long to fasten it to the fore-mast and to lead clear of the headgear. In an ordinary gale the sea-anchor rope is sometimes fastened to the end of the jibboom, but I strongly deprecate this practice when a real, heavy storm is raging.

12. How to Bring a Small Vessel's Head to Sea Without Shipping Heavy Water.

This is done on the same principles as No. 4. When the boat is head to sea put the sea anchor out and set storm-riding-sail.

13. How a Small Vessel Should Lie, Under a Sea Anchor and Riding Sail, in a Heavy Gale, so as to Keep Dry and Comfortable.

Your boat should lie straight head to sea, or nearly so. The sea anchor is out about a hundred and fifty feet ahead and fifteen feet below the surface, kept there by its cork buoy. The riding sail is set over the stern with the sheet hauled in flat. If the vessel be provided with a bobstay, put a tackle on the mizzen-boom and haul the sail a little to that side which is opposite the anchor rope hawse. To explain it thoroughly: if the anchor rope plies out over the starboard bow, haul the mizzen-boom to the port side. In that way your boat will lay a trifle off the wind which, far from being a disadvantage, will prevent chafing of the bobstay and headgear. The mizzen or riding sail should be made of strong canvas, and in order to keep it set flat put a preventer-stay from the mizzen masthead forward.

All blocks, ropes and strops as well as the sail, and everything else should be of the very best. For when a small boat is hove to under a sea anchor the riding sail will shake heavily at times, as if electric shocks were passing through it. This is very hard on the gear and the sail itself.

A ketch, schooner-ketch, yawl, or schooner-yawl are the best small vessels in which to make an ocean cruise. For all these carry a mizzen-sail, which is ever ready and avoids the necessity of having an extra riding sail when hove to.

14. How to Secure the Rudder When Hove To Under Sea Anchor and Riding Sail.

When a small vessel is hove to under sea anchor and riding sail she will have stern way, and the swinging about of the stern as caused by breaking seas at times will be hard on the rudder. Through neglecting precautions, I have on two different occasions lost the rudder post while hove to in the above way. To avoid breaking the rudder post, fasten two heel ropes to the upper back of the rudder blade, one to each side, and haul them up over the quarter: then place the rudder at midships, haul the heel ropes tight and fasten on deck. The tiller, on the other hand, should remain entirely unlashed.

15. The Drift of a Small Vessel When Hove To Under Sea Anchor and Riding Sail.

Not counting prevailing ocean currents the drift will always occur in a direction opposite to the wind, *i.e.*, if the wind is north the vessel will experience a southerly drift. A small vessel hove to in a gale under sea anchor and riding sail will in this way drift at a rate of about one and a quarter miles per hour when out at sea. In a bay or a similar place where no ocean swell is perceivable the drift will be faster.

In speaking about the drift of a vessel in a heavy gale I have been asked on many occasions: What are you going to do when you have no sea room?

To this I answer: he who is in charge of any vessel on an ocean voyage should thoroughly understand to interpret the indications of an approaching storm. He must take care to bring his vessel timely into such a position as to weather the storm in safety.

16. How to Cross Surf Breakers in a Boat or Launch.

Whether a boat be propelled by an engine, sail, or oars, drag a sea anchor behind the stern and let her go in slowly and straight before the breakers. You will be surprised to see how nicely she will raise her stern to the combers.

In case of a launch or tug towing another small vessel across surf breakers towards the shore, have a sea anchor over the towed boat's stern and proceed as above. But it is most essential to have a strict understanding with the man in charge of the towboat beforehand, as to go 'slow,' and there will be no trouble similar to that I witnessed on the Wanganui Bar, New Zealand.

17. What Gear Should Be Carried in Lifeboats Aboard Ships, for the Safety of Shipwrecked People.

Apart from what the Board of Trade and other regulations prescribe, the following should be provided for each lifeboat:

> A complete sea-anchor outfit as described in Nos. 10 and 11.
> A small mast to set a riding sail, including the latter.
> Two tins of oil and two oil bags.
> Two trained men who understand how to handle boat and gear.

Owing to the many shipping disasters of recent years and the loss of life involved, the question how to obtain a sufficient number of competent men to take charge of the lifeboats in case of a shipwreck has become acute. As I may, perhaps, claim to possess more experience than the average boat sailor, and trusting that it will serve a good purpose, I take the opportunity of giving here my opinion on the subject.

On various occasions I have witnessed lifeboats being lowered from passenger vessels in a harbour and in dead calm weather. And in spite of there being from twelve to twenty-four men at the oars and an officer at the helm they were absolutely unable to control the boat. We can easily imagine what would happen to such a lifeboat at sea, in bad weather and when loaded with passengers. I think it quite safe to say that when it comes down to a case of dead earnest nine out of ten lifeboats on passenger vessels are manned on the same lines. My suggestion, therefore, is that all steamers should have on board two trained lifeboatmen for each boat.

However, here the question crops up: How are such men to be secured? My own idea is that this may be arranged for in the following way:

There are many lifeboat stations in all quarters of the globe where provision could be made to train able-bodied men, have them pass an examination, and then provide them with a certificate to the effect that they are capable of taking charge of a ship's lifeboat at sea. Men in possession of such certificates, whether they be deckhands, firemen, stewards or whatever else, should be and naturally would be given preference in shipping; the required number should receive a little extra payment. And in a few years there would be ample trained men, which would prove of great advantage to themselves as well as to shipowners and the travelling public. In addition, there could be appointed in each passenger ship an officer or other competent seaman also holding a certificate to be in charge of all lifeboat gear. One of his chief duties would be to arrange for a drill from time to time to keep his men up to the standard.

Ships' lifeboats, according to existing regulations, are provided with some sort of a sea anchor, but even if it were of the best kind, a boat without a riding sail will not lay head to sea in a seaway. Therefore, the fate of such a boat loaded with women, children and inexperienced men, when swinging sideways up against a breaking sea may be considered sealed. The occupants will go with the roll of the frail craft, which is sure to ensue, and the boat will capsize in spite of the sea anchor being out. But this will not happen when all the rules of properly heaving to are observed.

18. Various Indications of the Typhoon Which Appeared on August 31st, 1912, its Violence, the Seas Encountered, etc.

August 27th.—An unusually large swell was setting through from the south-east, accompanied by squally and rainy weather.

August 28th.—The weather cleared up during the day, a moderate breeze blowing from the east. But as the south-easterly swell was getting larger and the barometer falling very slowly, I gradually came to the conclusion that a typhoon was approaching.

August 29th.—The moderate easterly breeze and clear weather continued until nine o'clock. Then an extensive and heavy ring of varied fiery colours formed round the sun. The atmosphere became exceedingly sultry and a dense bank of clouds of a threatening appearance arose on the horizon. These conditions lasted until four o'clock when the sun disappeared behind the cloudbank on the horizon. Between sunset and dark the clouds covering the sky assumed a fierce yellow tone, which gradually became grey as darkness set in. At eight o'clock the barometer stood at twenty-nine eighty, and went down slowly. The temperature during the night was warm and pleasant; the ocean swell, however, increased, while some of the seas almost came to a break.

AUGUST 30TH.—This day opened with a light baffling wind alternating between east and south and accompanied by a dark cloudy sky. At six o'clock the wind settled into the south-east with increasing force and occasional heavy rain squalls. Barometer twenty-nine forty-five. The wind and squalls increased during the day and the following night, until on

AUGUST 31ST, at about nine in the morning, the typhoon had attained its full strength. The tremendous force of the wind lashed the sea up to such a height and confusion that oil became utterly useless, leaving not the slightest trace on the troubled waters.

The barometer meanwhile continued falling until it stood at twenty-eight twenty-five. A short time after we entered the centre of the typhoon where dead calm prevailed. The glass then kept steady till the wind started to blow again, when it commenced to rise. The second half of the typhoon blew hard for about four hours and then gradually moderated to a fresh breeze.

19. HOW TO MANAGE A SMALL VESSEL IN A TYPHOON.

If you feel sure that a typhoon is approaching prepare to meet it, because it is a tough customer to deal with.

First of all, as in an ordinary gale, have your sea anchor and riding sail in readiness. As the force of the wind is much greater than in even the heaviest gale, unbend all sails except the riding sail and strip the vessel as much as possible. All running gear should be unroved, the foregaff and boom lashed on deck, also the top masts, if there are any. If you should be unlucky enough to have your sea-anchor gear carried away, don't hesitate to cut away the fore-mast to lessen head pressure. This latter measure, if taken in time, may prevent your vessel from being blown on beam ends or, which is worse, capsizing, as happened to the *Sea Queen*. However, be careful not to lose the mast.

20. THE EFFECT OF OIL ON BREAKING SEAS IN HEAVY GALES, AND WHAT KIND MAY BE EXPECTED TO GIVE THE BEST RESULTS.

If a vessel is hove to in the proper way under a sea anchor and riding sail she will only ship spray even in the worst of gales. I was never particular about a few drops of water taken over, and therefore in small vessels, with a few exceptions for experimenting purposes, and while on the *Sea Queen* in the first stage of the typhoon, I hardly ever used oil during my cruises. However, throughout my five years of sealing in the North I employed oil on many different occasions, and have found that that obtained from the fat of hair seals, fur seals, and sea lions gave the best results. Next to this comes fish oil, which is nearly as satisfactory. The former is difficult to procure, while fish oil may be bought in almost any port.

To utilise a small quantity of oil to best advantage proceed as follows: A canvas bag a little smaller than a fifty-pound flour bag is loaded with loose oakum, woollen rags or waste until about three parts full. A few small holes are then punched through the bag and the whole is saturated with oil and tied up. After securing a lanyard and adding a weight to prevent the bag from being blown back again, put it over the rail and lower to the water level; then make fast.

If your vessel is lying to a sea anchor and head on to the sea, put the bag over the bow. If she is hove to under storm sails and makes a square drift, or nearly so, put it over the weather bow. If the vessel be a long one, place one bag near the fore- and another one near the after-rigging.

A ship's lifeboat loaded with passengers and hove to under sea anchor and riding sail with the additional help of such an oil bag will lay dry and comfortable. On the other hand, when a vessel is lying to under storm sails or steam, and reaches ahead, oil will be useless. It is only good, and certainly works wonders, when a vessel is allowed to drift along with the wind and sea.

Oil will also render good service in case of large vessels running straight before a bad sea. One bag is placed on each side of the forward end while a long bight of a large rope is paid out over the stern and dragged along. By allowing the vessel to go slow under small sail, or, still better, under bare poles, she is in this way quite safe and may keep running before almost any gale as long as she steers well. The same course, when followed in the case of small vessels, will likewise prove a great help. However, if you want to be on the safe side, 'heave to.'

Some Remarks on Loading and Ballasting.

If iron or any heavy cargo is put into the lower hold of a vessel till she is down to the loading mark serious consequences may follow. From the quick, jerking roll ensuing and through shipping heavy seas she will most likely get dismasted or break up in the first gale encountered. If too much cargo is put in the between-deck or on deck she is liable to turn turtle. But if the cargo is property distributed in the lower hold, between-deck and on deck, whatever the case may be, and if then the vessel is handled in the right way, it will be surprising how easy her movements are in heavy gales and large seas.

When I made my first voyage in the *Prussia* as first mate, the ship being deeply loaded with coal, she behaved as badly as any vessel possibly could. No matter whether we were running, hove to or in a dead calm, she would roll about in an awful way. Old Captain Reynolds told me that I had put too much cargo into the lower hold.

The next time when we took a cargo of coal I filled up the between-decks and left a space in the lower hold empty, and with the same draught as on the previous voyage the vessel steered and sailed well and behaved much better in every way.

The same principle pertains to small vessels. The *Tilikum*, for example, I had to ballast well down in order to facilitate sailing with a beam wind or when close hauled. The result was that in running, especially with the wind and sea a little on the quarter, she would roll, roll—well, she would roll the teeth out of one's mouth. But as soon as I had placed my four hundred pounds of shifting ballast on the cabin deck, or still better, tied half of it in two bags to the main-mast about three or four feet above the deck, she would go along as steadily as a lumber-loaded ship. The latter, with their large deck loads, I have found to be the steadiest vessels as far as rolling is concerned.

REFLECTIONS ON STEAMSHIP DISASTERS.

As regards steamships I must say that my experience with them is limited, having sailed in engine-driven vessels as a passenger merely. However, I have crossed in steamers the North Sea and the Atlantic each four times, the Pacific once, not to mention voyages on smaller seas. Therefore, although I do not wish to attempt a full criticism, I may be allowed to say a few words on the management of some steamships in heavy storms as laid down in records.

Many times I have read in daily papers of steamships that have been smashed to pieces and foundered from the effect of large seas breaking on them. Then there were reports of other steamers which, deeply loaded, had lost their propeller or rudder and were absolutely beyond control. And while in that condition they had weathered most severe gales and by some means managed to make port with little or no damage to hull or cargo. This set me thinking. After carefully comparing my own notes with statements obtained from various shipmasters I deem it permissible, in spite of my inexperience with steamships, to pass an opinion on the subject.

Only lately I read an account of the terrible experiences of the SS *Narrung* in which I noticed that the most important points which led the captain to despatch a wireless SOS distress signal were the following:

'On December 26th, 1912, while the vessel was in the Bay of Biscay her head was kept towards a heavy gale, the waves broke over her with a relentless force which threatened to overwhelm her. Then a sea broke over the vessel, which literally wrecked the fore end of the ship. Plates were torn and twisted, rails carried clear away, two steam winches weighing several tons had been lifted bodily and tossed along the deck where they lay, a confused mass of bent and twisted ironwork. Water got into the hold and gave the ship a list to starboard. The vessel was then put round before the sea and, as she appeared out of danger, the captain replied to the news of coming assistance with the tidings that his ship was under control and that he could manage to return without assistance.'

Here is another report. The SS *Volmer* was lost on the same day with fifteen members of the crew twenty-five miles south of the Scilly Islands. The captain and one of the crew were saved.

'Although the waves,' so the captain's statement goes, 'mounted higher and higher we had to keep going full steam ahead in the teeth of the storm in order to be able to steer at all. All night we struggled, but at half-past ten on Boxing Day morning, when about twenty-five miles south of the Scillies, a tremendous sea broke aboard, sweeping away everything on deck, ripping off the bulwarks, and smashing in the hatchway. Water rushed in torrents into the hold and engine-room, putting out the fires and leaving the ship practically in a sinking condition. With hatches open, the vessel deeply loaded with coal, lots of water in the hold, and the fires out, the doomed vessel swung round and, absolutely out of control, kept afloat for five more hours in a heavy gale!'

How much longer would the vessel have kept afloat after she had received the deadly blow if the engines had been preserved in good condition and the ship continued heading into the gale? In my opinion, not five minutes! If the engines had been stopped when the *Volmer* was threatened with being overwhelmed the vessel may have drifted a little out of her course; but I am quite sure that she would have received, if any at all, only slight damage. And the same applies to the *Narrung*.

There is no better proof of the correctness of my assumption than the incident that befell the SS *Snowden Range*, which lost her rudder last winter in the North Atlantic. Deeply loaded and absolutely beyond control she weathered gale after gale, and eventually, after experiencing forty days of the worst weather, drifted into port with the cargo in first-class condition. Apart from having lost her rudder and a few small breakages the vessel appeared none the worse for all the wear and tear!

Only by comparing the above three cases, I think, any experienced seaman should become convinced that an engine-driven vessel in a heavy gale at sea acts precisely on the same principle as a sailing vessel, large or small, as explained in my narrative and record of experiences. And therefore I deem it advisable that a steamship, whenever she encounters a real heavy gale, should not be driven into a dangerous head sea just for the sake of keeping steerage-way on her, with the possible result that she gets badly damaged or even broken up. It is a far better plan to stop the vessel's headway dead, tell the engineers to take a rest, and, with the wheel down, let her drift where she likes. In that condition the vessel may swing about, probably as much as eight points, as she may lay with the wind on the quarter. But however she lies, she is bound to make a drift with the wind at the rate, I would judge, of about a mile or perhaps a little more an hour. Leave her wake to windward and she will be out of all danger. Besides this a few oil bags over the weather side will do no harm.

The above points on the management of steamships in heavy gales I have discussed with old experienced shipmasters, and in most cases they agreed with my views. Some, however, claimed that a steamship laying to in the trough of heavy waves would roll too much. The latter may be so if she be badly loaded. But if properly loaded, as every vessel should be when going on a voyage where there is a likelihood of bad weather, this will not happen. The force of the gale blowing up against her side and topwork, I am quite sure, will prevent her rolling excessively.